Religion, the Community, and the Rehabilitation of Criminal Offenders

Religion, the Community, and the Rehabilitation of Criminal Offenders has been co-published simultaneously as *Journal of Offender Rehabilitation*, Volume 35, Numbers 3/4 2002.

The *Journal of Offender Rehabilitation* Monographic "Separates"

Below is a list of "separates," which in serials librarianship means a special issue simultaneously published as a special journal issue or double-issue *and* as a "separate" hardbound monograph. (This is a format which we also call a "DocuSerial.")

"Separates" are published because specialized libraries or professionals may wish to purchase a specific thematic issue by itself in a format which can be separately cataloged and shelved, as opposed to purchasing the journal on an on-going basis. Faculty members may also more easily consider a "separate" for classroom adoption.

"Separates" are carefully classified separately with the major book jobbers so that the journal tie-in can be noted on new book order slips to avoid duplicate purchasing.

You may wish to visit Haworth's website at . . .

http://www.HaworthPress.com

. . . to search our online catalog for complete tables of contents of these separates and related publications.

You may also call 1-800-HAWORTH (outside US/Canada: 607-722-5857), or Fax 1-800-895-0582 (outside US/Canada: 607-771-0012), or e-mail at:

getinfo@haworthpressinc.com

Religion, the Community, and the Rehabilitation of Criminal Offenders, edited by Thomas P. O'Connor, BCL, BTheol, MS, and Nathaniel J. Pallone, PhD (Vol. 35, No. 3/4, 2002). *Examines the relationship between faith-based programs, religion, and offender rehabilitation.*

Drug Courts in Operation: Current Research, edited by James J. Hennessy, PhD, and Nathaniel J. Pallone, PhD (Vol. 33, No. 4, 2001). *"As one of the founders of the drug court movement, I can testify that Dr. Hennessy's book represents the highest level of sophistication in this field." (Michael O. Smith, MD, Director, Lincoln Recovery Center, Bronx, New York; Assistant Clinical Professor of Psychiatry, Cornell University Medical School)*

Family Empowerment as an Intervention Strategy in Juvenile Delinquency, edited by Richard Dembo, PhD, and Nathaniel J. Pallone, PhD (Vol. 33, No. 1, 2001). *"A hands-on book. . . . Provides detailed guidelines for counselors regarding implementation of the FEI curriculum . . . accurately describes the scope of counselor responsibilities and the nature of treatment interventions. Unique in its coverage of counselor competencies and training/supervision needs. Innovative and based on solid empirical evidence." (Roger H. Peters, PhD, Professor, University of South Florida, Tampa)*

Race, Ethnicity, Sexual Orientation, Violent Crime: The Realities and the Myths, edited by Nathaniel J. Pallone, PhD (Vol. 30, No. 1/2, 1999). *"A fascinating book which illuminates the complexity of race as it applies to the criminal justice system and the myths and political correctness that have shrouded the real truth. . . . I highly recommend this book for those who study causes of crime in minority populations." (Joseph R. Carlson, PhD, Associate Professor, University of Nebraska at Kearney)*

Sex Offender Treatment: Biological Dysfunction, Intrapsychic Conflict, Interpersonal Violence, edited by Eli Coleman, PhD, S. Margretta Dwyer, MA, and Nathaniel J. Pallone, PhD (Vol. 23, No. 3/4, 1996). *"Offers a review of current assessment and treatment theory while addressing critical issues such as standards of care, use of phallometry, and working with specialized populations such as exhibitionists and developmentally disabled clients. . . . A valuable addition to the reader's professional library." (Robert E. Freeman-Longo, MRC, LPC, Director, The Safer Society Press)*

The Psychobiology of Aggression: Engines, Measurement, Control, edited by Marc Hillbrand, PhD, and Nathaniel J. Pallone, PhD (Vol. 21, No. 3/4, 1995). *"A comprehensive sourcebook for the increasing dialogue between psychobiologists, neuropsychiatrists, and those interested in a full understanding of the dynamics and control of criminal aggression." (Criminal Justice Review)*

Young Victims, Young Offenders: Current Issues in Policy and Treatment, edited by Nathaniel J. Pallone, PhD (Vol. 21, No. 1/2, 1994). *"Extremely practical. . . . Aims to increase knowledge about the patterns of youthful offenders and give help in designing programs of prevention and rehabilitation."* (S. Margretta Dwyer, Director of Sex Offender Treatment Program, Department of Family Practice, University of Minnesota)

Sex Offender Treatment: Psychological and Medical Approaches, edited by Eli Coleman, PhD, S. Margretta Dwyer, and Nathaniel J. Pallone, PhD (Vol. 18, No. 3/4, 1992). *"Summarizes research worldwide on the various approaches to treating sex offenders for both researchers and clinicians."* (SciTech Book News)

The Clinical Treatment of the Criminal Offender in Outpatient Mental Health Settings: New and Emerging Perspectives, edited by Sol Chaneles, PhD, and Nathaniel J. Pallone, PhD (Vol. 15, No. 1, 1990). *"The clinical professional concerned with the outpatient treatment of the criminal offender will find this book informative and useful."* (Criminal Justice Review)

Older Offenders: Current Trends, edited by Sol Chaneles, PhD, and Cathleen Burnett, PhD (Vol. 13, No. 2, 1985). *"Broad in scope and should provide a fruitful beginning for future discussion and exploration."* (Criminal Justice Review)

Prisons and Prisoners: Historical Documents, edited by Sol Chaneles, PhD (Vol. 10, No. 1/2, 1985). *"May help all of us . . . to gain some understanding as to why prisons have resisted change for over 300 years. . . . Very challenging and very disturbing."* (Public Offender Counseling Association)

Gender Issues, Sex Offenses, and Criminal Justice: Current Trends, edited by Sol Chaneles, PhD (Vol. 9, No. 1/2, 1984). *"The contributions of the work will be readily apparent to any reader interested in an interdisciplinary approach to criminology and women's studies."* (Criminal Justice Review)

Current Trends in Correctional Education: Theory and Practice, edited by Sol Chaneles, PhD (Vol. 7, No. 3/4, 1983). *"A laudable presentation of educational issues in relation to corrections."* (International Journal of Offender Therapy and Comparative Criminology)

Counseling Juvenile Offenders in Institutional Settings, edited by Sol Chaneles, PhD (Vol. 6, No. 3, 1983). *"Covers a variety of settings and approaches, from juvenile awareness programs, day care, and vocational rehabilitation to actual incarceration in juvenile and adult institutions. . . . Good coverage of the subject."* (Canada's Mental Health)

Strategies of Intervention with Public Offenders, edited by Sol Chaneles, PhD (Vol. 6, No. 1/2, 1982). *"The information presented is well-organized and should prove useful to the practitioner, the student, or for use in in-service training."* (The Police Chief)

Religion, the Community, and the Rehabilitation of Criminal Offenders

Thomas P. O'Connor
Nathaniel J. Pallone
Editors

Religion, the Community, and the Rehabilitation of Criminal Offenders has been co-published simultaneously as *Journal of Offender Rehabilitation*, Volume 35, Numbers 3/4 2002.

The Haworth Press, Inc.
New York • London • Oxford

Religion, the Community, and the Rehabilitation of Criminal Offenders has been co-published simultaneously as *Journal of Offender Rehabilitation*™, Volume 35, Numbers 3/4 2002.

Cover design by Lora Wiggins

Library of Congress Cataloging-in-Publication Data

Religion, the community, and the rehabilitation of criminal offenders /Thomas P. O'Connor, editor.
     p. cm.
"Co-published simultaneously as Journal of offender rehabilitation, volume 35, numbers 3/4 2002."
Includes bibliographical references and index.
     ISBN 0-7890-1976-0 (hard : alk. paper) – ISBN 0-7890-1977-9 (pbk : alk. paper)
1. Criminals–Rehabilitation. 2. Religion and social problems. 3. Religious work with prisoners.
I. O'Connor, Thomas P. II. Journal of offender rehabilitation.
     HV9276 .R445 2003
     365'.66–dc21
                                          2002152630

Indexing, Abstracting & Website/Internet Coverage

This section provides you with a list of major indexing & abstracting services. That is to say, each service began covering this periodical during the year noted in the right column. Most Websites which are listed below have indicated that they will either post, disseminate, compile, archive, cite or alert their own Website users with research-based content from this work. (This list is as current as the copyright date of this publication.)

Abstracting, Website/Indexing Coverage . . . . Year When Coverage Began

- *CNPIEC Reference Guide: Chinese National Directory of Foreign Periodicals* **1996**

- *Criminal Justice Abstracts* **1986**

- *Criminal Justice Periodical Index* **1982**

- *e-psyche, LLC <www.e-psyche.net>* **1999**

- *ERIC Clearinghouse on Counseling and Student Services (ERIC/CASS)* **1983**

- *Expanded Academic ASAP <www.galegroup.com>* **1999**

- *Family & Society Studies Worldwide <www.nisc.com>* **1996**

- *Family Violence & Sexual Assault Bulletin* **1992**

- *FINDEX <www.publist.com>* **1999**

- *Gay & Lesbian Abstracts <www.nisc.com>* **2001**

(continued)

(continued)

Special Bibliographic Notes related to special journal issues (separates) and indexing/abstracting:

- indexing/abstracting services in this list will also cover material in any "separate" that is co-published simultaneously with Haworth's special thematic journal issue or DocuSerial. Indexing/abstracting usually covers material at the article/chapter level.
- monographic co-editions are intended for either non-subscribers or libraries which intend to purchase a second copy for their circulating collections.
- monographic co-editions are reported to all jobbers/wholesalers/approval plans. The source journal is listed as the "series" to assist the prevention of duplicate purchasing in the same manner utilized for books-in-series.
- to facilitate user/access services all indexing/abstracting services are encouraged to utilize the co-indexing entry note indicated at the bottom of the first page of each article/chapter/contribution.
- this is intended to assist a library user of any reference tool (whether print, electronic, online, or CD-ROM) to locate the monographic version if the library has purchased this version but not a subscription to the source journal.
- individual articles/chapters in any Haworth publication are also available through the Haworth Document Delivery Service (HDDS).

Religion, the Community, and the Rehabilitation of Criminal Offenders

CONTENTS

ABOUT THE EDITORS

Thomas P. O'Connor, BCL, BTheol, MS, is administrator of religious services for the Oregon Department of Corrections where he manages and evaluates the implementation and impact of a broad array of faith-based programming and religious services for over 10,000 incarcerated men and women in thirteen prisons around the state. He also serves as president of the Center for Social Research in Maryland, an organization that assists government and non-profit agencies in the development and evaluation of social programs. His degrees are in law, philosophy, theology, and pastoral counseling. An attorney in his native Ireland, he has worked on religious and treatment issues in the U.S. criminal justice system since 1990. Prior to his work in the U.S., he was a friar of the Carmelites (Catholic Religious Order) for nine years, working in Ireland, Scotland, and France. He is a member of the Editorial Advisory Board of the *Journal of Offender Rehabilitation.*

Nathaniel J. Pallone, PhD, editor of the *Journal of Offender Rehabilitation*, is University Distinguished Professor (Psychology), Center of Alcohol Studies, at Rutgers–The State University of New Jersey, where he previously served as dean and as academic vice president.

Religion, the Community, and the Rehabilitation of Criminal Offenders. Pp. 1-9.

Introduction:
Religion-Offenders-Rehabilitation:
Questioning the Relationship

THOMAS P. O'CONNOR

Oregon Department of Corrections

SUMMARY This overview situates the essays and studies in this collection in the current cultural and religious context of faith-based initiatives from the White House and from a number of religious groups that affect the justice and correctional system in the U.S. The paper creates a unity among the articles by organizing them around four different but interconnected levels of inquiry concerning the relationship between religion, the community and offender rehabilitation. First, questions of intelligibility such as, *what is it?* Second, questions of truth such as, *is it so?* Third, questions of ethics such as, *is it good?* Fourth, religious questions such as, *is it loving?* By exploring some of the answers to these questions by the authors, the paper shows how the collection of articles advances our knowledge about the relationship between religion, the community, and offender rehabilitation. In addition, the insights of the authors help to reframe the current public debate about whether there is a positive role for faith-based programs in the justice system to a debate about how to foster and ensure the authenticity of that role. *[Article copies available for a fee from The Haworth Document Delivery Service: 1-800-HAWORTH. E-mail address: <getinfo@ haworthpressinc.com> Website: <http://www.HaworthPress.com> © 2002 by The Haworth Press, Inc. All rights reserved.]*

KEYWORDS Religion, faith communities, rehabilitation of offenders, faith-based initiatives

One cannot overestimate the role of religion in shaping the character and mission of the American penal system. Religion has taken its place beside other cultural forces–mythical, political, economic, philosophical, sexual, familial, racial–in an ongoing public discourse around crime, power, justice, and social order that has created and shaped the various systems of punishment and rehabilitation that have operated in this country. This interplay between religion and the developing U.S. penal system has been part of a more general dialogue between religion and culture that is essentially historical in nature in that it takes its meaning from and reflects the broad social forces of a given culture at a particular time. These broad social forces inform the operation of any given system of punishment and/or rehabilitation through a developing public discourse about the nature of the human person and community, the nature of crime, the structure of society and the structure of society's response to crime.

The Puritan settlers in the Massachusetts Bay area in the 1600s were Calvinists who placed great emphasis on the concept of obedience to law for it was the external law that helped keep "sinful" human beings in right relationship with God. Although church and state were somewhat separate–church ministers could not be elected to civil office–both church and state answered to the same authority of the Christian scriptures at that time. Thus it became the job of the clergy, the people who were the authorities on the Bible, to keep order among the various communities and to be the final arbiters of the law. So began the history of the dialogue between religion, the community and the justice system in the U.S. This evolving dialogue reached a critical and different point in the late 1800s and early 1900s when a less "sinful" or more optimistic Christian view of the person provided momentum for the construction of the first penitentiaries in America. The Quakers in Pennsylvania believed that penitentiaries and their penal regimes (which included religious instruction, practice and reflection) could bring about an internal spiritual conversion that would restore criminals to virtue and honesty.

Throughout the 19th and 20th centuries, under the influence of Enlightenment ideas and other broad-based cultural and political developments, the U.S. Penal system became less self-consciously directed by religious views of the person and society and developed a more secular and social scientific rationale to guide its development. This viewpoint, which tended to rely on reason alone, helped to change "penitentiaries" first to "reformatories" and then to "correctional institutions" that relied on a varying mixture of punishment and treatment programs to bring about rehabilitation.

Today, however, there is an emerging public discourse, which is at times contentious, about whether society might benefit from recovering a more explicit role for religion in addressing issues of crime, punishment, and rehabilitation. Indications of the diversity and vitality of this latest chapter in the religious-rehabilitation-punishment dialogue include: the formation by President Bush of a White House Office for Faith-Based and Community Partnerships in the first two weeks of his term; a call from the U.S. Catholic bishops (recently endorsed by the Pope on American soil) for an end to capital punishment; the growth of the restorative justice movement which often draws on Biblical notions of justice; the widespread influence of Islamic, Native American and other religious practices such as Transcendental and Buddhist meditation among the prison population; and the growth of faith-based prisons or prison units in several states such as Texas, Ohio, and the Federal prison system which explicitly place the role of religion at the center of the correctional process. One could easily argue that society has arrived at another critical point in the dynamic relationship between faith, crime, and rehabilitation.

Twelve years ago when I began to work directly on the topics of religion and spirituality and their interaction with correctional systems in this country, there were very few empirical or academic studies that dealt directly with the question of spiritual development and offender rehabilitation. Now, a new body of research on this topic is forming as the academic community seeks to keep pace with and inform current developments in the ongoing dialogue between religion and corrections. This collection of articles represents that growing body of research through the discoveries and thoughts of a number of distinguished scholars from a variety of disciplines. The articles in this collection are organized around four different but interconnected levels of inquiry.

- The first level of inquiry or questioning seeks to understand or develop ideas about the phenomenon: what is the current nature of the relationship between religion, the community and rehabilitation? Answers to this type of question give us a variety of conceptual ways of understanding the topic.
- The second level of questioning asks: which of the variety of possible ways of understanding the phenomenon are true or correct? Does the relationship work the way people think it works? This second level of questioning raises the need for empirical or critical studies that move beyond and test descriptive studies and the hypotheses they raise. For example, does a prisoner's interaction with religion actually result in better adjustment to prison life?

- Having discovered something about the impact, truth or reality of the relationship we need to ask: is this relationship a good one? This third level of questioning concerns the ethical or moral nature of the relationship, between religion and corrections. For instance, this level of questioning could take us into the debate over values between people who view issues of church and state differently in society.
- The final or fourth level of questioning carries us beyond the moral realm and into the religious realm when we ask: is the relationship a loving one? All of the major world religions promote love as a central religious act and so if we are to understand the relationship between religion, the community and corrections from a religious perspective we must ask: does the interaction with religious concepts and groups make the justice system and those who are affected by it more loving? Or, to put it another way, is there anything truly religious about the phenomenon we are seeking to understand?

The papers in this volume therefore begin to ask four kinds of questions about the relationship between religion, the community and offender rehabilitation: First, questions of intelligibility such as, *what is it?* Second, questions of truth such as, *is it so?* Third, questions of ethics such as, *is it good?* Fourth, religious questions such as, *is it loving?*

The first five articles tell us a great deal about the nature of the relationship between religion and corrections today. *O'Connor and Perreyclear* reveal that religion in corrections is extremely varied and extensive. Almost 50% (779 of 1597) of the prison population in a large medium-to-maximum security prison for men in South Carolina attended, at varying levels of frequency, more than 800 religious services or meetings that were offered during a one-year period. These services were offered by a large variety of denominational and religious groups including various Protestant denominations, Catholics, Jehovah Witnesses, Muslims, and Alcoholics Anonymous. Because this extensive level of faith-based programming is largely conducted by trained volunteers from the community under the guidance of prison chaplains, it costs far less than most other correctional programming–$150 to $250 compared to $12,000 to $14,000 per person served.

Dammer uses an ethnographic methodology to explore some of the reasons why inmates attend religious services in such high numbers. According to a consensus of prisoners and correctional staff, the reasons for religious involvement differ among inmates across a "sincere" to "insincere" continuum. People who are sincere in their religious practice derive motivation, direction and meaning for their life, hope for the future, peace of mind, positive self-esteem and a change in lifestyle. As one inmate stated, "Religion is a guide to not get out of hand, it gives you a straight path." Insincere people practice religion for different reasons: to gain protection, to meet other inmates, to interact with women volunteers and to gain access to prison resources. Relating these findings to deprivation theory, Dammer theorizes that religion helps to mitigate the psychological and physical deprivations of being incarcerated for both the sincere and insincere religious practitioner.

Sundt, Dammer, and *Cullen* explain and elucidate the historical and contemporary role of the prison chaplain in bringing about the potentially positive relationship between religion and offender rehabilitation. Chaplains do this through their direct ministry and by bringing the community into the prisons when they organize volunteer religious services. We learn from a national study that correctional chaplains are well educated and experienced in correctional work. They also focus on the rehabilitative aspects of their work, and use treatment methods that have been associated with reducing recidivism.

Dix-Richardson's and *Close's* social context approach documents the way in which race, religion, and inmate culture have worked together to foster growth among the various traditions in the prison system that claim a relationship to Islam. They tell of the role played by the Nation of Islam in changing some of the discriminatory and unethical practices of the penal system toward non-Christian religions and African-Americans. At first, Nation of Islam adherents were basically denied the right to practice their religion until their successful lawsuits were instrumental in establishing the right of all prisoners to practice the religion of their choice. They posit that Islam continues to exist behind the prison walls in part because it helps African-American inmates to address the economic, social, and political inequalities they face.

In a second article by *Dix-Richardson*, we also learn that this history of interaction between Islam and offenders has been different for African-American women who have not been as involved as men in the Muslim faith. She examines the different social and religious contexts that exist for female and male African-American prisoners both before and during their incarceration. As compared to men in the African-American community, women are more likely to attend Christian church services and to gain status in those churches. Thus they have more to lose should they convert to Islam. Other factors, such as different experiences with racial issues, the lack of experience with Islamic female role models, and a comparative lack of access to Islamic prison ministry opportunities may also affect the disparity between male and female involvement.

All the opening papers suggest that given their understanding of the nature of the relationship, religion should have a positive influence on offender rehabilitation. The next set of articles addresses the question of whether or not this is so. Does religion influence rehabilitation? *Clear* and *Sumter* give an intriguing and nuanced affirmation to the question of whether religion works to help offenders adjust in positive ways to prison. Overall, high religiosity among inmates in their study of 20 prisons in 12 states around the country was related to fewer in-prison infractions and to better overall psychological adjustment (via less depression) in somewhat surprising ways. In some prisons religiosity was related to better infraction rates but not to better psychological adjustment, and vice versa. In other words, the positive effects of religion on adjustment were prison specific and the article concludes with a discussion of the individual and situational factors that might explain this finding.

Benda and *Toombs* argue that religiosity among young offenders in a group-camp situation is not an isolated variable but one that interacts with many other variables such as attachment to caregivers. Benda and Toombs build a model of how these different variables interact and find that religion is indeed part of a model that explains reductions in juvenile delinquency. As indicated, O'Connor and Perreyclear also addressed the question of whether or not religion facilitates rehabilitation, finding an inverse relationship between level of religious involvement among inmates and in-prison infractions. Findings by Clear and Sumter seem congruent, since the amount of involvement in religion or religious meetings varied inversely with infractions, even when controlling for a number of demographic and criminal risk variables by means of logistic regression analysis. Together, these articles make a strong case that religion does indeed "work" to influence rehabilitation in positive ways.

In the final paper in this section, *Ellis* assesses whether religious affiliation prevents delinquency by investigating denominational differences in self-reported criminal behavior in a large sample of North American college students. Students who identified with conservative Protestant denominations had lower rates of illegal drug use when compared with members of other groups, including atheists/agnostics. But Ellis also finds that there were few other differences in offending across denominations, particularly among males. His findings call into question the belief that variant religious teachings and denominations have varying, or even substantial, effects on core criminal offenses. It may be that only so-called "victimless" crimes like illicit drug use are deterred by religiosity.

The third and final set of articles in this collection tend to relate more to ethical questions and questions of compassion or love. *Skotnicki* challenges researchers who are studying religion among prisoners to reflect on whether or not their standard sociological research methods are good enough or sufficient to reveal the reality they purport to study. Skotnicki uses methodological insights from social philosophy and hermeneutics about how one should properly approach the study of religion to show that some studies that claim to describe the religious experience of prisoners actually are more descriptive of the worldview of the researchers and conceal the religious voice of the prisoners.

Jensen and *Gibbons* use research methods (as did Dammer) that endeavor to address some of the concerns that Skotnicki raises and they seek to allow ex-inmates in the process of reentry to speak about how their religious experience assisted them in that process. The authors give us a fascinating account of how the subjects in their study work with themes of forgiveness, shame, and change as they struggle to reintegrate into a society that can actually be rejecting, or at least obstructive, of their efforts to change. For many of the subjects in the study, their religious worldview proved to be an integrative factor that played an important role in their successful reentry process.

The last three articles make a strong case for the central and vital role of community and by implication love in the process of rehabilitation. If the building of community is not an essential part of the criminal justice process then love cannot exist within that process and therefore rehabilitation cannot really take place. *Erickson* describes transformative encounters that take place among a community of educators, prisoners and volunteers who explore social theory and sacred texts together in a way that is liberating for all involved. Erickson points out how some of the standard rituals of justice are neither good nor loving for they only serve to degrade people. In contrast, the program run by the New York Theological Seminary for inmates at Sing-Sing Prison has found a way to develop a mutual relationship of dignity and respect among teachers and students with indications of good results for ex-inmates in terms of reduced recidivism (and increased employment). *Gorringe* also uses a religious perspective to question the morality and level of compassion exhibited by the criminal justice system as it seeks to rehabilitate prisoners. Gorringe shows how an abuse of the Old Testament religious ritual of the Scapegoat and the concepts the ritual embodies can be used to support the removal of a person from community to the detriment of all involved. More authentic readings of scripture, however, suggest the possibility and necessity of enhancing community between people who are outside and inside the prison walls. Gorringe argues that religious notions that enable society to remove prisoners from community are inauthentic because they are based on an incomplete reading of sacred texts. If Christianity is to help society redeem and rehabilitate prisoners, therefore, Christians need to retrieve a fuller understanding of the essentially communal nature of the Christian God and Christian churches.

Again from a Christian perspective, *Grimsrud* and *Zehr* directly question the criminal justice system as to whether or not it is a loving system. The authors find that the justice system is lacking in love because it is dominated by a retributive or punitive understanding of justice that does not meet the criteria for Christian justice according to their reading of the biblical view of justice. To create a truly just, loving, and effective justice system which must heal all elements of the community that are broken by crime including victims and offenders, society must recover an understanding of biblical justice that is far more reconciling than punitive of people, and far more creative than destructive of community between community members, offenders, and victims of crime. The examples and approach of the cases they present in which a justice system is following this healing-of-brokenness approach stand in stark contrast to the approach of so many U.S. justice systems that are caught up in the prison-building boom.

The public debate fostered by President Bush's faith-based initiative has suffered, in my experience, from two generalized sources of error. First, a tendency by some commentators to exaggerate the positive nature of research findings about the impact of faith-based programs. Second, a tendency to claim that faith-based programs are the only programs that "work." There is absolutely no support for either of these positions in the research literature. Therefore, in times of Presidential and cultural initiatives for recovering a more explicit role for religion in addressing issues of crime, punishment and rehabilitation, it is all the more important for academics across all of the human sciences to help inform public debate and policy on every aspect of the interplay of these forces. It is vital that the public have a thorough understanding of what the interplay is, know whether and to what degree the interplay is effective, know whether the interplay is both moral and loving. Collectively, the authors have advanced our knowledge at each of these levels of questioning. Perhaps more importantly, however, the carefully researched insights of the authors help to reframe the current public debate from whether there is a positive role for faith-based programs in the justice system to a debate about how to foster and ensure the authenticity of that role.

AUTHOR'S NOTE

Tom O'Connor is an administrator of religious services for the Oregon Department of Corrections where he manages and evaluates the implementation and impact of a broad array of faith-based programming and religious services for over 10,000 incarcerated men and women in 13 prisons around the state. He also serves as president of the Center for Social Research in Maryland, an organization that assists government and non-profit agencies in the development and evaluation of social programs. Tom is an attorney from Ireland who has worked on religious and treatment issues in the U.S. criminal justice system for the past 12 years. Prior to his work in the U.S., Tom was a Carmelite friar (Catholic Religious Order) for nine years, working in Ireland, Scotland, and France. He has degrees in law, philosophy, theology, and pastoral counseling. He has published articles on religion and corrections and has presented papers at the American Sociological Association, American Psychological Association, and the American Society of Criminology. He is completing PhD dissertation research at the Catholic University of America, Washington, DC, on "Religion and Culture in the American Penal System–A Sociological and Hermeneutical Study of the Influence of Religion on the Rehabilitation of Inmates."

The author thanks Crystal Parikh and Frank Quillard, who made a substantial contribution to the organization of this collection of articles, and Aislinn Adams and Joe Garcia for their assistance.

Address correspondence to Thomas P. O'Connor, Oregon Department of Corrections, Religious Services, 2575 Center Street NE, Salem, OR 97310-0470 (E-mail: tom.p.oconnor@doc.state.or.us).

Religion, the Community, and the Rehabilitation of Criminal Offenders. Pp. 11-33.

Prison Religion in Action and Its Influence on Offender Rehabilitation

THOMAS P. O'CONNOR

Oregon Department of Corrections

MICHAEL PERREYCLEAR

Center for Social Research, Silver Spring, Maryland

SUMMARY A theory of religious conversion, social attachment, and social learning guides this study of prison religion and its influence on the rehabilitation of adult male offenders. The study found the religious involvement of inmates in a large medium/maximum security prison in South Carolina was extremely varied and extensive. During a one-year period 49% of the incarcerated men (779 out of 1,579) attended at least one religious service or program. Over 800 religious services or meetings, across many different denominations and religious groups, were held during the year. Two prison chaplains, four inmate religious clerks and 232 volunteers who donated about 21,316 hours of work to the prison (the equivalent of 11 full-time paid positions) made this high level of programming possible. The estimated yearly cost of these religious services was inexpensive at between $150 to $250 per inmate served; in contrast, other effective correctional programs cost around $14,000 per person. Controlling for a number of demographic and criminal history risk factors, logistic regression found an inverse relationship between intensity of religious involvement and the presence or absence of in-prison infractions. As religious involvement increased the number of inmates with infractions decreased. The findings of the study provide greater insight into the nature of religion in prison setting and support the view that religion can be an important factor in the process of offender rehabilitation. *[Article copies available for a fee from The Haworth Document Delivery Service: 1-800-HAWORTH. E-mail address: <getinfo@haworthpressinc.com>*

KEYWORDS Religious conversion, social attachment, social learning, prison religion, offender rehabilitation

There is a deeply held belief among many in the U.S. that religion plays a profound and necessary role in the creation and maintenance of a moral and law-abiding community. Indeed this kind of belief in the social effects of religious practice has inspired a great deal of religiously motivated social action aimed at rehabilitating criminals in the U.S. and was influential in the very creation of the U.S. prison system (Colson, 1979; Colson & Van Ness, 1988; McKelvey, 1977; O'Connor & Parikh, 1998; Skotnicki, 1992). This study takes that belief in the efficacy of religion seriously and examines the influence of prison religion on the rehabilitation of adult prison inmates. Is there, in fact, a relationship between religion and the rehabilitation of prisoners and what is the nature of that relationship?

There is no doubt that religion is widely practiced among the nearly two million prisoners in the U.S. Almost every prison has a chaplain who presides over the constitutional right of incarcerated people to practice their religion, and a 1991 survey found that about one out of every three inmates (32%) participate in worship services, Bible study groups and other religious activities, making religious involvement one of the most common forms of "programming " in U.S. state prisons (U.S. Department of Justice, 1993). Despite the extensive historical influence and widespread practice of religion in prisons, very little research of good methodological quality has been done on the meaning and practice of religion in prison, or on whether that religious practice actually contributes to the rehabilitation of offenders. Reviews of the criminological literature point out that while a substantive body of work has been published on the influence of religion on the level of crime in the general population, especially among juveniles, there has been little published that directly concerns the influence of religion on the rehabilitation of inmates or ex-offenders, especially among adults (Clear et al., 1992; Gartner et al., 1990; Johnson, 1984; Sumter & Clear, 1998).

In general, the reviews of the broader literature on religion and the prevalence of crime in the general community conclude that while most studies have found a significant inverse relationship between religious involvement and crime, the methodological weaknesses of these studies tend to make their findings somewhat inconclusive (Baier, 2001; Ellis, 1985; Evans, Cullen, Dunaway, & Burton, 1995; Gartner, Larson, & Allen, 1991; Knudten & Knudten, 1971; Sloane & Potvin, 1986; Tittle & Welch, 1983). For example, Sumter (1998, 30) found that 18 of 23 studies published since 1985 produced evidence of an inverse relationship between different measures of religiosity and various indicators of deviance but summarized her findings in the following way:

> Although associations have been detected, the studies have not been successful in establishing evidence of causal relations between these measures which primarily results from two inherent problems (research design and measurement error) and other methodological flaws in studying religiosity and deviance.

The few studies that have looked directly at the influence of religion on adult offender rehabilitation tend to follow the same pattern as the wider body of literature–some evidence of a significant relationship between religious involvement and rehabilitation, accompanied by methodological weaknesses that leave unanswered questions and inconclusive findings. These studies of the influence of religion on adult offender rehabilitation all tended to use either in-prison infractions or recidivism as their measure of rehabilitation. Three studies have provided evidence of a positive relationship between religion and offender rehabilitation, two studies failed to find evidence of such a relationship, and one yielded mixed evidence.

RELATED STUDIES

Johnson (1984) found neither a significant correlation nor relationship in a path analysis between self-reported religiosity, church attendance, or prison chaplain's rating of inmate religiosity and amount of time spent in confinement for disciplinary infractions (controlling for race, age, offense type, maximum sentence, denomination, and religious conversion) among 782 men in a minimum security prison who were serving their first term of incarceration.

Young et al., however, did find a significant long-term impact of a Federal prison ministry program known as the Washington, DC Discipleship Seminars on adult criminal recidivism. These Seminars were sponsored and run by Prison Fellowship Ministries (PFM) which was founded in 1975 by Charles W. Colson, a former presidential aide to Richard M. Nixon, following his own incarceration in Federal prison on a conviction of obstructing justice. Young et al. identified 180 men and women who had participated in the seminars and used a stratified proportional probability sampling method to select a matched control group of 185 Federal inmates from a cohort of 2,289 inmates who were released around the same time as the PFM inmates. The two groups were carefully matched on age, race, gender, and Salient Factor Score (a risk index that is predictive of recidivism). The study examined the re-arrest patterns of the two groups over a period of eight to 14 years after each person's release from prison. Logistic regression analyses with recidivism (yes or no) as the dependent variable, controlling for race, gender, age at release, risk level, and time on the street, showed that the PFM group had a significantly lower rate of recidivism.

Survival analysis also showed that the PFM group who did recidivate took significantly longer to recidivate compared to the comparison group recidivists. Further analyses revealed that most of the program effects were concentrated in PFM women (white and black) and in white PFM men who were in the low risk of recidivism category. Compared to their respective controls religious women had much lower rates of re-arrest than the religious men. No impact of the program could be discerned among white men in the high risk category or among black men across all risk categories. These findings indicate the importance of controlling for gender, race and risk factors when examining the influence of religion on offender rehabilitation. Beside the issue of self-selection or self-motivation, which affects all the studies on this topic because of the inability to randomly assign subjects to religious and non-religious groups, an important methodological weakness of this study lay in the fact that the subjects in the religious program group were selected for participation according to strict criteria. This meant that the PFM group could have succeeded because the basis on which they were selected rendered them prone to succeed rather than because of their participation in the program. However, the essence of the selection criteria was that the subjects be heavily involved in religious participation prior to the program. Thus the subjects in this study were highly involved in religious activity and it may be that the intensity of their religious involvement combined with the program was responsible for their success.

Clear and his co-investigators (1992, 1995) also found a significant relationship between religiosity and rehabilitation. Clear's study used in-prison adjustment (a psychological measure of how well an inmate was able to cope with the deprivations and difficulties of prison life) and in-prison infractions as its measure of rehabilitation. Clear and his associates studied 769 men in 20 prisons across 12 states in the U.S. chosen to represent different regions of the country as well as different security levels of prisons. This was a non-random sample of subjects as each subject volunteered to be in the study. Clear et al. reasoned that religion might interact with other personal and situational variables within the prison context to affect in-prison adjustment as well as in-prison infractions. Religiosity was measured using a self-report instrument that included 33 questions from the Hunt and King scale (a measure of religious beliefs through assessing symbolic religious commitment) and a set of 12 questions about what the inmates would do in different prison situations of conflict. The subjects also answered questions on depression, self-mastery, self-esteem, demographics and criminal histories. In-prison adjustment was measured using the Wright (1985) adjustment scale. Infractions were measured by the self-reported number of disciplinary infractions. Although adjustment and infractions scores were significantly correlated with each other, analysis showed that these two variables were measuring different constructs.

Clear et al. found strong significant correlations between high religiosity and both adjustment and infractions at a bivariate level. Controlling for demographic and criminal history variables ordinary least squares regression revealed that high religiosity directly predicted fewer infractions and indirectly predicted better adjustment. Religiosity was one of the strongest predictors of the number of infractions along with variables like number of priors and age. Religiosity fell out of the regression equation on adjustment when the control variables were introduced, but was indirectly related to better adjustment through depression. Of particular interest is that the study findings were "prison specific"–the religious effects on adjustment and infractions were found in some but not all of the prisons. Furthermore, the two effects were not found together, but depending on the prison there was either a religious effect on adjustment *or* on infractions. Religious factors, therefore, can interact with other variables and produce different results. This means that context is a vitally important variable for the study of the relationship between religion and rehabilitation. A second study by Sumter (1999) using some of the data from the Clear et al. (1992) study found that a religious vs. non-religious dichotomy did not predict post-release success for the subjects. However, this study did find that the more motivated offenders were involved in religious activities in prison and the more they believed in a transcendent God, the less likely they were to be rearrested after release to the community.

A study by O'Connor, Yang, Ryan, Wright, and Parikh (1996) found that religious involvement had no relationship to the presence or absence of in-prison misconducts but had some relationship to recidivism. This study controlled for self-selection bias by using a multivariate matched sampling procedure to draw a one-to-one matched control group from over 40,000 inmates from the general population based on their propensity to self-select into the religious program. Over 200 men who had participated in a religious ministry program in four New York prisons did not differ from the matched comparison group on whether or not they had a prison misconduct. This study also compared the prison ministry and comparison groups on recidivism and found no overall difference between the two groups on whether or not they were rearrested or on time to rearrest. The study did, however, find some significant differences in recidivism, when it compared those who had high rates of ministry participation to those who had low or no ministry participation and controlled for level of risk of recidivism. A weakness in this study was the relatively small amount of information presented on the overall religious participation of the program group and the complete absence of information on the religious participation of the comparison groups. Because the study had no way of telling for sure that the comparison group was not involved in religious activities the study may even have been comparing religiously involved inmates to other religiously involved inmates.

A secondary analysis of the data from the O'Connor et al. study by Johnson, Larson, and Pitts (1997) was essentially confirmatory and also found no evidence of a significant overall difference between Prison Fellowship participants and "non-religious" controls on either in-prison infraction or rearrest within one year. The Johnson group did find some evidence of a significant relationship between high program attendance and lower rates of recidivism.

Pass (1999) did not find any influence of self-reported religiosity on in-prison infractions among 345 randomly selected inmates from the prison population at Eastern Correctional Facility in New York. Subjects were asked about their agreement or disagreement with three statements: (1) Religion is important; (2) Religion gives people special privileges; and (3) Some people in religious groups joined for protection. Pass also used a 10-item "Intrinsic Religious Motivation Scale" (Hoge, 1972) to measure religious motivations. The motivation scale seeks to measure how much a person's religiosity is motivated by internal reasons (using religion to find meaning in life) or external reasons (using religion to develop social relationships) (Hoge, 1972). Pass hypothesized that only internalized religion would lead to a reduction of in-prison infractions.

Pass found that a higher number of people reported a religious affiliation since prison than before prison and fully one third of the sample reported a change of affiliation once in prison. Using ANOVA, Pass also found that religious motivation scores differed significantly among the religious groups. Muslims were the most internally religiously motivated, followed by Protestants, Other religionists, Catholics, and those with No religion. Logistic regression revealed that levels of internal motivation were not significantly related to the presence or absence of infractions within a three-month period prior to the survey when religious affiliation, importance of religion, views on protection and privilege, race, age, educational level, and first offender versus multiple offender status were controlled for.

Each of the foregoing studies has strengths and weaknesses. As a group, the studies have helped us to understand more about the nature and impact of prison religion. Prison religion varies in its meaning and practice across individuals, prisons, and different religious groups. Intensity of involvement (or "dosage " in treatment jargon) seems to be a crucial factor in whether or not it has an impact on offender rehabilitation. Furthermore, other variables such as gender, race, risk level for recidivism, and prison context influence both the kind and depth of impact that religion may have on rehabilitation. Certain things are needed to make these intimations of how religion "works" more conclusive: future studies need to be more informed by theoretical considerations, become more precise in their measurements of religion, and model the impact of religion on rehabilitation using better research designs and statistical methods.

The present study seeks to build upon the knowledge gained in previous studies of religion and offender rehabilitation by overcoming many of the methodological difficulties that rendered their findings somewhat inconclusive. The study sought to determine whether level of religious involvement influenced rehabilitation as measured by in-prison infraction. The setting was Lieber Correctional Institution (Lieber), a large medium/maximum security prison for men in South Carolina. During 1996, we worked with the South Carolina Department of Corrections (SCDC) Research division, the Pastoral Care division, and the chaplain's office at Lieber Correctional Institute (LCI) to collect sign-up sheets for every religious activity that occurred in the prison. The chaplains and their clerks at Lieber prison entered this data into a computerized system that maintained a count of times each person attended any religious program by month. In addition, they recorded what activities were held on what dates of every month. (There may be some minor errors in the data, because inmates did not always sign in when they attended programs, and occasionally volunteer program leaders failed to turn in sign-in sheets. But chaplains and their clerks made every effort to monitor the data, and we feel satisfied that the data adequately represent the actual attendance of inmates at religious programming.)

The SCDC Division for Resource and Information Management then provided us with additional demographic, criminal history and infraction data on all 1597 inmates who spent any part of 1996 in LCI. (Many who do not attend services may nonetheless be "religious" persons; hence, this study is not a study of religiousness per se but instead of religious involvement.) This was the entire population of inmates at Lieber in 1996 and included both those inmates who had and who had not attended religious programs. Confidentiality was maintained by using the data in aggregate form only. This design for collecting data meant that there was no "selection bias" in our data, since participation was voluntary. Selection, after inmates had volunteered, proceeded without specific criteria. Because there was nothing resembling either "random selection" or "random assignment" into "religious" or "non-religious" groups once inmates had volunteered to participate, we nonetheless need to recognize the likely link between self-selection and motivation.

GUIDING THEORY

The theory underlying the study is based on a theological understanding of religious conversion and faith development (Fowler, 1981; Lonergan, 1972) and a criminological understanding of how rehabilitation comes about through a process of social attachment (Sampson & Laub, 1993) and social learning (Andrews, 1995; Bandura, 1977). The theory of religious conversion holds that we are spiritual beings as well as physical, emotional, social, and intellectual beings. Our spiritual nature means that we are capable and desirous of having an ultimate and meaningful sense of connectedness or relationship with other people, our world, and God. The extent to which we have not fully achieved this connection or union is the extent to which we are in need of religious conversion or development. Saint Paul gives us a Christian understanding of the source of religious conversion when he says "The love of God has been poured out in our hearts through the Holy Spirit who has been given to us" (Rm:5:5). Just as a parent's love awakens life within a child, God's free gift of love is constantly awakening and deepening life within us. From this perspective spirituality is the integrative principle of our lives. One inmate at Lieber prison involved in religious programming seems to be referring to this sense of spiritual conversion or awakening when he says: "Before [prison], it was all me. Now I know life is also about relationships. I have to think of others and God. If you're serious about God, you have to take on the nature of God, and God cares about other people too." The lack of a spirituality was expressed by another inmate who was not religiously involved when he insisted: "Life is dog eat dog, and I will do anything I have to–lie, cheat, steal, or kill–to stay out of here [prison] when I get out." Religious faith and belief can free up a part of who we are, and these inner resources can lead to changed attitudes and behaviors.

Social attachment theory holds that the more attached a person is to the major social institutions of life (family, education, work, politics and religion), the less likely he or she is to commit crime, for he or she has something of value to lose by committing crime. Social learning theory believes that criminal behaviors are learned behaviors in a given social and cultural context. Because criminal behaviors are learned behaviors, offenders are capable of learning noncriminal behaviors should their given context change. Both of these processes–increased social attachment and new social learning–are likely to be accelerated when an inmate becomes immersed in the religious milieu of a prison, for this milieu places an inmate among chaplains and volunteers who are very attached to the major social institutions of life and who are very committed to pro-social learned behaviors. A national study of correctional chaplains found that 79% had a Master's degree or higher. In addition, prison chaplains had an average of 10 years of correctional experience and believed strongly in a philosophy of rehabilitation. The chaplains spent most of their time counseling inmates and used methods of counseling that treatment studies have found to be effective in reducing recidivism. The chaplains were highly-skilled role models and advocates for inmates, and they were also responsible for coordinating the work of the thousands of religiously motivated volunteers who work in prisons (Sundt & Cullen, 1998).

An exploratory study in South Carolina surveyed 82 ministry volunteers and found they were moved to work in the prison system by two major motivations: (1) to act on their faith and (2) to make a difference. When the study compared these volunteers to the general population of the Southeast region, it found that the volunteers had the same gender and ethnicity demographics as the general population, but tended to be older. The volunteers were also more involved than the general population with the major social institutions of life. For example, the volunteers earned more, were more likely to be married (80% versus 54%), had more education (57% versus 23% had some college education), were more involved in politics (86% voted versus 64%), and 90% of the volunteers compared to 30% of the general population went to church once a week or more. The volunteers were also happier than the general population–47% versus 31% "very happy" (O'Connor, Parikh, & Ryan, 1997). In other words, the volunteers were a group of people who had learned how to successfully negotiate and derive satisfaction from the different worlds of work, family, education, politics, and religion. In contrast, offenders tend to have trouble negotiating these areas of life, and we know that problems in these areas are predictive of crime and recidivism. One inmate explained how the modeling of religious volunteers (some of whom were successful ex-offenders) provided him with hope by their example of overcoming adversity:

> I have to come to my own place of healing . . . I've seen myself do some things, or think some things, or say some things, or act in a manner that I know was inappropriate. And still it makes me unhappy. And so, the question still comes to me, why did I do that? So what do they [the volunteers] do? The hope, the hope says that these people [the volunteers] have changed their lives, and if they can do that so can I.

The chaplains and volunteers are a tremendous resource as role models and teachers of the very skills and lifestyles that many offenders lack but desire. It seems natural and theoretically valid from a "what works" correctional treatment point of view to hypothesize that the social attachment and learning which takes place between the chaplains, volunteers and offenders in each area of life, not only in the religious domain, is likely to aid the process of offender rehabilitation. Awakening the religious or spiritual domain in a person brings additional inner hope, motivation, and resources for learning how to address the domains of work, family, education, church and politics in a pro-social manner. Thus our hypothesis for the study was: The greater the level of religious involvement, the greater the influence of religion on the rehabilitation of adult offenders as measured by in-prison infractions.

NATURE AND PRACTICE OF PRISON RELIGION AT LIEBER

During the course of 1996 the chaplain's office recorded 23 different kinds of religious programming at LCI, most of them offered on a weekly basis. These programs include worship services, Bible studies, religious seminars and retreats, alcoholics and narcotics anonymous, and fellowship gatherings. The religious services are offered by many different denominations or church groups such as Catholics, Protestants, and Muslims. Volunteers from outside the prison lead the majority of the programs, while a few are run by the chaplain's office or by inmates themselves. There is a religious program of some kind offered every day of the week. Table 1 lists these religious activities, their general type, the frequency of their meetings, and the total number of meetings held in 1996.

Many of these religious programs attract a similar group of attendees, while a few are notably distinct. Using data from the month of July, those who attended Alcoholics Anonymous were highly likely to also attend Narcotics Anonymous, but both groups were less likely to attend any other religious programming. The Muslim community also tended to be a separate group unto themselves, as did the Jehovah's Witness attendees and Catholics.

During the year, 779 of the 1,597 inmates–49%–attended at least one religious program or service. This is a very high level of religious involvement given that the estimated average attendance at religious services in state prisons throughout the country is only 32% (U.S. Department of Justice, 1993). The fact that Lieber prison is located in the "Bible Belt," a highly churched region of the U.S., probably helps to explain this high level of inmate attendance, together with the fact that the religious program at Lieber seems to be well organized.

Of the total 779 inmates who attended any religious programming, 12% participated mostly in non-Protestant programs, while 88% participated mostly in the Protestant programs. Attendees at any of the Protestant worship services or Bible studies were likely to also attend other Protestant worship services or Bible studies. Using a cut-off correlation of .30 as an indication of a meaningful relationship, the weekend worship services showed relationships with the largest number of other programs and were most highly correlated to each other. That is, inmates who attended one worship service were likely to attend other worship services and also a Bible study or two during the week.

On average, those who went to religious services in Lieber went to about six meetings every month. (Since some of the men entered LCI

☐ **Table 1: Religious Programs at LCI During 1996**

Activity	Type of Program	Meeting Frequency	Number
Alcoholics Anonymous	12-Step	Every Thursday	36
Catholic communion	Worship	First and third Friday	22
Christians in Action	Christian fellowship	3 or 4 times a month	38
Christmas programs	Worship / fellowship	Several in December	6
Evening Light Fellowship	Bible study	Every Saturday (canceled 10/24/96)	40
Faith, Praise and Worship	Bible study	Every Sunday (June to 10/24/96)	20
Full Word Fellowship	Bible study	Every Sunday (canceled 10/24/96)	35
Jehovah's Witness	Education / worship	Every Sunday	51
Kairos Choir	Choir	Approximately twice a week for practice and fellowship	90
Kairos Journey	Bible study	Every Thursday	45
Kairos Reunion	Fellowship	Monthly	13
Kairos weekend	Retreat / worship	Two weekends a year	8
LCI Choir	Choir	Approx. 1 practice and 1 service per week	102
Muslim community	Education / worship	Once to twice a week	50
Narcotics Anonymous	12-Step	Every Tuesday	37
Prison Fellowship Bible Study	Bible study	Every Monday	44
Prison Fellowship seminar	Retreat / fellowship	Three weekends a year	8
Prison Fellowship Starting Line	Retreat / fellowship	One weekend	3
Revival meeting	Evangelism	One weekend	2
Saturday night service	Protestant worship	Every Saturday	46
Sunday morning service	Protestant worship	Every Sunday	50
Sunday night service	Protestant worship	Every Sunday	38
Sunday school	Protestant teaching	Every Sunday	41
Through the Bible in Three Years	Bible study	Every Thursday	41
Wednesday Bible Study	Bible study	Every Wednesday (ended 1/31/1996)	3
TOTAL MEETINGS			**869**

after January 1996 and some left before December of the same year, not everyone had the same numeric opportunity to attend.) In all there were 23 different kinds of religious services or programs operating in the prison. Amazingly, there were more than two religious meetings every single day of the year (a total of 869 meetings). The fact that prison becomes almost like a monastic setting for some inmates can be discerned in a comment from Shawn, one of the inmates at Lieber:

I guess when I was out in the world . . . I was raised where I went to church, was in the church. The difference is out there I didn't have the time to stop, think, study, get a chance to know who Jesus was, and what He was about. Whereas back here you got nothing but time.

The type of spiritual reflection taking place here seems to be about personal transformation or spirituality and not just rote religious attendance.

The religious activities at Lieber were made possible through the services of two full-time prison chaplains, four inmate clerks to the chaplains, several inmate religious leaders, and approximately 232 volunteers from the community. The 232 volunteers donated about 21,316 hours of work to the prison: the equivalent of 11 full-time paid positions. The estimated yearly cost of these religious services could be considered a bargain at about $150 to $250 per inmate served. In contrast, Joan Petersilia estimates that effective correctional programs cost about $14,000 per inmate per year (Petersilia, 1995). Thus, some of the main findings of this study are that religious and spiritual involvement in prison is extremely varied and extensive, and costs the Department of Corrections very little.

FINDINGS ON THE IMPACT OF RELIGION ON INFRACTIONS

When we compared the religious attendees to the non-religious attendees on their demographics and criminal histories, we found some interesting similarities and differences. There were no significant differences between the two groups on marital status, having children, or race. Thirty-five percent of the inmates reported that they had been or were married, over half (60%) reported having at least one child, with a range of 0 to 18, and an average of one, and the majority (68%) were Black, with virtually all of the rest being White. Nor were there any differences on the number of prior sex or violent convictions, the number of current offenses, or the number of current offenses which involved alcohol or drugs.

The religious and non-religious attending groups did differ significantly on the following variables. The religious attenders tended to be younger than the non-religious attenders with an average age of 33 compared to 34, and to be a little more educated with an average of 11 years of education compared to 10 ($p < 05$). The "religious" inmates had an average of five prior convictions, compared to an average of four for the "non-religious," and were more likely both to have a current sex offense (24% versus 15%) and a current violent offense (61% versus 52%). These differences mean that the religious inmates were probably more in need of rehabilitation that the non-religious inmates, as they have more serious criminal histories. In other words, the religious programs were not "creaming" the easiest inmates to work with.

For a variety of reasons, such as new incarcerations, completion of sentences, changes in custody level, lockup, administrative needs, court hearings and parole, inmates are moved in and out of LCI regularly. Therefore, most of the inmates in our study did not spend the entire 365 days of 1996 in LCI. They averaged 230 days, with a range of 0 (full days) to 365. The religious inmates had been in LCI for a significantly longer part of 1996, averaging 276 days, while the rest of the inmates averaged 186 days. This probably means that the longer a man is in a particular prison, the more likely he is to attend religious programming or services at that prison, at least once or twice.

To look at the impact of religious programming, we needed to calculate a rate of attendance at religious programs. We wanted to be able to distinguish between those religious inmates who were highly involved and those who were not so highly involved in religious programs or services. The movement of inmates in and out of LCI and the varying number of religious sessions per month complicated calculating a reasonably accurate rate of attendance at religious programs. The rate needed to reflect the actual number of meetings attended divided by the number that could have possibly been attended during the time that individual was in LCI.

In addition, to look at the impact of the religious programming, we narrowed the window of opportunity to only the time period the person was in LCI following their first appearance at a religious program in 1996. We wanted to be sure that we were only considering infractions that took place after the men had been involved in religious programs. The number of days spent in Lieber was corrected for the "religious" inmates to reflect only the days in the institution since they first attended a religious program. (The estimate of days spent in the institution may be underestimated, because the starting date was measured only to the level of months rather than days. Thus, when a month was subtracted to account for a difference in the beginning of a program, 30 days were lost, when the real number may have been something less than that. However, such an underestimate is consistent across cases and is never more than 30 days.) Therefore, the religious participation rate is the number of religious sessions attended by an individual in 1996 at LCI, divided by the number they personally could have attended since their first appearance at a religious activity in 1996. (We estimated the number of meetings an inmate could possibly attend by adding the number of religious sessions per month from the first month he appeared at a religious meeting through his last month in the prison. The procedure somewhat overestimates, since the person may have had some movement in and out of LCI between their first and last month that prevented attendance, other activities or restrictions may have sometimes prevented attendance, and the first and last month may not have been full months for that person. Overestimating this value means that the rates of attendance may be somewhat below the most accurate value.) By definition, the participation rate of the inmates who did not attend any religious sessions is always zero.

An infraction is any incident of breaking of institution rules for which the inmate is caught and found guilty. It could be anything from assaulting someone, to being caught in a restricted area, to having contraband in one's possession, to escaping. The majority of LCI inmates (78%) had no infractions in 1996. The mean number of infractions is 0.43, with a range of zero to 16. No escape infractions were reported. Only 1% of the inmates incurred an infraction that was classified as violent.

To analyze the impact of religious programming on infractions we took a two-tiered approach. First of all we examined whether a wide variety of variables had any relationship to predicting infractions taking each variable one at a time. As far as possible, given the data we had to work with, we used the literature on infractions and recidivism to guide us in selecting those variables that are known to be in some way related to predicting infractions (Alexander & Chapman, 1981; Andrews et al., 1990; Bailey, 1966; Law, 1993; Motiuk, 1983). Our question was: Does the extent of involvement in religious programming help to predict infractions in addition to other variables that predict infractions? The following characteristics were statistically unrelated to infractions at a bi-variate level: race, self-reported highest level of education completed, count of prior convictions, count of violent prior convictions, use of alcohol or drugs during the commission of a crime, having a current conviction on a sex offense, and having a prior conviction on a sex offense.

Eight non-religious characteristics were significantly related to whether or not a person had infractions. Inmates who had a current conviction on a violent offense were more likely to have an infraction (24%, compared to 18%). The same was true for inmates with any prior violent crime convictions (27%, compared to 20.6%). In addition, the more current convictions an inmate had, the more likely he was to have an infraction. Those who were either currently married or had been at one time were less likely to have an infraction than those who had never been married (13%, compared to 26%). The familial tie of having children was also important. Those with no children were more likely to have an infraction than those who had at least one child (26%, compared to 19%). Age had an inverse relationship with infractions–the older an inmate was, the less likely he was to have had an infraction. Also, the higher maximum sentence length an inmate had and the more days he spent in LCI in 1996, the more likely he was to have an infraction.

Finally, a bi-variate analysis of religious involvement and infractions found two things. First, when religious inmates were compared to non-religious inmates, there was no difference in the propensity to have infractions. Secondly, when we looked at rates of participation in religious programming, higher rates were always associated with less chance of infractions. The more religious programming sessions an inmate attended, the less his chance of having infractions. This gave us a clue to the fact that religious involvement had an impact on infractions. However, these results might be an artifact of the religious inmate's different amounts of time in LCI than the non-religious inmates or to the fact that religious inmates were different from non-religious inmates in certain ways, as pointed out above. We needed to include these non-religious demographic and criminal history variables as controls for religious participation in a multivariate analysis. All items mentioned above, regardless of whether or not they were individually related to the presence of infractions, were included as possible controls in forward conditional logistic regression. We were particularly aware that we needed to control for the time spent in LCI in 1996, since there was a significant difference between the religious and non-religious groups on this important variable.

When we did this and compared all religiously involved inmates who attended any type of religious program to the non-religiously involved inmates, the independent variable did not reach statistical significance to enter the final logistic regression model. That is, there was no difference between the religious and non-religious groups in their likelihood of having an infraction.

However, we did find that the more religious sessions an inmate attended, the less likely he was to have an infraction. Thus, the findings supported our hypothesis. As previous studies have found, the intensity of religious programming seems to help reduce infractions. The impact of religious programming derives not from the fact of attending religious programs but from going to religious programs more often. In

Table 2, the final logistic regression model shows that an inmate's chance of committing an infraction goes down as his rate of attendance at any religious program goes up, within categories of current age, ever married, and days spent in LCI. What Table 2 tells us is that the more religious sessions the men attended the better the chance that they had no infractions.

Logistic regression enables one to say whether or not a variable of interest is related to a dichotomous dependent variable. However, logistic regression is not very helpful when it comes to interpreting the meaning of that relationship. To help us get a glimpse of what it means to say that the more often inmates attended religious programs the less infractions they had, we looked at the percentage of inmates who had little or no religious involvement and found that 21% of them had infractions during the study period. By way of contrast only 11% of those inmates who had a medium or a high level of involvement with religious programs had infractions during the study period. One must exercise caution in interpreting the meaning of these differences, for the model indicates that such a difference may be attributable to a number of variables, including rate of religious participation.

DISCUSSION

The two main findings of the present study are (1) religious practice in the Lieber prison setting was extensive, varied, and inexpensive to conduct; and (2) when a number of demographic and criminal history variables are controlled for, the intensity of religious practice was inversely related to the presence of in-prison infractions.

□ **Table 2: Final Model of Forward Conditional Logistic Regression Analysis of Infractions (Yes/No) by Religious Rate of Participation**

Variable	B	S.E.	Wald	Df	Sig.	R	Exp(B)
Rate of religious participation	−4.3828	1.158	14.3099	1	.0002	−.0906	.0125
Current age	−.0450	.0101	19.9963	1	.0000	−.1095	.5420
Ever married	−.6125	.1737	12.4333	1	.0001	−.0834	
Days spent in LCI	.0062	.0006	104.7743	1	.0000	.2617	1.0063
Constant	−1.1135	.3360	10.9806	1	.0009		

- Model Chi-Square = 187.463, df = 4, Cox & Snell R^2 = .115

These findings expand the literature on religion in corrections by providing the first detailed empirical description of the actual practice of religion in a prison setting, and by deepening our understanding of the influence of religion on rehabilitation. Religious practice in prison can be very extensive with about 50% of inmates attending religious services an average of six times per month. Religious practices spread themselves across more spiritually-based programs such as AA and NA, and more formal religious programs such as worship and Jumuah services that are Protestant, Catholic and Muslim. Because of the heavy involvement of hundreds of volunteers in running these programs they cost as little as $150 to $250 per inmate per year to run. The presence of so many volunteers who gave over 21,000 hours of programming to the prison also means that religious programming is a major source of pro-social role modeling in the prison setting, for these volunteers appear to be very attached to and involved with the major social institutions of life–family, work, education, church and politics. The work of the chaplains, volunteers and religiously involved inmates insures that the life of faith or the spiritual dimension of life is brought into being in the prison setting. Religion may help to bring into the correctional setting the much needed element of hope and motivation to change, and introduce important ethical and religious ideas of forgiveness and the love of one's neighbor. The involvement of members of the "outside" community also helps to normalize the prison experience and ameliorates the sense of isolation from the community that incarceration brings. Isolating people from the community can actually cut off offenders from the pro-social sources of behavior and support they need to learn how to live without crime, and such a practice of isolation is directly contrary to most theologies which emphasize the importance of active participation in a faith community in helping people live a good life. The pro-social benefits of this human interaction between volunteers and offenders in a prison setting ought not to be underestimated.

If inmates are to benefit from this human interaction and communal experience, it seems they must become involved at a certain level of intensity. Mere attendance at the odd worship service, Bible study, or Jumuah prayer simply is not enough to bring about change or development. As with other correctional programs, religion is not a panacea, rather religion works for some people in some circumstances. One of these circumstances seems to be a certain level of attendance at the religious programs.

The findings suggest that correctional theory and practice ought to include active religious participation among those factors that are predictive of in-prison infractions such as age, criminal history and other risk factors like attachment to work and family. And because research is finding that the factors that are predictive of in-prison infractions also predict recidivism, the findings also suggest that religious participation may be an important variable in predicting recidivism. In short, the study supports the widely held view that religious involvement is positive as an influence on the rehabilitation of adult offenders.

As is usual, there are methodological limitations to this study, which means that we must interpret its findings carefully. The major threat to the validity of these findings arises from what is called self-selection bias or specification error and the fact that the subjects in our two groups–religious and non-religious attenders–were not randomly assigned, in the experimental fashion, to those two groups. This means that we may have failed to measure both groups on some crucial variable that relates to reduced levels of infractions, such as motivation to change, and so have a spurious effect with regard to religious participation and reduced levels of infractions.

Following Heckman, we believe that the lack of random assignment is not a critical methodological limitation. "Selection bias arises because of missing data on the common factors affecting participation and outcomes. The most convincing way to solve the selection problem is to collect better data. This option has never been discussed in the recent debates over the merits of experimental and econometric approaches and has only recently been exercised" (Heckman, 1979). Collecting better data is precisely what we did in this study. We were able to account for the religious participation level of a very large number of inmates–1,597 over a one-year period–in a setting or context that was the same for each of the subjects over that one-year period. Unlike previous studies, which either relied on self-reported religiosity or very incomplete measures of participation in religious programming, we tied our measure of religiosity to a concrete behavioral measure and gained a complete picture of the in-prison religious programming involved for each of the subjects in our study. In addition, we collected as much information as possible on the demographics and criminal history risk factors of our subjects to control for all the factors that might influence participation and outcomes.

One important variable that we were not able to collect information on was involvement in other programming during the study period. The lack of other program involvement data is a weakness in the design of our study. Such involvement could be related to participation in religious programs and to our outcome variable of infractions. Unfortunately, this data was simply not available. However, this lack of information is not crucial in this study because, due to budget cutbacks, Lieber had very little programming available beyond basic work assignments. Given the foregoing limitations, our research design was methodologically sound. Our study was guided by a theory, collected thorough data, used a quasi-experimental design that included a longitudinal element so as to look at the issue of causality, and used multivariate statistical measures and controls. In summary, the research design strengthens the findings of the study.

The study looked at religion from a global perspective and did not make any distinction between different types of religious programming among different religious groups. We suspect the influence of different types of religious programming on rehabilitation is not uniform. Undoubtedly, based on such factors as training, style, content, frequency and quality of leaders or presenters, there will be different effects of various religious programs on the rehabilitation process of offenders. We leave the question of the differential impact of different kinds of religious programs to future studies. What is valuable about this study is that we were able to discern patterns of a global religious impact on reducing infractions. In this way, the study supports the widely held cultural belief in the U.S. that religion plays a role in the creation and maintenance of a law-abiding community, and argues that the religious variable is an important one that must be considered in the mix of variables and "best correctional practices" related to offender rehabilitation.

The theology of redemption essentially examines the process of turning evil into good or transforming a bad situation into a good situation. Rehabilitation is often thought of as the movement of a person from committing infractions or crime to not committing infractions or crime. But of course, such a purely functional definition of rehabilitation does not do justice to the profound change that can take place in a person's life or situation as he or she turns from crime. Ultimately religion in a correctional setting seeks to influence offenders not only to desist from crime but also to grow in living well and justly. That such a transformation from selfishness to self-giving may be taking place among the religiously-involved men incarcerated at Lieber can be discerned in the findings of this study and the words of one of the subjects:

> Before [being in prison], it was all me. Now I know life is also about relationships. I have to think of others and God. If you're serious about God, you have to take on the nature of God, and God cares about other people too.

REFERENCES

Alexander, J., & Chapman, W. R. (1981). *Adjustments to prison: A review of inmate characteristics associated with misconducts, victimization, and self injury in confinement.* (Classification Improvement Project, Working paper 10, 1986. Prison Crowding: Search for Functional Correlations): State of New York Department of Correctional Services.

Andrews, D. A. (1995). The psychology of criminal conduct and effective treatment. In J. McGuire (Ed.), *What Works: Reducing Criminal Reoffending* (pp. 35-62). New York: John Wiley.

Andrews, D. A., Zinger, I., Hoge, R., Bonta, J., Gendreau, P., & Cullen, F. T. (1990). Does correctional treatment work? A clinically relevant and psychologically informed meta-analysis. *Criminology, 28,* 369-404.

Baier, C. (2001). If you love me, teach my commandments: A meta-analysis of the effect of religion on crime. *Research in Crime & Delinquency, 38* (1), 3-21.

Bailey, W. C. (1966). Correctional outcome: An evaluation of 100 reports. *Journal of Criminal Law, Criminology, and Police Science, 57,* 153-160.

Bandura, A. (1977). *Social Learning Theory.* Englewood Cliffs, NJ: Prentice-Hall, Inc.

Clear, T., & Myhre, M. (1995). A study of religion in prison. *IARCA Journal on Community Corrections, 6* (6), 20-25.

Clear, T., Stout, B., Dammer, H., Kelly, L., Hardyman, P., & Shapiro, C. (1992). *Prisoners, Prisons, and Religion: Final Report.* Newark, NJ: School of Criminal Justice, Rutgers University.

Colson, C. (1979). *Life Sentence.* Richmond, VA: Chosen Books.

Colson, C., & Van Ness, D. (1988). *Convicted: New Hope of Ending America's Crime Crisis.* Westchester, IL: Crossway Books.

Ellis, L. (1985). Religiosity and criminality: Evidence and explanations surrounding complex relationships. *Sociological Perspectives, 28,* 501-520.

Evans, T. D., Cullen, F. T., Dunaway, R. G., & Burton, V. S. (1995). Religion and crime reexamined: The impact of religion, secular controls, and social ecology on adult criminology. *Criminology, 21,* 29-40.

Fowler, J. (1981). *Stages of Faith: The Psychology of Human Development and the Quest for Meaning.* San Francisco: Harper & Row.

Gartner, J., Larson, D. B., & Allen, G. D. (1991). Religious commitment and mental health: A review of the empirical literature. *Journal of Psychology and Theology, 19*(1), 6-25.

Gartner, J., O'Connor, T., Larson, D., Young, M., Wright, K., & Rosen, B. (1990). *Rehabilitation, Recidivism and Religion: A Systematic Literature Review.* Baltimore, MD: Loyola College in Maryland.

Heckman, J. J. (1979). Sample selection bias as a specification error. *Econometrica, 47*(1), 153-161.

Hoge, D. R. (1972). A validated intrinsic motivation scale. *Journal for the Scientific Study of Religion, 11,* 369-376.

Johnson, B. R. (1984). *Hellfire and Corrections: A Quantitative Study of Florida Prison Inmates.* Unpublished Doctoral Dissertation, Florida State University.

Johnson, B. R., Larson, D. B., & Pitts, T. C. (1997). Religious programs, institutional adjustment, and recidivism among former inmates in prison fellowship programs. *Justice Quarterly, 14*(1), 501-521.

Knudten, R. D., & Knudten, M. S. (1971). Juvenile delinquency, crime, and religion. *Review of Religious Research, 12*, 130-152.

Law, M. A. (1993). *Predicting Prison Misconduct*. St. John, NB: University of New Brunswick.

Lonergan, B. (1972). *Method in Theology*. New York: Seabury Press.

McKelvey, B. (1977). *American Prisons: A History of Good Intentions*. Montclair, NJ: Patterson Smith.

Motiuk, L. (1983). *Antecedents and Consequences of Prison Adjustment: A Systematic Assessment and Reassessment Approach*. Ottawa: Unpublished Ph.D. dissertation, Carleton University.

O'Connor, T. (1995). The impact of religious programming on recidivism, the community and prisons. *IARCA Journal on Community Corrections, 6*(6), 13-19.

O'Connor, T., & Parikh, C. (1998). Best practices for ethics and religion in community corrections. *ICCA Journal on Community Corrections, 8*(4), 26-32.

O'Connor, T. P., Parikh, C., & Ryan, P. (1997). *The South Carolina Initiative Against Crime Project: 1996 Volunteer Survey* (Evaluation). Silver Spring, MD: Center for Social Research, Inc.

O'Connor, T., Ryan, P., Yang, F., Wright, K., & Parikh, C. (1996, August). *Religion and Prisons: Do Volunteer Religious Programs Reduce Recidivism?* Paper presented at the American Sociological Association Convention, New York.

Pass, M. G. (1999). Religious orientation and self-reported role violations in a maximum security prison. *Journal of Offender Rehabilitation, 28* (3/4), 19-134.

Petersilia, J. (1995). A crime control rationale for reinvesting in community corrections. *The Prison Journal, 75*(4), 479-496.

Prison, F. (1991). *Beyond Crime and Punishment*. Washington, DC: Prison Fellowship.

Sampson, R. J., & Laub, J. H. (1993). *Crime in the Making: Pathways and Turning Points Through Life*. Cambridge, MA: Harvard University Press.

Skotnicki, A. (1992). *Religion and the Development of the American Penal System*. Berkeley, CA: Unpublished Doctoral Dissertation, Graduate Theological Union.

Sloane, D., & Potvin, R. (1986). Religion and delinquency: Cutting through the maze. *Social Forces, 65*, 87-105.

Sumter, M. T. (1999). *Religiousness and Post-Release Community Adjustment*. Tallahassee, FL: Unpublished Ph.D. Dissertation, Florida State University.

Sumter, M. T., & Clear, T. (1998, March 14). *An empirical assessment of literature examining the relationship between religiosity and deviance since 1985*. Paper presented at the Academy of Criminal Justice Sciences Conference, Albuquerque.

Sundt, J., & Cullen, F. T. (1998). The role of the contemporary prison chaplain. *Prison Journal, 78*(3), 271-298.

Tittle, C. R., & Welch, M. (1983). Religiosity and deviance: Toward a contingency theory of constraining effects. *Social Forces, 61*(653-682).

U.S. Department of Justice (1993). *Survey of State Prisoners, 1991*.Washington, DC: Bureau of Justice Statistics, U.S. Government Printing Office.

Wright, K. N. (1985). Developing the prison environment inventory. *Journal of Research in Crime and Delinquency, 22*(3), 257-277.

AUTHORS' NOTES

Tom O'Connor is the administrator of religious services for the Oregon Department of Corrections and the president of the Center for Social Research headquartered in Silver Spring, Maryland.

Michael Perreyclear is a research associate, Center for Social Research. Active in prison ministry for a decade, he is currently studying pastoral ministry with the Independent Study Institute, Southern Baptist Convention, Nashville, Tennessee.

Financial and other support for this research was provided by the Center for Social Research, the South Carolina Department of Corrections, Prison Fellowship Ministries, and the Oregon Department of Corrections. The authors would like to acknowledge the contribution of the following to the study: Director Michael Moore, Chaplains Terry Brooks, Robert Shaver, James Brown, and Richard Ittner and their clerks (Michael, Stacy, and Kamathaii), Dr. Lorraine Fowler, Ms. Meesim Lee, Ms. Mei-chu Tang, Ms. Barbara Simon, and Ms. Deanne Williams, South Carolina Department of Corrections; Dr. Karen Strong, Mr. Fred Kensler, and Mr. Jimmy Stewart, Prison Fellowship Ministries; and Ms. Patricia Ryan and Dr. Crystal Parikh, Center for Social Research.

Address correspondence to Thomas P. O'Connor, Administrator, Religious Services, Oregon Department of Corrections, 2575 Center Street NE, Salem, OR 97310 (E-mail: Tom.P.Oconnor@doc.state.or.US).

Religion, the Community, and the Rehabilitation of Criminal Offenders. Pp. 35-58.
© *2002 by The Haworth Press, Inc. All rights reserved.*

The Reasons for Religious Involvement
in the Correctional Environment

HARRY R. DAMMER

University of Scranton

SUMMARY This paper discusses the reasons for inmate religious involvement in the correctional environment. Participant observation and seventy individual interviews were employed to gather the ethnographic data in two large maximum-security prisons located in the northeast United States. Content analysis and constant comparison methods were used to develop analytic categories and to compare results across research sites and between denominational groups. It was revealed that inmates practice religion for a variety of reasons depending on the sincerity of their intentions. The results introduce insight into why inmates practice religion in prison, provide valuable information for those who administer religious programs, and are shown to be theoretically linked with findings of prior research conducted in the correctional environment. *[Article copies available for a fee from The Haworth Document Delivery Service: 1-800-HAWORTH. E-mail address: <getinfo@haworthpressinc.com> Website: <http://www.HaworthPress.com> © 2002 by The Haworth Press, Inc. All rights reserved.]*

KEYWORDS Ethnography, religion, inmate, meaning, social support, prison

The influence of religion as a treatment alternative in the correctional setting is as old as the history of prisons. The early Christian church, beginning in the days of Constantine, granted asylum to criminals who would otherwise have been mutilated or killed. Soon thereafter, imprisonment under church jurisdiction became a substitute for corporal or capital punishment. In medieval times, monastic cells served as punishment places for many miscreants (Hoyles 1955).

Early Americans brought with them the customs and common laws of England. With this came the "treatments" of the pillory, the stocks and the whipping post. Also, the idea of an offender being locked up in isolation from fellow prisoners became accepted correctional philosophy. The prisoner was encouraged to become penitent over his sins, thus the term penitentiary was derived. Even during the 19th century when work (by day) was initiated by the Auburn System, solitary confinement (by night) was the norm in correctional practice (Rosenblatt 1982). The forced solitary confinement was thought to serve the same repenting purpose as the older penitentiary.

Today, the use of religion as a correctional program or treatment modality is commonplace in most jails and prisons throughout the United States. In fact, of the many types of programs offered in prisons, religion is among those with the highest degree of participation. One study by the U.S. Department of Justice reported that 32 percent of sampled inmates were involved in religious activities such as Bible study and church services (BJS, 1993). Previous research has stated that religion even surpasses education as the most frequently represented program in jails and prisons throughout the United States (Corrections Compendium 1983).

Religion in corrections currently varies from a single chaplain to "hear personal problems" to a multi-staffed religious program which serves a variety of denominational groups. Evidence of the acceptance of religion in the correctional setting is supported by the growth of numerous prison ministry programs. One such program is the Prison Fellowship Program which was founded in 1975 by Charles Colson. The program is actively involved in prison ministry throughout the fifty states, and in a number of foreign countries.

In spite of the historical significance and prevalence of religion in prison, the topic has generally been largely untold in criminological research. A surprisingly limited amount of scientific research has been conducted in the area, and what has been attempted is mostly non-empirical, topical, and highly subjective. What is encouraging is the recent interest that social scientists have taken in the issue of religion in corrections and its effect on rehabilitation. Clear et al. (1992a, 1992b) and Johnson (1984, 1987a, 1987b) are among those who have studied the influence of religion on inmate prison behavior and recidivism. Johnson and his colleagues (1997) advanced the research on the topic with their study of religious programs, adjustment, and recidivism among inmates who participate in the Prison Fellowship Program.

This paper, then, will attempt to add to this current interest in the study of religion in the correctional environment. It is hoped that the information provided will help to narrow the void in the current state of knowledge of the practice of religion in the correctional environment. More specifically, this paper will discuss the reasons for religious involvement in the correctional environment.

METHOD

The data for this paper were derived from a year-long ethnographic study of two religious programs in two large male prisons located in the northeast United States. The sites were selected because they were maximum security institutions, representative of the type, with an active group of religious inmates. The primary research site where the majority of the data were collected was a maximum security institution with over 1,500 inmates, herein coined Western Prison. The second institution, to be called Eastern Prison, served as a check for validity and to provide generalizability of the results to other prison settings. At least two different denominations served as a control for the analysis of the religious groups.

The research was conducted in two concurrent phases. Phase one included a nine-month participation period to study the different religious activities at both prisons. The second phase, which lasted three months, consisted of seventy individual-intensive interviews with inmates and staff. From the participant observation phase, questions and theoretical propositions were developed. Global sorting was employed to place the questions and propositions into uniform categories. Respondents for the individual interviews were chosen on a volunteer basis. Purposive sampling was used to obtain a cross-section of religious and non-religious inmates and to produce a sample of the various denominational groups.

The research produced two types of data: field notes and intensive interview transcripts. Field notes were developed into a descriptive ethnography. Content Analysis was used to develop analytic categories from the intensive interviews. The constant comparison method (Glaser and Strauss 1967) was used to compare analytic categories across research sites and between denominational groups.

To describe the frequency or strength of the responses, specific terms are employed to give the reader a more definitive picture of the results.

Consensus is used to reflect a situation in which most (over 75%) of the inmates and correctional officers respond in kind. *Most frequent* is used when over half (50%) respond similarly, but below consensus. When below half respond similarly, but above one fourth (25%), the term *often responded* is utilized.

FINDINGS

To grasp the reasons for religious involvement in prison, two questions were asked of inmates and correctional officers. The two questions were, respectively, *Why do inmates become involved with religion in prison?* and *What are the reasons for your involvement with religion in prison?* From the beginning of the data collection and concurrent data analysis, it was clear that there was a consensus concerning the responses to these questions. The consensus was that the motivations of the sincerely religious respondents must be explained separately and distinctly from the motivations of those who were labeled insincere. More simply, the sincere inmates often had different reasons for religious involvement than the insincere inmates.

It is important here to clarify the terms *sincere* and *insincere* as defined by the respondents. The "sincere" inmates were said to be more legitimate or genuine in their religious belief and practice; they found religion a motivating factor for their lives. In contrast, the "insincere" inmates were more likely to be involved in religion for manipulative purposes; their behavior did not reflect the rules or norms of any formal religion although they might claim to be religious inmates.

Understanding the reasons for religious involvement within this sincere-insincere model is important for two reasons. First, the sincere-insincere description for religious involvement is clearly representative of what the respondents feel is integral to understanding the meaning of religion in prison; it is how they view their world. Clearly documenting these perceptions is consonant with the ethnographic approach of explaining a particular culture in the words and feelings of those involved.

The second important feature of the sincere-insincere description is that the respondents' remarks are theoretically linked to a large and important body of literature in corrections.

The *deprivation theory of imprisonment* was first developed by Sykes (1958) but since has been tested frequently in the correctional environment. Discussion of the deprivation perspective and its relevance to the findings of this research will come later in this paper. First, we turn to a detailed discussion of the reasons for religious involvement using the sincere and the insincere model described by the respondents.

Sincere Reasons for Religious Involvement

Results of this research indicated that, among the inmates who practiced religion while incarcerated and were labeled "sincere," a number of specific psychological and behavioral conditions were present. Among those conditions gained from religious practice were motivation, direction and meaning for life, hope for the future, peace of mind, positive self-esteem, and change in lifestyle.

In the analysis of the reasons for sincere involvement, a common pattern emerged at both research sites. The respondents most frequently said that the sincere inmates would gain some form of motivation, direction, and meaning for their life from the practice of religion while in prison. The sincere inmate, one respondent said, "would live life for God, not for himself."

Many inmates felt that, because of their incarceration and the way they had lived life prior to incarceration, their future is gloomy. A life of crime and imprisonment is what they have come to expect out of life. In this way, life for many inmates is in fact hopeless. But the practice of religion provides the opportunity to change that situation. Different religious denominations often provide doctrines or rules that persons can follow to lead them through life. These rules and ways of living can be found in the various writings of different religious groups. For example, the Christian denominations have the Bible, Jews the Torah, Muslims the Koran. In each of these books believers are told to follow certain rules and behaviors and told to avoid others. These rules teach how to live a "better" life, and how to avoid acts that will lead one astray and towards the path of "sin" or self-ruin. So with the help, direction, and structure of religious practice, inmates can search for a life that is better than their present life condition.

Two types of responses were most frequently given to reflect the motivation, direction, and meaning that came from the practice of religion. The first was the frequent use of phrases that related religion as providing "direction" to the life of the sincere inmates, such as these:

- Religion helps lead someone in the right direction. You can't help but make your life better. (W15)

- Religion is a guide to not get out of hand, it gives you a straight path. (W23)
- It (religion) is a way of life, it is a road map, a way to be constantly aware of bad habits. (W28)

A by-product of providing direction for inmates is that religion provides hope for those who are incarcerated. Inmates need hope to keep them optimistic about the future and the possibility of being released. Some inmates hope that when released they will be reformed from a life of crime and future imprisonment. The various denominational groups, the correctional officers, and the non-religious samples often responded that the more sincere inmates would express hope from the practice of religion. They believed that religion would provide hope for reform from a life of crime as well as from a life of imprisonment. The feeling of hope was expressed in numerous conversations and in statements like these:

- (Religion) gives them hope.
- Religion keeps hope alive.
- Religion gives them (the inmates) something to look forward to.
- The sincere inmate has hope for the future, for a better life than being in prison.

In addition to direction and hope, a second set of comments that reflected motivation, direction, and meaning were those expressed from a limited group of inmates in the religious sample. Five inmates indicated that their situation of being incarcerated was in fact "what God wanted for them," being in prison was "God's will" and that full acceptance of his will was essential for being truly sincere in one's faith. They felt that incarceration was part of a plan that God held for them and it was their responsibility to live out that plan. This finding is interesting because it expresses a faithful response to the difficult situation of being incarcerated. The following responses express this attitude:

- Whatever happens I put my trust in God. (W11)
- I don't look at prison as prison but as a monastery to do God's work. The only thing that is lacking in here is freedom of movement and women, but that is only a state of mind. I've seen some guys who don't really realize that they are in prison because it is not the prison that they see it's the walk with God. Prison doesn't bother them anymore. (W1)

Respondents also stated that the sincere inmate could also achieve a certain "peace of mind" from religious practice. In fact, both inmates and officers often responded that the religious inmate would often gain some inner peace or peaceful mind from the practice of religion:

- A very peaceful mind, a peaceful heart. A positive outlook. I am looking at a very long time in an institution. Without that positive outlook, it would be very devastating to attempt spending one's life like that. (N2)
- Peace of mind. Not only in prison, in the world because prison is just a small population of what's out in the world. I've seen guys who don't really realize that they are in prison because it is not prison that they see it's the walk with God. Prison doesn't bother them anymore. In my opinion it gives you peace of mind. (W1)

Having peace of mind was stated to be important for the psychological survival of inmates because they are often facing a very long time in an institution. Inmates surely see their current life situation as a "very difficult time." While incarcerated, inmates are often forced to deal with intense feelings such as guilt, fear, rejection, and personal failure. Without having some level of "peace of mind," inmates would find it difficult to handle these feelings. Religion helps to provide "peace of mind" because different religious denominations often teach that it is important to accept the will of a higher power and to accept as best as possible the conditions life has provided. Religion helps inmates deal with the pains of imprisonment and provides a framework for accepting their current circumstances no matter how bad they may appear. In gaining "peace of mind" inmates are better able to deal with the frustrations and day-to-day pressures of being incarcerated. Without religion inmates may choose to vent their frustration in aggressive fashion either through harming themselves or others.

Another important reason for why inmates become involved with religion while incarcerated is to improve their negative self-concept, or to feel better about themselves. Having a negative self-concept is a common problem with correctional inmates. Many inmates feel they have been a "failure in life" as compared to the standards of those who have not been incarcerated. This self-concept may have been formed by poor education and work performance, remorse from criminal acts, or from the pain of a dysfunctional family background. Because the core of many religious beliefs includes acceptance and love from a higher being and from the religious group, inmates can feel better about themselves if they become involved with religion while incarcerated. It must be noted, however, that relatively few (less than 25%) of the respondents stated that improving one's self-concept was a reason for religious involvement by inmates. While some did imply this reason to be important, it was not often verbalized. The development and interpretation of this reason is primarily derived from inferences made by the respondents but is formulated by this researcher.

The respondents in all sample groups often responded that the sincere inmates would derive a behavioral change or "change in lifestyle" from the practice of religion. If an inmate was sincere in his religious practice, his behavior would reflect that sincerity. The respondents noticed that an inmate's sincerity could be seen in his actions taken (or avoided) on a regular basis. The respondents gave the following two examples of sincere religious inmates: "They are different in how they carry himself," and, the "sincere inmate displays 'civil' behaviors like a positive attitude, politeness, humility, calmness or self-control."

Finally, inmates and staff often responded that because of the rules and discipline that the serious practice of religion requires, inmates can learn to develop self-control. Self-control is obviously very useful in preventing behavior that can lead to problems in correctional facilities and after being released. Increased self-control can help inmates avoid confrontations with inmates and staff, and assist them in complying with institutional rules and regulations. In some cases inmates can learn to become less aggressive and violent. It was stated that the sincere inmate would often "avoid questionable behavior such as homosexuality, drug dealing, and the use of bad language."

To this point, this paper has explored some of the reasons why inmates labeled as "sincere" practice religion while incarcerated. It is important to mention that these reasons "to obtain peace of mind, direction and meaning in life, self-esteem, and to change behavior" are not meant to be a definitive or exhaustive description of why inmates choose to practice religion. There were other reasons mentioned by the respondents that could be placed in the sincere category. However, because of the limited number of the responses in any one category, they were eliminated from inclusion in this analysis.

Insincere Reasons for Religious Involvement

The findings also indicated with consensus from the respondents, that among inmates who practiced religion while incarcerated there were a considerable number that were "insincere" in their religious practice. As mentioned earlier in this paper, these inmates were more likely to be involved in religion for what were viewed as negative or manipulative purposes. The reasons for insincere religious involvement were: protection, inmate convergence, interaction with women volunteers, and access to prison resources.

Protection

In both formal and informal interviews, it was found that a consensus of inmates, officers, staff and volunteers consistently responded that protection was the most significant reason why the insincere inmate becomes involved in religion. Information pertaining to this issue was even received when unsolicited. When the purpose of the study was mentioned as be "To find out the meaning of religion in prison," individuals would immediately respond with, "Most do it (religion) only for protection." It can be stated that throughout the data collection period, hardly a day passed without the mention of religion for protection by a guard, inmate, staff or volunteer.

The reason why inmates chose religion for protection was usually spelled out in the following manner: If an inmate hoped to "be safe" while in prison, he needed a group to protect him physically from other individuals or groups. Without this protection, inmates believed that they would be subject to economic and sexual exploitation and physical confrontations. It was assumed that the religious group would then provide the protection necessary to avoid such difficulties.

The finding that inmates often seek protection from other inmates is hardly novel. The need and search for protection while incarcerated has been mentioned frequently in criminological literature (Carroll 1974). What is important, however, is the finding that membership in a religious group would serve such a purpose. The significance of this finding is the apparent dissonance between the concepts of religion and protection. This dissonance becomes clear when we consider that conventional religion is believed to reinforce the establishment of a personal moral relationship with transcendent moral beings or a "God" (Reiss and Rhodes 1970). As a result of this relationship with a transcendent moral being or "God," it is assumed that the behavior of a "religious" individual will be pro-social in nature.

It appears strange, then, that inmates who are "religious" are involved in activities which would be connected with protection and aggressive behavior which are antithetical to pro-social behavior. Findings also indicated that the role of religion as protection was entangled in other prison issues like race, the past criminality of the inmate, and sexual preference of the inmate.

Race. At Western Prison, the Muslim denomination was the most frequently mentioned religious group that practiced religion for protection. This quotation is a typical example of an inmate's search for protection:

> When you come to jail there is only three things you can be to establish yourself. That is, you can be tough, you have to know someone, or be a fag. Those are the only three things you can be. You can be a guy who gets pushed around. If you are not tough or a fag you need a group. Everyone has to be a part of something. They get protection. The Islamics (Muslims) are good for protection. Islamic people will help one another. He (another Muslim) will jump in and help you. It's their job. (W21)

This importance of gaining protection from within the Muslim prison community was affirmed by all of the other religious denominations. Even the members of the Muslim group agreed to the statement that their denomination was most commonly associated with protection. The Muslims interviewed, however, qualified their remarks. They often responded that the protection was only for those who were treated unjustly. If a Muslim is acting in consonance with the teachings of the faith, it is the responsibility of fellow brothers to assist and, if necessary, to protect him:

> Being a Muslim will benefit you spiritually, your soul, and then there are other aspects like protection. Muslims are obligated to protect another Muslim if they aren't doing anything wrong. We don't support anything that is wrong. If the guy is weak and we know he is weak and we realize that he's becoming a Muslim because he is weak, we are obligated to protect him and help him grow spiritually because we don't know what is in his heart. So we have an obligation to protect him and see that he grows spiritually. (W19)

The Muslims interviewed took exception to the implication that their group was a "gang." They often responded that to refer to the group as a gang was a misconception developed, in part, by many of the newer Muslim inmates. When new inmates would enter the group with this misconception, the "true" Muslims would become very insulted. Further, they felt it was a responsibility to correct misinformed inmates of the purpose of their mission.

The findings of this research do not suggest that the Muslim inmates were *in fact* more aggressive in their protection than other religious groups. But what can be stated is that membership in the Muslim denomination at Western Prison was undoubtedly connected with racial affiliation. Almost all the Muslim inmates at Western Prison were African-American. On only one occasion was the participation of a white inmate witnessed at a Muslim religious function.

The large number of African-American inmates involved in the Muslim faith is largely a cultural one. Coming from similar economic, geographic and cultural settings, the African-American inmates identify with the Muslim group because it provides them with the chance to associate with those of like backgrounds. This finding has support in the literature that suggests African-Americans in prison develop a more supportive social system than whites (Carroll 1974). Likewise, African-Americans are more likely to become involved in political, social, and religious groups that allow them to show solidarity because of their shared experience of racism and discrimination (Reasons 1974; Jacobs 1976). The issue of protection for religious inmates was also important for the Protestant denomination. However, the Muslims definitely received most of the consideration. Very rarely was there mention of the other groups being associated with protection.

Past Criminality. Another finding related to protection is that past criminality would often determine whether an inmate would need protection while incarcerated. For example, if an inmate was incarcerated for certain sex offenses, like child molestation or sexual assault of an older woman, he was stigmatized as a deviant among deviants. The label used to describe those who committed such crimes was "skinner." The "skinner" was the least respected of all the inmates; he was forever subject to verbal and physical abuse.

Inmates, officers and even chaplains often responded that many of the "skinners" would become involved in the Christian denominations for protection because religious involvement would allow the "skinner" some respite from the fear of attack from other inmates. The protection was provided in the form of a "safe haven" of the religious services. Inmates felt that those involved in religious services were less likely to be overtly aggressive. On this point, one inmate said that the "religious services police themselves because no one wants to ruin the opportunity to practice religion for the other inmates." Others stated:

- Anybody with a sex beef (conviction) or child beef will find himself in Christian programs. Anybody who is looking for something in prison one step away from protective custody. It's sad because that is what happens. Most cases they are not sincere. They got to have some friend who is going to hang out with them, and only the other Christians will do that. (W25)
- The sex offenders who show up in the Christian group so they won't get hurt. They need to get protected. The ones who aren't really strong or the ones who aren't sincere fall right out. They need protection. The Muslims, the 5%ers, the Roman Catholic, the Protestants, the Born Again Christians. They are using it for protection. (W28)

Sexual Preference. Inmate and officer respondents often stated that many inmates who practice homosexuality attend religious services for protection, a concept somewhat related to the previous issue of protection for the sex offender. Again, it was felt that inmates could use the religious services as a safe haven. Two inmates did admit to engaging in homosexual activity during the intensive interviews. In both instances, the inmates involved acknowledged homosexual behavior, but stated that they had "changed their ways" with the help of religion.

Also significant was the mention of religious services as a possible haven for those with (HIV) AIDS. In informal conversations, inmates and staff said that the religious services were the only place where some inmates could interact with other inmates in a relatively safe and positive fashion. On most occasions, inmates with AIDS are treated with disdain and cruelty by the other inmates, but in religious services, the inmate can receive much needed support from religious inmates and chaplains. This finding is important because it suggests that religious services in prison provide an essential psychological service for those who are infected with AIDS.

Inmate Convergence

After protection, the most common reason for the religious involvement by the insincere was to take advantage of the opportunity to converge with fellow inmates. Inmates and staff at both institutions often responded that this was true. The opportunity to attend religious services is available to all inmates who are in the general prison population. Because of daily job schedules, evening school programs and security restrictions it was possible for the inmates not to see each other for weeks. Religious services assured them of weekly contact. If they attended all the religious programs, one could see fellow inmates two or three times a week:

> I wanted to see a friend of mine that was in another unit. I wanted to correspond with him at that certain time. It was the only place we could meet. Sometimes it is just a meeting place to see someone you know. I would imagine it's also just to get out of the unit. (E14)

Even those with limited access to the general population were allowed to attend religious services in many cases. At Western Prison, the D-Block Unit was reserved for inmates awaiting placement into the general prison population or transfer to another institution. During the interim, the inmates were not allowed out of their cell except for one hour of recreation in the yard and for religious services. Consequently, many would take advantage of the chance to attend religious services. One officer responded:

> In D-Block, each day is different religion. D-Block is a transient unit. You have Protestant services one day, Catholic the next, Muslim the next, Spanish the next. But the thing is that each of these guys have nothing to do, so they all go to each service. You will see the same person at all services. They go just to get out. (W7)

Respondents explained and observations confirmed that two reasons exist for inmates taking advantage of religious services as a place to converge. The first, and most obvious reason, is social in nature; the second, attendance at religious services provides an opportunity to pass contraband.

Social Reasons. It is not surprising that inmates, like people outside prison, enjoy regular social interaction with those whom they consider friends. The different religious services distinctly served this purpose. Frequently, the services were the social event of the day. These activities were informally publicized and accepted as a time to meet with friends, "hang out," or "see your home boy."

Numerous examples of such social interactions between inmates were witnessed. It was not unusual for inmates to sign up to attend religious services, and then spend most of the service outside the chapel smoking cigarettes or conversing with fellow inmates. As much as could be determined, the conversations were most often unrelated to religious activity (e.g., the discussion about the quality of spaghetti "gravy" by two inmates of Italian background).

It was also apparent during many religious services that the back of the room or chapel was often occupied by those who came to socialize. During almost every Sunday service at both institutions, a large number of inmates, who were not regulars to the group, would sit in the back and talk. On more than a few occasions the talking became quite disturbing and the Chaplain would ask the inmates to be quiet. These discussions among inmates would occur most frequently during a long speech by a Protestant Chaplain/Volunteer or immediately after Communion during the Catholic Mass.

In the correctional literature there have been numerous accounts of the need for inmates to become involved in groups while incarcerated (Giallombardo, 1963; Davidson, 1974). More recently, Johnson (1987) has said that inmates need to find their own "niche," one that is compatible with their interests and which will serve to assist the inmate in "negotiating the stress of prison." Becoming involved in religion while in prison provides another formal mechanism for inmates to find an acceptable niche through improved social identity.

The inmates' need for social interaction was evident because they often responded that they detested the idea of staying in their cells any longer than absolutely necessary. It was not unusual for an inmate to try to occupy his time by working by day and attending an educational or religious program in the evening.

Pass Contraband. The second reason why insincere inmates converge at religious services is for the purpose of passing contraband, a reason most frequently mentioned by the inmates for attending religious services. The inmates indicated that the contraband passed was usually in the form of food, candy, written messages, and cigarettes:

> Some come just to get out of their cell. Some come to meet their homeboys. Pick up cigarettes, pick up food or exchange photos, get addresses. (W2)

A consensus of the correctional officers indicated the passing of contraband was a major reason for religious involvement. According to the officers, however, the type of contraband passed by inmates was more likely to be drugs or weapons than food or cigarettes. In an informal interview, one officer stated that inmates use religious services to "set up hits and transactions for drugs."

The passing of contraband that was observed did not appear to be illegal or dangerous. Nor did the inmates seem to mind being watched. Only once out of the estimated fifty times in which such interactions were witnessed did the inmates seem to be passing contraband in a clandestine manner. As far as could be determined, the contraband passed was innocuous. It is possible that within the pack of cigarettes, a handwritten message, rolled up newspaper or candy wrapper, there could be dangerous contraband. But if that were the case, the inmates surely did not make an attempt to hide it.

Women Volunteers

After protection and inmate convergence, the next most common reason for inmates to become involved in religion was the opportunity to meet the women volunteers. Inmates and officers at both research sites and in each denominational group often responded that this was the case. For most of the Catholic and Protestant weekly services and all of the large group seminars, civilian women volunteered time to visit the prison to assist in religious instruction. For obvious reasons, the inmates' interactions with women are limited to contacts with an occasional visitor or one of the few female staff members. Consequently, the inmates would look forward to coming to religious services to meet the volunteers. One inmate made this observation:

> Because a lot of women come from the outside. If there are a couple of nice cuties coming in, the word gets around. They have been in jail so they want to see the women. (W18)

During the course of the research, a number of different respondents said that the inmates often tried to persuade the women volunteers to become romantically involved with them. If the women were mothers, the inmates would try to meet or contact the daughter. The goal was apparently either to get a female to visit them on a regular basis or to begin a letter-writing relationship. One interesting story about an inmate who eventually convinced a volunteer to marry him is noteworthy here:

> I know one guy that went to a seminar and there was a woman there and he ran a line on this woman that he prayed to God that he would find a woman, a mate for him and his prayer was answer through her and he convinced her that Jesus wanted them to get

married and they got married. All he really wanted was jelly beans (sex). He told me so. (W7)

Again, it must be noted that no situations were observed that would provide evidence for the belief that volunteers became romantically involved with inmates. Furthermore, the women volunteers were always treated with considerable respect by most, if not all, the inmates. The reason for this respect was an unwritten inmate rule that, if broken, could result in retaliation, as is evident in this response:

> If you disrespect some of the women these guys will take it personally. They say that woman could have been my mother, that could have been my sister. You disrespecting her is like disrespecting my family. In jail especially if you are someone who molests women or anything, you can get in trouble. I think that has a big role to play. If some guy like you who does some shit like that to some woman in the street, I would break your neck because she could have been my family. (W16)

Prison Resources

A final reason for insincere involvement apparent in the results was the opportunity to access prison resources that were available only to the religious inmate: free goods such as food, religious greeting cards and books, music and musical instruments, and individual favors from the Chaplain.

Free Goods. During many of the special religious services (e.g., seminars, holidays) coffee, cookies and donuts were supplied for the inmates who attended religious services. It was clear that the attendance was largest when food was provided. In fact, inmates, chaplains, and staff agreed that attendance was better if cookies and coffee were served:

> The big thing is that everybody knew that the Father was bringing in cookies and cakes and doughnuts and so forth. So, naturally everyone wanted to come. (W7)

Similarly, certain religious holidays seemed to "motivate" numerous inmates to become involved in certain denominations. These holidays were always associated with special food privileges. At Western Prison, during the Muslim holiday Ramadan, the Islamic inmates were allowed a special diet. Forty to fifty inmates regularly attended weekly Muslim services on Friday afternoons; over ninety requested the diet during Ramadan. Likewise, the same phenomenon occurred with the Jewish inmates during the holiday Purim. Although the regular Jewish congregation meetings on Thursday afternoon numbered an average of eight to ten inmates, over twenty signed up to participate in the special meal which would come at sunset during the week-long holiday.

The free goods given to inmates were not limited to food. Often the Chaplains or volunteers would provide holiday cards for the inmates. This occurrence was usually publicized in advance and the numbers in attendance at services were larger than usual. Many of the inmates who attended these services were not "regulars." On one occasion, an inmate was seen peering into the classroom where Christmas cards were being given out during the break of a Bible-study class. After a while, he entered, acquired two to three cards, and left before the class resumed study.

Music. Inmates from all the sample groups, except the Muslims, said that music was an important reason for their religious involvement. The Muslim services did not include music. The Protestant services at Western Prison often included a segment of gospel music. The large number of inmates sitting in the back of the chapel, who prior to that point in the service did not appear to be too interested or involved, would often enthusiastically clap and sing during certain gospel songs. On one occasion, an inmate was asked why he attended Monday evening seminar and not the Sunday service. He responded: "On Sunday morning I sleep, I come on Monday night because the music is good."

A similar situation existed at Eastern Prison. One evening each week a special group of religious volunteers entered the prison to give a "concert" for the inmates. The inmates who attended this concert were often different from those who attended Sunday morning mass. And like the services at Western Prison, services with music were often the most well-attended and the audience participation most intense. It was also observed that inmates at Western Prison were able to secure musical instruments to bring back to their cell to practice for religious services. This resource was provided by the chaplain who would purchase the instruments out of his religious program budget. It appeared that the inmates who were able to obtain these musical instruments were very fond of their possessions and were not likely to lend them to other inmates.

Favors from Chaplain. The use of religion to gain favors from the Chaplain was also mentioned as a contributor to religious involvement.

The Chaplain was an important person for inmates because he was able to provide two valuable resources for inmates: phone access and written recommendations for parole or transfer.

While incarcerated in a maximum security institution, the inmate's resources for making phone calls are often limited. He is allowed to use the phone only during certain times, for a limited amount of time (five minutes), and then he can only call collect. As a result, any unforeseen occurrence, family disturbance, marital discord, or legal problem must wait until the inmate can get to a phone. His only other option is to use the phone of a staff member. The Chaplain is the most likely choice because he is often sympathetic to the needs of the inmates and has a phone in the privacy of his own office.

Inmates also felt that the Chaplain was a good person to ask for a letter of reference before a parole board hearing. With that in mind, an inmate would likely attend religious services immediately prior to his parole hearing. On one occasion, evidence surfaced of a letter written by a Chaplain in support of an inmate who "found religion" just prior to his parole hearing.

Another reason to gain favor with the Chaplain was to obtain a transfer to another prison. Because Western Prison was part of a large prison system, inmates were often transferred throughout the state to different institutions. This was not an unusual situation and it occurred often for security reasons. However, if an inmate belonged to a certain religious group, and was recommended by the Chaplain, he could be transferred to a specific prison for "religious reasons." The transfer would be to an institution with a special religious program, similar to the faith of the inmate. What was interesting was the finding that many of the inmates who sought this "religious transfer" were raised or had relatives residing nearby the institution that possessed this special religious program.

THE DEPRIVATION PERSPECTIVE

The reasons for religious involvement just discussed are related to a large and important body of literature in both corrections and religious behavior: the deprivation perspective. Because of the relevance of deprivation to our findings, a more detailed discussion of the theory is necessary. The discussion will be followed by an explanation of how the theory is relevant to the findings of this research.

Theories linking religious activity and deprivation outside the prison are common in the literature of religious behavior (Argyle and

Beit-Hallahmi 1975). The relationship between religion and deprivation is best explained by Davis (1948) who stated:

> The greater man's disappointment in this life, the greater his faith in the next. Thus the existence of goals beyond this world serves to compensate people for frustrations they inevitably experience in striving to reach socially acquired and socially valuable ends. (p. 42)

Deprivation theory was first fully developed in the correctional literature by Gresham Sykes in *The Society of Captives* (1958). Sykes explained that the inmate subculture was a functional adaptation to five types of deprivation in prisons: deprivation of liberty, deprivation of goods and services, deprivation of autonomy, deprivation of security, and deprivation of heterosexual relationships. He stated:

> The inmate's social system is not simply the social order decreed by the custodians, but also the social order which grows up more informally as men interact in meeting the problems posed by their particular environment. (p. xix)

The deprivation perspective has arguably been the most often tested theory in corrections. Researchers have studied deprivation theory relative to the inmate counter-culture (McCorkle and Korn 1954; Tittle 1972); an effect on time served (Wheeler 1961); facility type (Akers, Hayner, and Gruninger 1977; Sieverdes and Bartollas 1986); institutional dependency (Goffman 1961; Meisefelder 1985); and post-release outcome (Goodstein 1979). Deprivation theory has been refuted by many as simplistic (Carroll 1974; Jacobs 1977) and it has been seen to be working conjunctively with importation theory (Thomas 1977). (For a more complete discussion of the research on deprivation in corrections, see Wright and Goodstein 1989.)

Deprivation theory, although tested extensively in the prison setting, has not been previously linked with the practice of religion in the correctional environment. The findings of this research imply that deprivation theory can be applied to the reasons for inmate religious involvement.

Most of the deprivations that a correctional inmate must face are physical in nature. The most obvious is the deprivation of liberty. The findings of this research indicate that inmates are most likely to become involved with religion soon after being incarcerated. The timing of their involvement with religion implies that inmates may turn to religion because of the immediate deprivation of liberty and the serious nature of their current condition in life.

Another physical deprivation is the inmates' inability to obtain goods and services. However, religious involvement can mitigate this deprivation because when inmates attend religious services they can obtain coffee, food, or musical instruments, or other contraband that can lessen the deprivation of good and services.

The most common reason for "insincere" religious involvement by respondents was stated to be protection. So then, it is not surprising that religion as a form of protection is closely connected with the deprivation of security. The lack of heterosexual relationships is a final physical deprivation that can be mitigated by religious participation in prison. As stated by the respondents, attendance at religious services for the purpose of meeting women volunteers is common in correctional institutions. Although these interactions are generally limited to brief meetings at religious services, subsequent meetings in smaller group sessions and one-to-one discussions can provide inmates with valuable contact with the opposite sex.

In addition to the physical deprivations that are mitigated by religious involvement, inmates also obtain psychological relief from religion in prison. They often stated that prison was very demeaning to their self-worth. The inmate is labeled as a criminal, placed in an institution with others who are "bad, evil or corrupt" and is then treated with contempt by those around him. He is removed from all the things in his life, "family, friends, and work," things that enhance self-esteem.

Inmates obtain psychological relief from religious involvement because it (religion) provides meaning to their lives. Because of religion, the inmate can attempt to answer existential questions, such as "What is the purpose of my life" and, "Why am I in prison." Without religion, he would find it difficult to deal with the cruel reality of his predicament. Further, religion provides a vehicle for improved self-esteem. Through meeting inmates, volunteers and Chaplains who are often very affirming, the religious inmate feels better about himself. He feels that, through religion, he is doing something useful, for even those on the outside encourage religious involvement.

RELIGION FOR EARLY PAROLE

It is important to mention findings pertaining to the statement that inmates attend religious services for the purpose of obtaining early parole release. The common belief is that inmates "find religion" with the hope that prison administrators and parole authorities will think they have become moral and law-abiding citizens worthy of release. This belief is probably the most commonly accepted reason for inmate religious involvement. Correctional literature has contributed greatly to this belief for decades (Barnes and Teeters 1951; Mannheim 1965).

The results of this research provide minimal support for this belief. Of the inmates interviewed at Western Prison, very few (less than five) even mentioned the possibility of obtaining early parole by using religious observance as a means to manipulate the parole board. Many inmates indicated that the parole board "doesn't care about religion."

To a sightly greater extent the inmates at Eastern Prison felt that "religion for parole" was a motivating factor for religious involvement. After further exploration into the issue, it was evident that the inmates felt being involved in religion was looked upon as a positive factor at Eastern Prison because the Warden was "supposed to be a Born Again Christian." What is interesting, however, is that the correctional system of Eastern Prison was located in state with determinate sentencing and no parole.

More significant are the responses of the officers on the issue of religion for parole. At both prisons officers often responded that religion for parole was definitely a reason why inmates are involved with religion. They were adamant in stating that the inmates either manipulate the Chaplain for a positive recommendation or hope that some volunteer at a religious service will "put in a good word for them" with the Chaplain or Superintendent.

It appears there are two reasons for the evidence presented by the officers. *First*, it is possible that officers have personally witnessed inmates who have professed to be religious, but who have then acted to the contrary or who are repeat visitors to the institution. Subsequent to these observations, the officers develop certain attitudes about the religious inmate, and they then look for instances which support their frame of reference.

Second, correctional officers are deeply influenced by their own subculture (Lombardo 1977; Kauffman 1985). This subculture, as with other cultures, has certain beliefs which are accepted as truth and, passed among the officers, they often go unchallenged. Religion as a vehicle for early release is one of those unchallenged beliefs. This perception has no supporting empirical evidence. What is accepted as "truth" is in fact unproven speculation and individual perception. It is possible that the opinions of the officers, although never empirically studied, do have some validity. However, it is suggested that the reasons for religious involvement of inmates are not limited to one or even two simplistic responses. Correctional officers, Chaplains and prison administrators would be professionally enriched by being open to the range of reasons for religious involvement.

DISCUSSION

This exploration into the reasons for religious involvement of inmates has introduced some light upon a subject that has previously been unexplored in criminological research. This article explains that there are numerous reasons for religious involvement in prison and they are tied to whether the inmates are sincere or insincere in belief and practice. These reasons introduce fresh insight into why the practice of religion is important for inmates in prison. Chaplains and correctional administrators can use this information to improve religious programs. Having a better understanding of the value of religious programs can assist the correctional administrator in making more informed decisions during difficult financial times. In addition, the findings display a theoretical link to a body of literature that has received considerable support in the disciplines of corrections and religious behavior: the deprivation perspective. The findings here clearly imply that religion serves to mitigate the psychological and physical deprivations created by imprisonment.

Finally, the findings indicate some evidence that the belief of "finding religion for parole release" has minimal empirical support among correctional inmates. Very few inmates, religious or non-religious, felt that inmates join religious programs for the benefit of early parole release. However, on numerous occasions, the correctional officers said that one of the major reasons for religious involvement was to secure an early parole date. It is suggested that the beliefs on the part of the officers have been passed down through the prison literature and correctional officer subculture.

As mentioned earlier, despite the historical significance and frequency of religion in prison, the topic has been neglected in criminological and sociological research. It is hoped that this paper has helped to fill at least part of the void in the current state of knowledge of religion in the correctional environment.

REFERENCES

Akers, R., Hayner, N., and Gruninger, W. (1974). Homosexual and Drug Behavior in Prison: A Test of the Functional and Importation Models of the Inmate System. *Social Problems,* Vol. 21.

Argyle, M., and Beit-Hallahmi, B. (1975). *The Social Psychology of Religion.* London: Routledge and Kegan.

Barnes, H., and Teeters, K. (1951). *New Horizons in Criminology.* 2nd Edition. Englewood Cliffs, NJ: Prentice Hall.

Bureau of Justice Statistics (1993). *Prisoners Profile.* Washington, DC: Bureau of Justice Statistics.

Carroll, L. (1974). *Hacks, Blacks, and Cons.* Boston: Lexington Books.

Clear, T.R., Stout, B.D., Dammer, H.R., Kelly, L., Hardyman, P.L., and Shapiro C. (1992a). Does Involvement in Religion Help Prisoners Adjust to Prison? *NCCD FOCUS*, pp. 1-7.

Clear, T.R., Stout, B.D., Dammer, H.R., Kelly, L., Hardyman, P.L., and Shapiro C. (1992b). *Final Report: Feasibility Study of the Impact of Religious Involvement on Prisoners.* Published by School of Criminal Justice, Rutgers University, for the Justice Fellowship Inc., Washington, DC.

Corrections Compendium (1983). Religious Programs, Volume 7.

Dammer, Harry R. (1992). Piety in Prison: An Ethnography of Religion in the Correctional Environment. Ann Arbor, MI: University Microfilms International.

Davidson, J. (1975). Glock's Model of Religious Commitment: Assessing Some Different Approaches and Results. *Review of Religious Research*, Vol. 16, 2:83-93.

Davis, K. (1948). *Human Society.* New York: Macmillan.

Donahue, M. (1985). Intrinsic and Extrinsic Religiousness: Review and Meta-analysis. *Journal of Personality and Social Psychology*, 49:400-419.

Giallombardo, R. (1965). *Society of Women: A Study of a Women's Prison.* New York: John Wiley and Sons.

Glaser, B., and Strauss, A. (1967). *The Discovery of Grounded Theory: Strategies for Qualitative Research.* New York: Aldine De Gruyter.

Goffman, E. (1961). *Asylums: Essays on the Social Situation of Mental Patients and Other Inmates.* New York: Anchor Books.

Goodstein, L. (1979). Inmate Adjustment to Prison and the Transition to Community Life. *Journal of Research on Crime and Delinquency,* 16:246-272.

Hoyles, J. (1955). *Religion in Prison.* London: Epworth Publishers.

Jacobs, J. (1977). *Stateville: The Penitentiary in Mass Society.* Chicago: University of Chicago Press.

Johnson, B.R. (1987a). Religiosity and Institutional Deviance: The Impact of Religious Variables Upon Inmate Adjustment. *Criminal Justice Review,* 12:21-30.

Johnson, B.R. (1987b). Religious Commitment within the Corrections Environment: An Empirical Assessment. In *Crime, Values, and Religion*, edited by J.A. Day and W.S. Laufer. Norwood, NJ: Ablex. Pp. 193-210.

Johnson, R. (1987). *Hard Time: Understanding and Reforming the Prison.* Belmont, CA: Brooks/Cole.

Kauffman, K. (1985). *Prison Officers and Their World*. Unpublished doctoral dissertation, Harvard University.

Lombardo, L.X. (1978). The Correctional Officer: A Study of a Criminal Justice Functionary in His Work Place. Unpublished doctoral dissertation, State University of New York at Albany.

Mannheim, C. (1965). *Comparative Criminology*. New York: Houghton-Mifflin.

McCorkle, L., and Korn, R. (1954). Resocialization Within Walls. *Annals of the American Academy of Political Science*, 293:88-98.

Meisenfelder, T. (1985). An Essay on Time and the Phenomenology of Imprisonment. *Deviant Behavior*. 6:39-56.

Reasons, C. (1974). Racism, Prisons, and Prisoners' Rights. *Issues in Criminology*, 9:3-10.

Reiss, A., and Rhodes, A. (1970). The Religious Factor and Delinquent Behavior. *Journal of Research in Crime and Delinquency*, 7:83-89.

Sieverdes, C., and Bartollas, C. (1986). Security Level and Adjustment Patterns in Juvenile Institutions. *Journal of Criminal Justice*, 14:135-145.

Sykes, G.M. (1958). *The Society of Captives: A Study of a Maximum Security Prison*. Princeton, NJ: Princeton University Press.

Thomas, C. (1977). Theoretical Perspectives on Prisonization: A Comparison of the Importation and Deprivation Models. *Journal of Criminal Law and Criminology*, 68, 135-145.

Tittle, C. (1972). Institutional Living and Self Esteem. *Social Problems*, 20:65-77.

Wheeler, S. (1961). Socialization in Correctional Communities. *American Sociological Review*, 26:697-712.

AUTHOR'S NOTE

Harry Dammer is an associate professor in the Department of Sociology and Criminal Justice at The University of Scranton, PA. He received his BS and MS degrees from the University of Dayton and his PhD from Rutgers University. His major research interests are corrections, and international criminal justice systems. He is the author of *Religion in Corrections* (American Correctional Association, 1999) and co-author (with Erika Fairchild) of *Comparative Criminal Justice* (Wadsworth/Thompson Press, 2000) and co-author (with Todd R. Clear) of *The Offender in the Community* (Wadsworth/Thompson Press, 2003). Dr. Dammer was a Fulbright Scholar during 1993-94.

The research reported in this article was supported by the Pew Charitable Trust Foundation.

Address correspondence to Dr. Harry Dammer, Sociology and Criminal Justice Department, University of Scranton, Scranton, PA 18510 (E-mail: dammerh2@scranton.edu).

Religion, the Community, and the Rehabilitation of Criminal Offenders. Pp. 59-86.

The Role of the Prison Chaplain
in Rehabilitation

JODY L. SUNDT

Southern Illinois University, Carbondale

HARRY R. DAMMER

University of Scranton

FRANCIS T. CULLEN

University of Cincinnati

SUMMARY Since the inception of the penitentiary, prison chaplains have played an integral role in the lives of inmates. Research has been limited, however, that explores the involvement of chaplains in offender treatment. This research examines chaplains' historic and contemporary roles in correctional counseling, the degree to which chaplains are supportive of rehabilitation, and the content of chaplains' counseling sessions. The findings reveal that chaplains are highly supportive of rehabilitation, spend the majority of their time counseling inmates, and utilize a combination of religious and secular methods of counseling. Further, it was found that chaplains view offender adjustment and rehabilitation as goals of their counseling and generally employ methods and styles of correctional treatment that have been associated with reductions in recidivism. *[Article copies available for a fee from The Haworth Document Delivery Service: 1-800-HAWORTH. E-mail address: <getinfo@haworthpressinc.com> Website: <http://www.HaworthPress.com> © 2002 by The Haworth Press, Inc. All rights reserved.]*

KEYWORDS Chaplain, rehabilitation, inmate, counseling, recidivism, religion, prison

A number of trends have, of late, converged to bring religion to the forefront of counseling. In particular, a growing awareness and appreciation of multiculturalism have lent a degree of acceptance to the incorporation of religion into mainstream counseling. Similarly, specifically religious counseling is gaining wider recognition as a viable method of treatment. In fact, in a recent review of research on religion and counseling, Worthington, Kurusu, McCullough, and Sandage (1996, p. 448) observe that "the acceptance of some role of religion in counseling has ... exploded into the mainstream of counseling and clinical psychology over the last decade." The expanded role of religion in mainstream counseling has also been encouraged by economic constraints. As health insurance companies have become less willing to pay for their patients' mental health needs, more clients have turned to the clergy for help, since ministers rarely charge for their services (see Worthington et al., 1996). The increased acceptance of and demand for religious counseling has encouraged a vigorous research agenda that seeks to examine the theoretical and practical significance of religion to counseling.

A related line of inquiry has recently gained momentum within the field of criminal justice. There is an emerging research agenda to assess the effect of religious programming on inmate prison adjustment and recidivism. With reports that approximately one in three inmates participates in religious programs (U. S. Department of Justice, 1993; Religious programs, 1983), these questions have become germane. Although tentative and preliminary, a handful of studies have concluded that participation in religious programming improves institutional adjustment and reduces recidivism among certain inmates (Clear, Stout, Dammer, Kelly, Hardyman, & Shapiro, 1992a, 1992b; Johnson, 1987; Johnson, Larson, & Pitts, 1997; O'Connor, Ryan, & Parikh, 1997; Young, Gartner, O'Connor, Larson, & Wright, 1995). Moreover, renewed enthusiasm for religious programming has spurred the establishment of faith-based prisons in Texas, Brazil, and Ecuador and similar programs are being developed in Oklahoma, Kansas, Iowa, England, Wales, and Scotland (Prison Fellowship, 1999). While religious programming in prison is certainly not a new phenomenon and has long been tied to the rehabilitation of offenders (as we will discuss below in greater detail), it is safe to say that we are witnessing a resurgence of interest in this area.

Somewhat surprisingly, little attention has yet to be given to the role of the prison chaplain in facilitating inmate adjustment and rehabilitation. This neglect is noteworthy for several reasons. First, the chaplaincy has historically provided inmates with a range of religious and secular services aimed at meeting inmates' religious, institutional, and post-release needs (Sundt & Cullen, 1998). Second, chaplains are the only members of the prison work group, other than correctional officers, who regularly have contact with inmates in the tier area (Shaw, 1995). Unlike correctional officers, however, chaplains are not charged with the control of inmates and as such have the opportunity to substantially affect inmates. And third, a recent survey of prison administrators revealed that chaplains are responsible for providing counseling to inmates in *all* of the 49 jurisdictions that responded (*Religion Behind Bars*, 1998).

The chaplain's importance as an agent of social change has been suggested by Glaser (1964). In his classic study, *The Effectiveness of a Prison and Probation System*, Glaser found that, among inmates who attributed their post-release success to members of the prison staff, one-sixth cited the prison chaplains, although they constituted less than 1% of the prison employees. Further, chaplains were the second most frequently mentioned staff member credited with bringing about inmates' rehabilitation (1964, pp. 141, 145).

Despite chaplains' involvement in counseling inmates and hints about their efficacy, to date research has been limited that explores systematically the involvement of chaplains in the treatment enterprise. This research attempts to address this oversight by exploring the role of the prison chaplain in offender rehabilitation. In doing so, we will examine the degree to which chaplains are supportive of rehabilitation as a goal of corrections. In addition, we will explore the chaplain's role in correctional counseling, the specific types of counseling methods employed by chaplains, and the extent to which they view their counseling as religious or spiritual. Finally, we will examine whether chaplains utilize counseling styles and methods that are associated with effective correctional treatment (Andrews & Bonta, 1994, p. 200; Andrews & Kiessling, 1980, pp. 462-463).

PRISON CHAPLAINCY AND OFFENDER REHABILITATION

Since the inception of the penitentiary, prison chaplains have played an integral, if changing, role in the lives of incarcerated offenders. Indeed, chaplains were arguably the first to provide inmates with services and, as such, are credited with being the first member of the prison staff responsible for the rehabilitation of prisoners (Keuther, 1951). Throughout the 1800s, much of the chaplain's time was spent visiting inmates in their cells, delivering short sermons to laboring prisoners, and providing religious services to inmates on Sundays (Adamson, 1992; Skotnicki, 1991). In addition to these religious duties, chaplains also performed a number of more secular tasks–most of which involved providing services to inmates. For example, chaplains were responsible for opening the first prison libraries and schools and took on full responsibility for educating prisoners. In addition, chaplains frequently led temperance revivals, created programs for discharged inmates, compiled statistical reports for the state legislature and philanthropic societies, and occasionally raised an intra-institutional voice against the maltreatment of inmates (Skotnicki, 1991).

During the 1900s, however, the chaplaincy's value to the prison was challenged. With the rise of rationalism and scientific positivism, the chaplain became a religious representative in a secularized institution of professionals. As a consequence, the chaplaincy was marginalized as religion moved from the center of penology to its periphery. This development had a number of effects on the chaplaincy. Most notably, the chaplain's role in the prison was diminished–duties that had traditionally been performed by the chaplain were taken over by trained professionals (Bates, 1938).

In response, chaplains attempted to recast their role in the prison by arguing that they could play an integral part in achieving central correctional goals. In other words, "the value of prison ministry came to be defined primarily by the extent to which it could advance central correctional goals as defined by the secular professionals administering the prison" (Sundt & Cullen, 1998, p. 274). Given the dominance of the rehabilitative ideal at this time, chaplains made the case that they could be instrumental in achieving this goal. This change was not a dramatic reinterpretation of the work of the chaplain; chaplains had a long history of providing services to inmates and the offender reformation was largely consistent with chaplains' religious beliefs about forgiveness and redemption. Still, this reorientation did solidify and reinforce the chaplain's (formal) role in offender treatment.

Thus, during the early 1900s, chaplains defined their role as educational (Scott, 1906; Thornton, 1903) as faith was placed in the ability of education to reform offenders (McKelvey, 1977). With the rise of the medical model, chaplains characterized themselves as "soul doctors" and "moral physicians" (Giesen, 1936). It was in the late 1930s, however, that the chaplaincy became most strongly oriented toward the rehabilitation of the offender. Again, this orientation was consistent with correctional trends, which likewise had gained additional focus on the classification and treatment (McKelvey, 1977; Rothman, 1980). It was common during this period for prison ministers to argue before the American Prison Association (now the American Correctional Association) that religion was essential to successful rehabilitation. In 1944, for example, Dr. C. E. Krumbholz asserted that "No rehabilitation can be complete without the spiritual therapy of religion" (1944, p. 170). A similar contention was made the following year by Rabbi Abraham Holtzberg:

> We fully endorse the attempt at vocational guidance and education in our penal institutions. But we are convinced that without God, the philosophy of morality and ethics which stem from such a concept, such a rehabilitation is not possible. (1945, p. 119)

In addition to these general statements, it was maintained that the chaplains could make "a special contribution including the remotivation, the substitution of pro-social for anti-social attitudes" (Powers, 1960, p. 197).

The 1950s and 1960s once more witnessed a renewed commitment to offender rehabilitation (McKelvey 1977), and following suit the prison chaplains–particularly those who were more liberal–renewed their commitment to theologically-oriented counseling. Clinical Pastoral Counseling, Transactional Analysis, and Gestalt therapy became the favored treatment strategies among chaplains. Not all chaplains embraced their rehabilitative role, however, and a rift began to develop between the more liberal, clinically trained clergy and the conservative sacramental ministers. As Taft observes (1978, p. 55), chaplains tended to focus either their attention on those few inmates who were interested in religion or they "schooled themselves in the late twentieth century's new religion: psychology." As the 1960s drew to a close, the chaplain's treatment role had been revitalized and even solidified.

As the hegemony of the rehabilitative ideal was attacked during the early 1970s, however, the chaplaincy found that their niche in the prison was challenged to some extent. In response, chaplains again reinterpreted their work by maintaining that they could play a key role in ensuring the newfound religious rights of inmates. Other correctional trends have similarly shaped the chaplaincy. For example, chaplains have recently argued that they can contribute to the management of inmates (Cook, 1994). Other recent accounts of the chaplaincy suggest that prison ministers should reassert their roles as correctional counselors and coordinators of religious programs and volunteers and place less emphasis on providing religious services or "doing church" (Fewell, 1995).

Although historical and contemporary accounts of the chaplaincy indicate that correctional counseling is an important part of prison ministry, as discussed above, there has been a paucity of empirical research examining the degree to which chaplains engage in and are supportive of the treatment of inmates. In addition, it is uncertain whether chaplains view their counseling as rehabilitative or primarily religious and spiritual. It is to these issues that we now turn.

METHODS

Sample

In the fall of 1997, we randomly selected a sample of 500 chaplains identified by the American Correctional Association as employed in the United States. Questionnaires were distributed to the sample following Dillman's (1978) "total design method." During the first mailing, each person in the sample was sent a questionnaire, a letter introducing the survey, and a postage-paid return envelope. A reminder letter was mailed to the entire sample one week later encouraging the return of the surveys. Three weeks after the initial mailing, replacement questionnaires were mailed to all those who had not responded. This process was repeated again five weeks after the first mailing. The original sample size of 500 was reduced to 402, however, when a number of surveys were returned undelivered because the respondents were either retired, no longer at the address listed, or deceased. Out of the 402 deliverable questionnaires, 232 were returned, for a response rate of 57.7%.

To further explore issues related to the content of chaplains' counseling sessions, a second sample of chaplains was obtained. In April of 1998, questionnaires were distributed to 45 chaplains attending a conference at Niagara University in Niagara, NY. Out of the 45 chaplains who were given surveys, 32 returned their questionnaire, for a response rate of 71%. Although of limited generalizabilty, this focused sample is nevertheless appropriate for exploring the specific methods and styles of counseling employed by chaplains.

The characteristics of both samples are presented in Table 1. The respondents in the national sample are predominately white males in their mid-50s with an average of 10 years of experience at the institution where they are employed. More than 90% of chaplains in the national sample are college graduates, and the vast majority of these individuals have completed a postgraduate degree. Further, 70% of the chaplains

☐ **Table 1: Demographic Characteristics (Percentages)**

Variable/Characteristic	GROUP	
	National (N = 232)	New York (N = 32)
Sex		
Male	85.2	87.9
Female	14.8	12.1
Race		
White	84.2	50.0
Black	10.4	40.6
Other	5.4	9.4
Educational Level		
High School Graduate	4.9	
Associate's Degree	3.0	
Bachelor's Degree	13.4	
Master's Degree	62.2	
Doctorate	16.5	
Training in Pastoral Counseling		
Yes	70.3	66.7
No	29.7	33.3
Religious Affiliation		
Protestant	69.4	38.7
Catholic	25.7	22.6
Jewish	0.9	3.2
Islamic	1.8	32.3
Other	2.3	3.2
Mean Age	56.5	50.5
Mean Years Experience	10.3	9.5
Mean Years of Education		17.0

report that they have received training in pastoral counseling. The New York sample differed somewhat from the national sample, particularly with regard to race and religious affiliation; compared to the national sample, Islamic and minority chaplains were overrepresented. Since so little is known about the chaplaincy, however, it is difficult to surmise what effect, if any, this discrepancy has on the results of this research.

Measures

To assess the role of the chaplain in offender rehabilitation we will examine the following: chaplains' support for rehabilitation, the extent to which chaplains are involved in counseling inmates, and the content of chaplains' counseling sessions.

Support for Rehabilitation. Chaplains' support for rehabilitation was measured with items derived from Cullen, Lutze, Link, and Wolfe's (1989) correctional orientation scale. The items included in this research tap the extent to which chaplains are supportive of offender treatment (see Table 2). For each statement, respondents were asked to indicate their degree of agreement or disagreement on a six-point Likert scale.

We are also interested in learning whether chaplains believe in the reformative ability of religion or credit treatment programs with the rehabilitation of inmates. To assess this issue chaplains were asked: *What do*

☐ **Table 2: Chaplains' Attitudes Toward Offender Rehabilitation (Proportions Reported)**

	Agree Strongly	Agree	Agree Somewhat	Disagree Somewhat	Disagree	Disagree Strongly	Mean
[1] Rehabilitating a criminal is just as important as making a criminal pay for his or her crime.	54.7	31.8	7.6	1.8	2.2	1.8	5.29
[2] One of the reasons rehabilitation programs often fail is that they are underfunded; if enough money were available, these programs would work.	5.1	21.2	27.0	10.4	27.5	8.1	3.43
[3] The most effective and humane cure to the crime problem in America is to make a strong effort to rehabilitate offenders.	17.9	44.4	18.4	8.1	9.4	1.8	4.48
[4] The rehabilitation of prisoners has proven to be a failure.	6.8	13.1	17.6	14.4	30.6	17.6	4.02
[5] All rehabilitation programs have done is to allow criminals who deserve to be punished to get off easily.	0.0	2.7	6.7	15.2	46.2	29.1	4.92
[6] The only way to reduce crime in society is to punish criminals, not to try to rehabilitate them.	1.4	0.9	3.6	5.9	44.6	43.7	5.23
[7] The rehabilitation of criminals just does not work.	1.3	3.6	10.3	13.9	42.6	28.3	4.78
[8] I would support expanding the rehabilitation programs with criminals that are now being undertaken in our prisons.	25.0	50.0	16.4	4.1	3.2	1.4	4.85

Note: Higher scores reflect stronger support for rehabilitation; mean of items 4-7 have been calculated from reversed scales.

you think is the best way to rehabilitate offenders? As summarized in Table 3, response categories included: *Give them a good education; teach them a skill that they can use to get a job when they are released from prison; help them with their emotional problems that caused them to break the law; change their values through religion.*

Chaplains' Role in Offender Rehabilitation. To measure the chaplain's role in offender rehabilitation, we comprised a list of activities in which chaplains engage. This list was derived from descriptions of the chaplaincy contained in essays and research (Cook, 1994; Fewell, 1994; Morris, 1961; Murphy, 1956; Shaw, 1995; Thompson, 1989; Williams, 1996), and includes those tasks that have been most frequently mentioned as duties of the chaplain (see Table 4).

☐ **Table 3: Chaplains' Views About Best Method of Rehabilitation**

Method	Number	Percent
Education	21	10.2
Teach Vocational Skills	27	13.1
Change Values Through Religion	124	60.2
Help with Emotional Problems	34	16.5

Respondents were asked: What do you think is the best way to rehabilitate offenders: give them a good education; teach them a skill that they can use to get a job when they are released from prison; change their values through religion; or help them with their emotional problems that caused them to break the law?

☐ **Table 4: Chaplains' Activities–Frequency of Performance and Assessment of Importance**

Task	Frequency		Importance	
	Mean	Rank	Mean	Rank
Counseling Inmates	6.910	1	2.022	1
Conducting Religious Services	5.413	4	2.482	2
Coordinating Religious Programs	6.247	2	2.960	3
Religious Education	4.482	5	3.412	4
Supervising Volunteers	5.491	3	3.592	5

Chaplains were asked to rate how much time they spent on each activity on a scale from 1 to 10, with 1 equal to no time and 10 equal to almost all of their time. Chaplains were also asked to rank the importance of the activities from 1 to 5, with 1 being the most important duty and 5 being the least important duty.

The list includes conducting religious services, counseling inmates, supervising volunteers, teaching religious education, and coordinating religious programs. For each of these tasks, chaplains were asked to indicate the amount of time they give to the activity on a scale from one to 10, with one equal to no time and 10 equal to almost all of their time. In addition to determining how chaplains spend their time, we also assessed the importance that they assign to these activities. This variable was measured by asking chaplains to rank the list of activities in importance from 1 to 5, with 1 the most important duty and 5 the least important.

As a final indicator of chaplains' involvement in offender treatment, we questioned chaplains about what they hope to accomplish through their work. Specifically, chaplains were asked, "In thinking about your work as a chaplain, what importance do you place on each of the following in terms of what you hope to accomplish through your work?"

The outcomes presented to the sample include helping inmates adjust to prison, rehabilitating inmates, and converting inmates to religious principles (see Table 5). Thus, these items provide an additional indicator of the extent to which chaplains view inmate adjustment and offender rehabilitation as important features of their work. Relatedly, this measure also provides an indication of whether chaplains view the purpose of their work as primarily religious or spiritual in nature.

☐ **Table 5: Importance Attributed to Prison Adjustment, Crime Prevention, and Conversion**

Objective	Very Important	Important	Mildly Important	Not Important
Helping inmates adjust to the harshness of living in prison; that is, making their lives less painful and more meaningful.				
	40.2	50.4	8.0	1.3
Helping inmates acquire the skills and attitudes they will need to be successful when they return to society.				
	50.5	44.6	4.1	0.9
Converting inmates to my religious principles so that they will be "saved" from a life in sin.				
	16.9	28.3	22.8	32.0

Question: In thinking about your work as a chaplain, what importance do you place on each of the following in terms of what you hope to accomplish through your work?

The Content of Counseling. As indicated earlier, this research also concerned the specific content of chaplains' counseling sessions and sought to determine whether chaplains utilize styles of counseling that are associated with effective treatment. These issues were explored with a number of measures:

- First, chaplains were presented with a list of counseling methods and were asked to report whether they currently use each approach when counseling inmates (see Table 6). In addition to listing the names of several treatment methods, we included a brief description of each counseling approach for reference (see Appendix). Finally, respondents were given space to write in any method that they used that was not included in the list.
- Second, we were interested in exploring the degree to which chaplains emphasize religion and spirituality in their counseling sessions with inmates. Chaplains were asked: "In thinking about your counseling sessions with inmates, what emphasis do you place on religion and/or spirituality?" Responses were measured on a scale from 1 to 10, with 1 equal to no emphasis and 10 equal to total emphasis.
- Third, two open-ended questions were posed to respondents. The first question asked chaplains to describe, in their own words, a typical counseling session with an inmate. Next, chaplains were asked to describe what their primary objective was when counseling inmates. Together these items provide a richer source of information about the content of chaplains' counseling sessions with inmates.
- Fourth, we constructed a measure to tap whether chaplains are employing styles of correctional counseling that are associated with treatment effectiveness. Andrews and Kiessling (1980) have found that styles of correctional counseling that are rooted in social learning theory are related to lower rates of recidivism. As Andrews and Bonta (1994, p. 200) explain,

Effective rehabilitative efforts involve workers who are interpersonally warm, tolerant and flexible, yet sensitive to conventional rules and procedures. These workers make use of the authority inherent in the position without engaging in interpersonal dominations (i.e., they are "firm but fair"), they demonstrate in vivid ways their own anticriminal-prosocial attitudes, values and beliefs, and they enthusiastically engage the offender in the process of increasing rewards for noncriminal activity . . . The alternatives [to criminal attitudes and behaviors] are demonstrated through words and actions, and explorations of the alternatives are encouraged through modeling, reinforcement and concrete guidance.

Our operationalization of the characteristics of effective correctional counseling are presented in Table 7. These items tap the extent to which counselors develop relationships with their clients that are open and enthusiastic, "firm but fair," and respectful. Further, we measure the degree to which counselors model and reinforce pro-social attitudes and behaviors and discourage pro-criminal attitudes and behaviors. Finally, these items assess whether counselors are advocates for inmates, refer inmates to needed services, and try to teach inmates to solve their problems. For each item, respondents were asked to indicate their degree of agreement or disagreement on a six-point Likert scale. (Although we do not analyze these measures as a scale, a reliable analysis indicates that the items contained in the effective correctional counseling scale are reliable, with a Cronbach's alpha of .76.)

FINDINGS

Support for Rehabilitation

Chaplains' attitudes toward rehabilitation were reported in Table 2, which reveals a high level of support for offender treatment. More than

□ **Table 6: Counseling Methods Used by Chaplains (in Descending Order of Frequency)**

Method	Percent	Rank
Reality Therapy	54.8	1
Group Counseling	54.8	1
Client-centered Counseling	51.6	2
Behavioral Methods	45.2	3
"Other"	38.7	4
Eclectic Counseling	35.5	5
Gestalt Methods	29.0	6
Rational-emotive Methods	29.0	6
Adlerian Counseling	25.8	7
Transactional Analysis	22.6	8
Psychoanalysis	9.7	9
Mean Level of Emphasis Placed on Religion or Spirituality	9.0	

Religious and Spiritual Emphasis scale ranges from 10-1, with high scores indicating greater emphasis on religion or spirituality.

☐ **Table 7: Chaplains' Utilization of Counseling Styles Associated with Treatment Effectiveness**

	Agree Strongly	Agree	Agree Somewhat	Disagree Somewhat	Disagree	Disagree Strongly	Mean
When interacting with inmates, I am open, warm, and enthusiastic.							
	34.4	40.6	21.9	3.1	0.0	0.0	5.06
I stress to inmates that criminal attitudes are wrong.							
	45.5	18.2	9.1	9.1	12.1	6.1	4.58
I try to develop relationships with inmates that are based on mutual respect and liking.							
	42.4	39.4	12.1	0.0	6.1	0.0	5.12
I am an advocate for inmates.							
	36.4	36.4	21.1	3.0	3.0	0.0	5.00
I try to teach inmates to solve their problems.							
	60.0	33.3	6.7	0.0	0.0	0.0	5.53
When inmates express poor moral judgment, I discourage this type of thinking.							
	53.1	34.4	9.4	0.0	3.1	0.0	5.34
An important part of my work is to refer inmates to agencies that can provide them with the services they need.							
	31.3	25.0	28.1	9.4	3.1	3.1	4.62
I stress to inmates that criminal behavior is wrong and harmful.							
	54.5	24.2	0.0	3.0	15.2	3.0	4.91
When inmates express good moral judgment, I reward and reinforce this type of thinking.							
	43.8	34.4	15.6	0.0	6.3	0.0	5.09
It is important to me to be "firm but fair" with inmates.							
	54.5	36.4	9.1	0.0	0.0	0.0	5.45
I try to be a role model of moral thinking and behavior to inmates.							
	63.6	30.3	6.1	0.0	0.0	0.0	5.58

90% of chaplains surveyed agreed, at least slightly, that treating offenders is as important as punishing them (item 1) and a similar number favored expanding rehabilitation programs (item 8).

In addition, an overwhelming majority of respondents rejected the idea that rehabilitation programs allow criminals who deserve to be punished to get off easily (item 5) and that punishing criminals is the only way to reduce crime (item 6). Four out of 5 respondents agreed that rehabilitation is the most effective and humane cure to the crime problem (item 3), and chaplains overwhelmingly disagreed that the rehabilitation of prisoners has proven to be a failure (item 4). The majority of chaplains also indicated that treatment programs could be improved with better funding (item 2) and soundly rejected the idea that the reha- bilitation does not work (item 7).

While these results indicate that chaplains are highly supportive of treatment, it is unclear whether prison ministers attribute the rehabilita- tion of offenders to the reformative ability of religion or to the success of treatment programs. To address this question respondents were asked to report on what they thought was the best method of treatment. The re- sults of this inquiry are displayed in Table 3. A clear majority of chap- lains (60.2 %) said that changing an offender's values through religion was the best method of rehabilitation. Teaching inmates a skill that they could use to get a job was the second most frequently selected response, closely followed by helping offenders with their emotional problems. Lastly, providing inmates with a good education was the least fre- quently selected response.

These findings advance the idea that chaplains not only support treat- ment, but also see religion and their spiritual work as rehabilitative. It is also instructive to note, however, that 40% of the sample did not select religion as the best method of treatment. Thus, a substantial minority of chaplains feel that secular methods are better suited to bringing about inmate change.

Chaplains' Role in Offender Counseling

Historical and contemporary discussions of the chaplaincy often mention that counseling inmates is a primary part of the chaplains' role (Acorn, 1990; Fewell, 1995; Morris, 1961; Murphy, 1956; Shaw, 1996; Religion Behind Bars, 1998; Thompson, 1989; Williams, 1996). The results presented here confirm these accounts (for a fuller discussion of the chaplain's role and task performance, see Sundt & Cullen, 1998). As summarized in Table 4, counseling inmates was the task that chaplains report spending the most time on and rate as their most important activ- ity. Coordinating religious programs was the second most frequently performed task, but was ranked third in importance. Conversely, con- ducting religious services was the third most frequently performed task, but was viewed by chaplains as second in importance. Finally, religious education and supervising volunteers were ranked fourth and fifth, re- spectively, in frequency of performance and importance.

In addition to assessing the amount of time and the importance that chaplains assign to these activities, we also questioned chaplains about what they hoped to accomplish through their work. In particular, respondents were asked to indicate the importance that they placed on helping inmates adjust to living in prison, helping inmates acquire skills and attitudes needed to be successful when returning to society, and helping inmates convert to religious principles to be "saved" from a life of sin. As summarized in Table 5, the vast majority of chaplains (more than 90%) reported that helping inmates to adjust to prison and preparing them for a successful return to society were important or very important goals of their work. Less consensus exists among chaplains regarding the conversion of inmates: 32% of chaplains felt that conversion was not an important objective of their work, close to 23% reported that converting inmates was a little important, 28% believed that this was important, and 17% said it was very important. These data indicate that chaplains are not only counseling inmates, but that they view prison adjustment and rehabilitation as important objectives of their work. It can also be argued that chaplains place more importance on inmate adjustment and rehabilitation than on religious conversion.

In sum, these findings reveal that chaplains spend a significant amount of their time counseling inmates. Further, chaplains viewed this task as their most important activity. Finally, evidence was found that chaplains consider inmate adjustment and rehabilitation to be important goals of their work.

Although these data are suggestive, the specific content of chaplains' counseling sessions with inmates remains unclear. For example, while these results can be interpreted to mean that chaplains are engaging in counseling to help inmates address their practical, emotional, and behavioral problems, it is also possible that these counseling sessions focus primarily on religious or spiritual issues. It may be that chaplains see religious and spiritual guidance as reformative in-and-of itself. In contrast, they may engage in counseling that employs secular methods. It is also possible that they may combine religious and secular philosophies, theories, and methods when counseling inmates.

The Content of Counseling

The results from the national survey indicate that chaplains are supportive of rehabilitation, see religion as reformative, spend a significant amount of their time counseling inmates, and place a high level of importance on this task. As discussed above, however, the content of chaplains' counseling sessions is ambiguous. Therefore, to further explore the specific nature of chaplains' counseling sessions with inmates, we administered follow-up surveys to a small sample of chaplains in New York. Our inquiry focused on examining the methods of counseling that chaplains used, the emphasis that they place on religion and spirituality, and the styles of counseling that they adopt.

As revealed in Table 6, over half of the chaplains in the New York sample reported that they employed reality therapy (54.8%), group counseling (54.8%), and client-centered counseling (51.6%). Behavioral treatment methods were also used by 45% of the respondents. Less frequently utilized methods of counseling include eclectic counseling, Gestalt therapy, rational-emotive therapy, Adlerian counseling, transactional analysis, and psychoanalysis. Finally, more than a third of the sample reported that they used another method of counseling. Notably, this research suggests that chaplains are utilizing treatment modalities that are associated with effective correctional intervention–namely, cognitive and behavioral approaches. Similarly, chaplains are using multiple methods of treatment, which again, is an approach that has been linked with reductions in recidivism (Andrews & Bonta, 1994; Andrews, Zinger, Hoge, Bonta, Gendreau, & Cullen, 1990; Palmer, 1992).

While chaplains report that they utilize established, secular methods of counseling, it should also be noted that they place a great deal of emphasis on religion or spirituality during their counseling sessions. As reported at the bottom of Table 6, on a scale from 1 to 10–with 1 equal to no emphasis on religion or spirituality during counseling sessions and 10 equal to total emphasis–the mean score for the New York sample is 8.97. Further, very little variation existed on this measure, with responses ranging from 7 to 10. On a related point, the counseling methods that chaplains favor tend to be those that are consistent with religious worldviews and emphasize personal responsibility, values and attitudes, and decision-making. Thus, together these findings suggest that prison chaplains utilize counseling techniques that combine secular and religious or spiritual content.

Chaplains in the New York sample were also asked to describe a "typical" counseling session in order to develop a fuller understanding of the content of chaplains' counseling. To aid in the interpretation of responses to this question, we drew on the work of Worthington (1986), who has hypothesized that three types of religious counseling techniques exist. These techniques include (1) the use of secular counseling theories and techniques to influence religious clients' worldviews to be more religious or spiritual, (2) the use of techniques derived from religion (e.g., prayer, meditation, and forgiveness) within counseling, and (3) the integration of secular approaches and religious content. In addition to *religious counseling*, chaplains may also engage in counseling in which religious and spiritual issues are excluded altogether (*secular counseling*), or they may employ *spiritual direction*, which focuses on clients' religious or spiritual life and not necessarily on his or her problems or behavior.

First, we found that none of the respondents' descriptions of typical sessions with inmates could be classified as exclusively religious in content. This finding, however, could be an artifact of the way that we worded this question, which asked chaplains to describe typical *counseling* sessions. It is possible that a different question would have revealed that chaplains also provide spiritual direction to inmates.

Second, we found that 16 chaplains (64% of those who responded to this item) described typical counseling sessions that did not include any mention of religious or spiritual issues and activities. For example, one chaplain wrote that

> The common counseling session [takes place in] a group setting. Inmates are given the opportunity to examine their behavior, analyze it and come up with self-corrective solutions. The inmate may solve his own problem or extract from the group discussion his resolution to his problem.

In a similar vein, another chaplain explains that

> A great deal of my counseling pertains to reality therapy. I believe an inmate must grapple with the reality of where he is and what brought him there. I also believe responsibility to do the right thing is paramount. Through reality therapy I then work through behavioral change and dealing with responsibility; I use the client centered approach at times for clarification.

Even though the majority of chaplains described counseling sessions in which no mention of religion or spirituality was made, this finding should be viewed cautiously in light of the finding that, when asked directly about this issue, all of the respondents reported that they placed a high level of emphasis on religion and spirituality during counseling sessions (see Table 6).

Third, the remaining nine chaplains described sessions that can be classified as "religious counseling." Among this group, none of the chaplains reported the use of secular theories to influence inmates' religious or spiritual orientations. Most of the responses that were classified in this group utilized methods of religious counseling that involved the integration of religious values, orientations, and practices, and secular counseling methods. The following description is illustrative of this approach:

> I use reality therapy to help inmates realize the importance of our decisions, our behavior and how we ultimately will answer to God for the choices we make in this life. My main text for *any* counseling session is the infallible word of God–the Holy Bible. I believe it has the answers to all of life's problems, because it deals with the inside of a man–his soul and spirit.

One respondent, however, indicated that his counseling sessions focused exclusively on techniques derived from religion:

> [A typical counseling session involves] a Bible-based approach to inmates, discovering Biblical moral principles and God's design for a spiritual healthy life. If an individual chooses or seeks help from this source, there is a broad base for the individual to have forgiveness, release from guilt, anger, helplessness as well as defined goals for his future. The spiritual base affects the physical, emotional, [and] behavioral aspects of the individual as well as the spiritual.

Viewed in conjunction with the results presented in Table 6, these narratives provide additional support for the assertion that prison chaplains utilize counseling techniques that combine secular methods with religious or spiritual content.

Aside from the methods of counseling described by chaplains, a number of noteworthy patterns warrant discussion. For example, eight of the respondents (32% of those who responded to this item) indicated that an important part of their counseling sessions involved listening to inmates' problems and concerns, or providing a "friendly ear." Further, six of the chaplains (24% of respondents) reported that they took a problem-solving approach to inmate counseling. Encouraging inmates to take responsibility for their actions and self, providing moral feedback, developing empathy for others, helping inmates in coping with grief, adjusting to prison and anger management, crisis counseling, and addressing family and relationship problems were also mentioned in this set of responses.

To further explore the content and nature of chaplains' correctional counseling, we asked chaplains to discuss their primary objective when counseling inmates. Responses to this question further support the conclusion that prison chaplains view religion and spirituality as life changing and rehabilitative. For example, the most frequently reported objective was to facilitate self-examination and insight, with nine chaplains (32% of those who responded to this item) indicating that this was their primary goal. As one chaplain explains:

> [My main objective is] to initiate the sense of self-examination, self-correction, and self-analysis; the spiritual, moral, and ethical resurrection of the individual.

Five chaplains also reported that their main objective was to help inmates solve their problems.

> [My main objective is to] identify [the] nature of [the] problem, identify feelings, and set goals and plan of action.

A number of chaplains (21% of respondents), however, specifically mentioned that offender change or rehabilitation was the primary objective of their counseling sessions. For example:

> As in education, the teacher has not taught until the student has learned. My primary objective is to see if he is motivated to make changes. If he cannot change the situation (often the case due to the powerlessness of inmates) then he must change himself, his attitude and perspective of his world. My job is to help him see that and if necessary five specific instructions on how to make changes. Change is the catch word. If he remains the same, I have not done my job. If he strives for change, I have been successful.

Similarly, another chaplain explains that:

> [My main objective is] to assist them in working though destructive learned behavior and guide them into a decision-making process dealing with responsibility. I believe spiritual commitment is imperative to this process.

Other objectives included encouraging inmates to take responsibility for their actions and themselves, helping inmates cope with grief, prison, and other problems, developing positive self-images, helping inmates achieve emotional stability, developing empathy, identifying serious problems and making referrals, providing an opportunity for catharsis, and promoting healing, forgiveness, and hope. Finally, one chaplain reported that the primary objective of counseling was exclusively religious:

> [The primary objective of my counseling sessions with inmates is] to give religious direction, Islamically.

Styles of Counseling. A final concern of this research is to explore whether chaplains utilize styles of correctional counseling that have been associated with treatment effectiveness (Andrews & Bonta, 1994; Andrews & Kiessling, 1980). Table 7 summarizes the results of this inquiry. Chaplains unanimously agreed that they try to teach inmates to solve their problems. All of the chaplains surveyed also reported that they try to be role models of moral thinking and behavior and place importance on being *firm but fair* with inmates. Similarly, more than 90% of the sample support an open, warm, and enthusiastic style of interaction, try to develop relationships with inmates that are based on mutual respect and liking, act as advocates for inmates, discourage poor moral judgment, and encourage good moral judgment. Finally, approximately three-fourths of the chaplains reported stressing that criminal attitudes and behaviors are wrong and harmful. Thus, these findings indicate that chaplains are highly supportive of counseling styles associated with effective correctional intervention.

Although little variation exists among responses to the items contained in Table 7, a few exceptions to this pattern should be noted. In particular, chaplains were slightly less supportive of stressing the wrongfulness of criminal attitudes and behaviors (items 2 and 8). It may be that some chaplains are not comfortable with making open judgments about their clients' criminal attitudes and behaviors, as this activity may conflict with their role as confidants, confessors, and grantors of absolution. In addition, less agreement was found among chaplains about the importance of making referrals for inmates (Table 7). This result may reflect a lack of services available in the prison setting for making referrals. In contrast, this finding is consistent with previous research on religious counselors, which has found a general reluctance among pastors to refer clients to secular professionals (Worthington et al., 1996).

DISCUSSION

In recent years, commentators have depicted the growing crisis in American prisons. Correctional institutions thus have become increasingly crowded and attempts have been made to toughen inmates' lives by taking away various amenities (e.g., college education, television). It also has been argued that prisons either are, or should be, places to warehouse offenders who pose a threat to society. In the midst of this "mean season" in corrections, it is easy to assume that prisons are devoid of humanity and efforts to better offenders. This picture of the nation's prisons, while true to a degree, risks being a caricature that masks the good works that often are done inside correctional facilities. For example, research suggests that wardens and correctional officers support the rehabilitation of offenders and do not view the mission of prisons as exclusively punitive or custodial (Cullen, Latessa, Burton, & Lombardo, 1993; Johnson, 1996). The current research confirms that chaplains are another source of "doing good" in prison.

Our research suggests several broad conclusions. First, chaplains are supportive of the rehabilitative ideal. This support is reflected by both their correctional ideology and by what they do inside prison. Chaplains feel strongly that rehabilitation is important, humane, and an effective means of reducing recidivism; they also support expanding treatment programs and disagree that rehabilitation lets inmates off too easily. While these views tend to parallel the attitudes of the public, who also endorse offender rehabilitation (Applegate, Cullen, & Fischer, 1997; Cullen, Applegate, & Fischer, in press), chaplains' support for treatment is notably high. These attitudes may be rooted in religious views about forgiveness and redemption. It is also possible, however, that chaplains' attitudes are shaped by their work experiences as ministers and counselors. In addition to supporting rehabilitation, many chaplains view prison work as a religious mission and a higher calling (Sundt, 1997). Thus, chaplains are potentially an important source for combating the ideas of penal harm and may be a humanizing presence in the prison.

Second, the present research reveals that in counseling offenders, chaplains integrate their religious and secular beliefs. Most prison ministers believe that offenders change due to religious transformation. But a sizeable minority of chaplains also believe that education, vocational training, and addressing emotional problems are the best way to change offenders. Further, prison ministers favor certain counseling styles that might be viewed as secular, yet they report that religion and spirituality are heavily emphasized during their counseling sessions. The methods of counseling adopted by chaplains similarly tend to mesh with their religious worldviews. Finally, although chaplains view the objectives of their counseling as helping individuals to gain insight into themselves and understand their place in the world, offender change and prison adjustment are also given primacy.

Third, chaplains appear to be utilizing methods and styles of correctional counseling that are associated with treatment effectiveness. Although it is unlikely that this is a planned strategy on the part of prison ministers, chaplains tend to *favor* approaches to correctional counseling that "work" with offenders. This tendency is likely due to the overlap between religious worldviews and certain treatment modalities. Chaplains favor approaches such as reality therapy and other cognitive-behavioral methods, which focus on the choices that people make, attitudes, and accountability. In other words, the treatment modalities that chaplains favor tend to converge with religious perspectives. Similarly, it was found that chaplains favor styles of counseling that emphasize modeling and rewarding pro-social moral attitudes and behaviors. Again, this is largely consistent with religious perspectives. In contrast, the methods of counseling that were not favored by chaplains, psychoanalysis for example, are less consistent with religious values.

Since the 1900s, chaplains have been marginalized in the prison. In response to this marginal status, chaplains have argued that, beyond their religious duties, they are central to meeting correctional objectives. One of the ways in which chaplains have done this is to maintain that they can play a key role in offender rehabilitation and adjustment. As religious counseling moves to the mainstream, it is possible that the role of the chaplain will similarly be afforded additional legitimacy. In addition, in the context of "penal harm" and the "no frills" prison movement (see, e.g., Clear, 1994; Finn, 1996), less emphasis is being placed on providing services to inmates. Thus, it is possible that chaplains and religious volunteers, in particular, will be increasingly called on to provide inmates with services at no or little cost–an expectation that is analogous to the general trend to rely on clergy for counseling at no cost to clients or health insurance providers.

This expectation is not purely speculative. For example, Prison Fellowship Ministries, the religiously-based prison reform group begun by Charles Colson (of Watergate fame), now administers an all-encompassing, faith-based prison community in a minimum-security Texas prison. Similar programs are in the process of being implemented in Oklahoma, Kansas, and Iowa. Prison Fellowship funds the program's staff and operation (but not the correctional officers or the inmates' living expenses) and relies on more than 350 volunteers to serve as mentors, instructors, small-group leaders, and administrators (Prison Fellowship

Ministries, 1999; Niebuhr, 1998; see also, the Internet site www.ifiprison. org).

Putting aside discussions about the appropriateness of this potential trend, there is a need to develop a fuller understanding about the importance of religion and religious counseling to offender adjustment inside and outside of prison, particularly as chaplains and religious volunteers are relied on more for providing inmates with services. There are some hints about the efficacy of religious counseling. For example, Propst, Ostrom, Watkins, Dean, and Mashburn (1992) report that a combination of pastoral counseling and cognitive-behavioral therapy reduces depression more than either method alone. Similarly, research in the area of criminal justice has provided some evidence in support of the effectiveness of religious programming (Clear et al., 1992a, 1992b; Johnson, 1987; Johnson et al., 1997; O'Connor et al., 1997; Young et al., 1995). Still, more sophisticated outcome research is needed in this area. For example, future research should examine whether religious counseling, or a combination of religious and secular counseling methods, is as effective as secular methods of treatment with correctional clients. Likewise, it will be important to determine if religious counseling "works" for a broad range of correctional clients, including those who are nonreligious. Finally, additional attention should be given to the role that religious volunteers play in providing support and treatment to inmates.

REFERENCES

Acorn, L. R. (1990). The challenges of ministering to a captive congregation. *Corrections Today, 52 (December)*, 97-98, 106-107.

Adamson, C. (1992). Wrath and redemption: Protestant theology and penal practice in the early American republic. *Criminal Justice History: An International Annual, 13*, 75-112.

Andrews, D. A., & Bonta, J. (1994). *The psychology of criminal conduct.* Cincinnati, OH: Sage.

Andrews, D. A., & Kiessling. (1980). Program structure and effective correctional practices: A summary of the CaVIC research. In R. R. Ross & P. Gendreau (Eds.), *Effective correctional treatment.* Toronto: Butterworth.

Andrews, D. A., Zinger, I., Hoge, R. D., Bonta, J., Gendreau, P., & Cullen, F. T. (1990). Does correctional treatment work? A clinically relevant and psychologically informed meta-analysis. *Criminology, 28*, 369-404.

Applegate, B. K., Cullen, F. T., & Fisher, B. S. (1997). Public support for correctional treatment: The continuing appeal of the rehabilitative ideal. *Prison Journal, 77*, 237-58.

Bates, S. (1938). *Prisons and beyond.* New York: Macmillan.

Clear, T. R. (1994). *Harm in American penology: Offenders, victims, and their communities.* Albany: State University of New York Press.

Clear, T. R., Stout, B. D., Dammer, H. R., Kelly, L., Hardyman, P. L., & Shapiro, C. (1992a). *Does involvement in religion help prisoners adjust to prison?* NCCD Focus (November).

Clear, T. R., Stout, B. D., Dammer, H. R., Kelly, L., Hardyman, P. L., & Shapiro, C. (1992b). *Prisoners, prisons, and religion.* Newark, NJ: School of Criminal Justice, Rutgers University.

Cook, J. R. (1994). Chaplaincy: A part of the inmate management team (pp. 61-64). *The State of Corrections,* Proceedings of the Annual Conferences of the American Correctional Association.

Cullen, F. T., Fisher, B. S., & Applegate, B. K. (in press). Public opinion about punishment and corrections. In M. Tonry (Ed.), *Crime and justice: A review of research.* Chicago: University of Chicago Press.

Cullen, F. T., Latessa, E. J., Burton, V. S., Jr., & Lombardo, L. X. (1993). The correctional orientation of prison wardens: Is the rehabilitative ideal supported? *Criminology, 31,* 69-92.

Cullen, F. T., Lutze, F. E., Link, B. G., & Wolfe, N. T. (1989). The correctional orientation of prison guards: Do officers support rehabilitation? *Federal Probation, 53,* 33-42.

Dillman, D. A. (1978). *Mail and telephone surveys: The total design method.* New York: Basic Books.

Fewell, T. (1995). The changing role of today's chaplain. *Corrections Today, 57 (July),* 16, 18, 20.

Finn, P. (1996). No-frill prisons and jails: A movement in flux. *Federal Probation, 60,* 35-44.

Giesen, A. F. (1936). Religion and reformation in the penal institution (pp. 187-197). Proceedings of the Sixty-Sixth Annual Congress of the American Prison Association.

Glaser, D. (1964). *The effectiveness of a prison and parole system.* Indianapolis: Bobbs-Merrill.

Holtzberg, A. (1945). Message from the president (pp. 117-119). Proceedings of the Seventy-Fifth Annual Meeting of the American Prison Association.

Johnson, B. R. (1987). Religiosity and institutional deviance: The impact of religious variables upon inmate adjustment. *Criminal Justice Review, 12,* 21-30.

Johnson, B. R., Larson, D. B., & Pitts, T. C. (1997). Religious programming, institutional adjustment, and recidivism among former inmates in prison fellowship programs: A research note. *Justice Quarterly, 14* (1),

Johnson, R. (1996). *Hard time: Understanding and reforming the prison.* 2d ed. Belmont, CA: Wadsworth.

Keuther, F. C. (1951). Religion and the chaplain. In P. W. Tappen (Ed.), *Contemporary corrections* (pp. 254-265). New York: McGraw Hill.

Krumbholz, C. E. (1944). Message from the president (pp. 170-172). Proceedings of the Seventy-Fourth Congress of the American Prison Association.

McKelvey, B. (1977). *American prisons: A history of good intentions.* Montclair, NJ: Patterson Smith.

Morris, A. (1961). What's new in the work of the church and the chaplain in correctional institutions? *Correctional Research Bulletin, No. 11.* Boston: United Prison Association of Massachusetts.

Murphy, G. L. (1956). The social role of the prison chaplain. Doctoral dissertation, University of Pittsburgh.

Niebuhr, G. (1998). Using religion to reform criminals. *New York Times*, January 18, Section 1, p. 16.

O'Connor, T. P., Ryan, P., & Parikh, C. (1997). The impact of religious programs on inmate infractions at Lieber prison in South Carolina. Report prepared for the South Carolina Department of Corrections.

Palmer, T. (1992). *The re-emergence of correctional intervention.* Newbury Park, CA: Sage.

Powers, S. B. (1960). The role of the chaplain on the institution treatment team (pp. 196-198). Proceedings of the Ninetieth Annual Congress of Correction of the American Correctional Association.

Prison Fellowship Ministries (1999). *The InnerChange freedom initiative: Background, fact sheet, history, faqs, and legal basis.* Washington, DC: Prison Fellowship Ministries.

Propst, L. R., Ostrom, R., Watkins, P., Dean, T., & Mashburn, D. (1992). Comparative efficacy of religious and nonreligious cognitive-behavioral therapy for the treatment of clinical depression in religious individuals. *Journal of Counseling and Clinical Psychology, 60*, 94-103.

Religion behind bars (1998). *Corrections Compendium, 23* (4), 8-21.

Rothman, D. J. (1980). *Conscience and convenience: The asylum and its alternatives in progressive America.* Boston: Little, Brown.

Scott, J. F. (1906). The prison chaplain (p. 138). Proceedings of the Annual Congress of the National Prison Association.

Shaw, D. R. (1995). *Chaplains to the imprisoned: Sharing life with the incarcerated.* New York: The Haworth Press, Inc.

Skotnicki, A. (1991). Religion and the development of the American penal system. Doctoral dissertation, Graduate Theological Union.

Sundt, J. L. (1997). Bringing light to dark places: An occupational study of prison chaplains. Doctoral Dissertation, University of Cincinnati.

Sundt, J. L., & Cullen, F. T. (1998). The role of the contemporary prison chaplain. *The Prison Journal, 78*, 271-298.

Taft, P. (1978, December). Whatever happened to that old time prison chaplain? *Corrections Magazine*, 54-61.

Thompson, E. A. (1989). Chaplains help inmates find freedom behind bars. *Corrections Today, 51*, 52, 82, 84, 86.

Thornton, S. W. (1903). The chaplain and his work (p.117-123). Proceedings of the Annual Congress of the National Prison Association.

U. S. Department of Justice (1993). Survey of state prisoners, 1991. Washington, DC: Government Printing Office.

Williams, V. L. (1996). *Dictionary of American penology: A revised and expanded edition*. Westport, CT: Greenwood Press.

Worthington, E. L., Jr. (1986). Religious counseling: A review of published empirical research. *Journal of Counseling and Development, 64*, 421-431.

Worthington, E., Kurusu, T., McCullough, M., & Sandage, S. (1996). Empirical research on religion and psychotherapeutic processes and outcomes: A 10-year review and research prospectus. *Psychological Bulletin, 119*, 448-487.

Young, M. C., Gartner, J., O'Connor, T., Larson, D., & Wright, K. (1995). The impact of a volunteer prison ministry program on the long-term recidivism of federal inmates. *Journal of Offender Rehabilitation, 22*, 97-118.

AUTHORS' NOTES

Jody L. Sundt (PhD, University of Cincinnati) is an assistant professor at the Center for the Study of Crime, Delinquency and Corrections, Southern Illinois University. Dr. Sundt has published in the area of correctional policy and public attitudes toward criminal justice.

Harry Dammer is an associate professor in the Department of Sociology and Criminal Justice at The University of Scranton, PA. He received his BS and MS degrees from the University of Dayton and his PhD from Rutgers University. His major research interests are corrections, and international criminal justice systems. He is the author of *Religion in Corrections* (American Correctional Association, 1999) and co-author (with Erika Fairchild) of *Comparative Criminal Justice* (Wadsworth/Thompson Press, 2000) and co-author (with Todd R. Clear) of *The Offender in the Community* (Wadsworth/Thompson Press, 2003). Dr. Dammer was a Fulbright Scholar during 1993-94.

Francis T. Cullen (PhD, Columbia University) is a professor of criminal justice at the University of Cincinnati. He is the former editor of *Justice Quarterly* and of the *Journal of Crime and Justice* and has served as president of the Academy of Criminal Justice Sciences. He is a Fellow of the Academy of Criminal Justice Sciences and the American Society of Criminology. His books include *Rethinking Crime and Deviance Theory; Reaffirming Rehabilitation*; *Corporate Crime Under Attack: The Ford Pinto Case and Beyond*; *Criminological Theory: Context and Consequences*; *Criminology*; *Combatting Corporate Crime: Local Prosecutors at Work*; *Contemporary Criminological Theory*; *Offender Rehabilitation: Effective Correctional Intervention*; and *Criminological Theory: Past to Present Essential Readings*.

An earlier version of this article was presented at the annual meeting of the Academy of Criminal Justice Sciences, Orlando, Florida, March 1999.

Address correspondence to Jody L. Sundt, PhD, Center for the Study of Crime, Delinquency, & Corrections, Southern Illinois University at Carbondale, Mail Code 4504, Carbondale, IL 62901-4504 (E-mail: jlsundt@siu.edu).

APPENDIX

The following descriptions of treatment modalities were provided to chaplains:

- *Adlerian Counseling:* In Adlerian counseling, abnormal behavior is seen as directly related to the client's feelings of inferiority. Therefore, the goal is to help the individual reduce his or her negative self-evaluations, correct perceptions of events, and help set new objectives, towards which the client can direct his/her behavior. Central to the process is helping the client understand the goal of his or her behavior and how that goal determines his or her disturbing attitudes, thoughts, and behaviors.
- *Behavioral Approaches:* The main emphasis is on how behavior is learned from interactions of the individual and the environment. This approach, which is rooted in learning theory, is concerned with observable behavior and does not take into account any inner reason for an individual's behavior. The counselor first will help to define the problem behavior, then the counselor and client will establish specific goals to help the client change.
- *Client-Centered Counseling:* In this method the counselor allows for the client to set the goals. It is believed that the client is self-motivated to change and seek self-actualization. Given the proper circumstances, the individual can develop and regulate his or her own behavior. The goal is to help the individual become more mature and to reinstitute the process toward self-actualization by removing the obstacles to this process.
- *Eclectic Counseling:* Eclectic approaches utilize theoretical principles from various schools of thought, keeping in mind their strengths and weaknesses as well as the situation/individual involved.
- *Gestalt Therapy:* The overriding objective of Gestalt therapy is to bring about an integration of the individual. A specific aim of counseling is to help clients discover that they do not have to depend on others, but can do many things for themselves. Since the sign of a healthy individual is the ability to regulate oneself, the objective of counseling is to move the individual from a state of dependence on others' judgments to a reliance on self-regulation. In ultimate terms, the goal is for the individual to be true to him or herself.
- *Group Counseling:* Because most problems for clients are acquired and maintained in a social context, it is believed that these problems can only be solved within a social (group) context. In the group setting it is believed that clients can gain understanding, empathy, and catharsis for their own problems in life. Different kinds of group therapies can be employed such as psychoanalysis, gestalt, behavior (learning), and transactional analysis. Psychodrama, the use of role playing, is also used in this setting.

- *Psychoanalysis:* The major goal is to bring into consciousness those repressed impulses that are causing the individual anxiety. The counselor must establish a situation that is threat-free, and individuals learn that they can express their thought without danger of being condemned. This freedom allows the individual to explore the appropriateness or inappropriateness of his or her present behavior and to consider new behaviors.
- *Rational-Emotive Therapy:* In Rational Emotive Therapy (RET) it is believed that people get into problems when they accept illogical and irrational ideas. In RET the counselor has one primary objective, to induce the client to accept a rational philosophy of life. The counselor is forceful in pointing out the specific basic irrational thoughts or processes that one may have learned from his parents or community.
- *Reality Therapy:* In reality therapy counseling involves teaching or training individuals what they should have learned earlier in life, most notably right and wrong, responsibility, and reality. The counselor establishes a warm and positive environment but also establishes that clients have the capacity to be responsible for themselves. Clients learn that happiness is the result of one's behavior, not because of external events. Success will come only if the client is willing to face reality and take responsibility for him/herself.
- *Transactional Analysis:* Transactional analysis (TA) views the development of personality, both normal and abnormal, as a result of transactions between different ego states the client passes through in life. The life path an individual chooses is the product of these transactions and once the individual makes a choice he or she sets about living his or her life to confirm this position. In many cases, the chosen life position and life script lead to inappropriate behavior. TA is primarily a contractual system for treating individuals within a group context.

Religion, the Community, and the Rehabilitation of Criminal Offenders. Pp. 87-107.

Intersections of Race, Religion, and Inmate Culture: The Historical Development of Islam in American Corrections

FELECIA DIX-RICHARDSON

Florida A&M University

BILLY R. CLOSE

Florida State University

SUMMARY Over the past decades, research on Islam in American prisons has failed to fully capture the essence of the prison Muslim movement because it has focused mainly upon religious rights and management issues. This paper articulates the real meaning of the Muslim prison movement by examining the historical development of Islam within the American correctional system using relevant literature, court cases, and other documents. First, the study presents various stages of Islamic growth in American prisons to illustrate the changes that the movement has encountered. Second, the paper uses a three-dimensional approach that combines race, religion, and inmate culture to identify the main factors that have contributed to the development of Islam in American prisons. The study concludes by addressing the significance of the prison Muslim movement for the reform possibilities of those who accept Islam while incarcerated. *[Article copies available for a fee from The Haworth Document Delivery Service: 1-800-HAWORTH. E-mail address: <getinfo@haworthpressinc.com> Website: <http://www.HaworthPress.com> © 2002 by The Haworth Press, Inc. All rights reserved.]*

KEYWORDS Muslims, Islam, prison, reform of offenders

Offender rehabilitation through religious efforts has been a major concern of researchers, prison officials, religious scholars, and others since the inception of American prisons. It has been thought that religion can have a positive impact upon the offender and prison administration. For example, religion seems to make the burden of serving time in prison less difficult for the inmate. In addition, religion has served as a rehabilitative tool, as it enables inmates to maintain ties with their families and administrators to run their prison systems more easily (Clear and Cole, 2000). However, these findings certainly do not hold true for the Islamic movement during its early developmental stages within American prisons. First, during the formative years of Islam in American prisons, Muslim inmates often discovered that practicing Islam made the burden of serving time in prison more difficult. Second, prison administrators did not consider Islam to be a rehabilitative tool. Instead, they viewed the religion as destructive and problematic. Third, Islam did not allow or enable administrators to run their prison systems easier, because prison officials were preoccupied with the belief that Islam presented a threat to prison security (*Cooper v. Pate*, 1967; *Fulwood v. Clemmer*, 1962; Irwin, 1980; Jacobs, 1977; Mann, 1993; and Yaker, 1962).

Why is there such a contrast between the rehabilitative perceptions and the historical developmental role of Islam and of Christianity in American corrections? This essay will address these initial disparities regarding the religious role and reformative abilities of Islam and Christianity through a social context approach.

Until recent decades, with regards to American prisons, religion was synonymous with Christianity. Thus, other religions, especially those that were considered as non-traditional, were not given research attention regarding inmate reformation. This lack of attention resulted, as I argue below, in part, because prisons were not forced to recognize these religions as legitimate groups. Through the successful religious rights challenges brought forward by Islamic inmates, religions formerly classified as "non-traditional" were granted legitimacy in American prisons. Thus, researchers eventually began to recognize that religions other than Christianity had become a permanent segment of the inmate society. This realization eventually led researchers to consider the impact and significance of other religions upon offenders and the prison system.

In a society where Christianity has been the dominant religion, one must consider how it is that, in the context of American corrections, other religions have grown to their present force behind prison walls; especially, when efforts of denying their existence was common practice. As noted by Butler (1978), Islam was once considered to be a passing fad. However, it is now relatively difficult to ignore Islam due to its high level of visibility behind prison walls. When addressing the issue of Islamic growth within American correctional institutions, one must consider not only the religion and those who convert. Consideration must also be given to contextual issues of race, the nature of incarceration, and the social realities of American society. In the literatures addressing Islam in the prison system, these approaches and topics are often lacking. Since the 1960s, researchers have begun to study various aspects of Islam within American prisons; however, their focus has been mostly limited to legal issues, prison adjustment, security issues, and descriptions of Islamic practices behind prison walls (Brown, 1965; Butler, 1978; Jones, 1983; Murdy, 1961; Palmer, 1991; Rigoli, 1990; Robbins, 1980; Rudovsky, 1988; Smith, 1993; and Yaker, 1962). This study will differ from such a limited scope by considering the Islamic influence upon religious reformation and the incarcerated African American male by incorporating the impact and contextual reality of race, religion, and inmate culture upon the prison Muslim movement.

In order to address questions relating to the possible reformative impact of Islam upon African American male inmates, one must consider the existence and evolution of the prison Muslim movement, because this movement reveals a unique story of prison, inmate culture, and religious reform. The need for this research is that an understanding of the Islamic existence, as it applies to African American male inmates, has not been completely provided in the existing literature. This is evident in the assertion made by Clear et al. (1992) that a study entailing the history of the Muslim movement in prison is needed to describe the extent to which a growing black religious consciousness has evolved into a religious prison movement.

An understanding of this movement will not only serve as a descriptor of a religious ideology, it can also lead to a more complete comprehension and appreciation of the impact of this movement upon American corrections. Thus, the purpose of this study is to provide a brief examination of the historical development of Islam within the American correctional system and its efforts at offender rehabilitation by utilizing the social context of race, religion, and inmate culture. This brief historical analysis will draw upon relevant literature, court cases, and documents.

This study will first begin by chronologically tracing the stages of Islamic growth in American prisons and the changes that the movement has undergone in order to provide background information for the basis of this research. Second, I will consider the impact of race, religion, and inmate culture upon the prison Muslim movement's evolution. This study will conclude by addressing the significance of this movement as it relates to reform possibilities of those who accept Islam while incarcerated.

EVOLUTION OF THE PRISON MUSLIM MOVEMENT

Islam has been present in American prisons since their inception in the early nineteenth century. This assertion is based upon the fact that many African Americans were descendants of Africans who attempted to maintain their Islamic beliefs once they arrived in the U.S. (Gardell, 1996; Goldman, 1989; Gomez, 1994; and Van Sertima, 1992). However, as a recognizable religion under the tutelage of Elijah Muhammad, Islam's beginning in American prisons can be traced to the 1940s (Butler, 1978). Although Islam has probably been present in American prisons from the very beginning, this study will begin by focusing upon the 1940s, when prison officials began to take notice of the Nation of Islam.

Religion Denied: Early Correctional Response to Islam

This stage of the prison Muslim movement brought forth prison officials' initial reactions toward Islam and Muslim inmates during the 1940s through the late 1950s. Throughout this era of correctional history, prison officials found themselves confronted by the beliefs and presence of Islam as practiced by the followers of Elijah Muhammad. At this time, prison officials assumed that Islam, as practiced by the Nation of Islam, would create problems within the prison.

This assumption was based upon the various religious beliefs of the Nation of Islam. This religious ideology presented a theology to its followers that was not only different from Christianity, it was different from traditional Islam as well. Not only were there issues concerning the theology of the Nation of Islam, there were also concerns regarding its position and opinions regarding American society and World War II. Believing that prison security would be compromised if inmates were allowed to accept and teach the philosophy of the Nation of Islam, prison officials became overly concerned about allowing Islamic practices within the prison.

While this may have been a legitimate concern for prison officials, during this era of correctional history, other factors must have contributed to this belief, since research has generally found that the teachings of the Nation of Islam did not cause any such immediate threat (Dell'Olio, 1966; Murdy, 1961; and Yaker, 1962). In this section, I will provide, through a contextual approach, a historical interpretation of the philosophy of the Nation of Islam and the broader social forces and existing attitudes that served as contributing factors for the denial of Islamic teachings behind prison walls.

Throughout the 1940s and 50s, the Nation of Islam was emerging in urban black communities across America. The momentum of this movement, coupled with the attractiveness of its message to many black Americans, began to capture public attention. The message that the Nation of Islam rendered caused enough concern and controversy that the FBI brought this group under close surveillance (Churchill and Wall, 1990; and Gardell, 1996). Why did the teachings and philosophies of the Nation of Islam create controversy and concern for the American government and its penal institutions? More interestingly, though, is why did these teachings create an element of hope for many urban black Americans? To grasp an understanding of these questions, the answers must be presented within their social context.

Islam, as it was practiced by the Nation of Islam, addressed controversial issues pertaining to racial inequalities imposed upon African Americans during a time in American history when black Americans were expected to behave passively and to exhibit a non-confrontational attitude toward the unjust mechanisms, such as Jim Crow laws and lynchings, that were used to govern and control them. Such laws and violent treatment represented a constant reality for many blacks. Black Americans knew that if they challenged these means of control, retaliation would be forthcoming.

To illustrate, Mann (1993) documented a study that reported between 1865 and 1955, approximately five thousand blacks were lynched by mobs. In addition, massacres of black townships in Tulsa, OK and Rosewood, FL certainly served as a reminder that the protection of the courts and police may not apply to black citizens. Thus, this era in American history represented a time of overt oppression and federal lawlessness for many blacks.

Even though blacks throughout America experienced racism, discrimination, and oppression during this era, blacks residing in the South often felt that their conditions were worse. After the abolition of slavery, the plague of the boll weevils on cotton crops, and growing frustration of a racist southern society, many blacks migrated to northern urban cities with aspirations for a better life and job opportunities

(Franklin and Moss, 1994). The North granted Southern blacks a limited new-found freedom. Yet to the surprise of many, the North was not exactly what they expected. Racism and job shortages for blacks were also a reality of northern life (Franklin and Moss, 1994; Drake and Cayton, 1993). Understanding the anguish and frustration of black Americans residing in urban cities, the Nation of Islam was able to captivate an audience who was willing to listen to its religious views and philosophies that addressed their needs of hope and feelings of despair. Soon, they discovered that not only were they willing to listen, there were many who were eager to convert as well. C. Eric Lincoln (1961) found that a significant number of the Nation of Islam's initial converts were recent migrants from the rural South. With a combined population of overly frustrated black Southern migrants and a black Northern underclass who continued to experience racism and oppression, the Nation of Islam discovered that the stage had been preset with an audience who might be willing to accept a religion that would address its specific needs.

As mentioned earlier, many blacks found solace in the teachings of the Nation of Islam. After practicing Christianity for many generations, why did many blacks begin to reject Christianity and accept the teachings of Elijah Muhammad? This issue has been addressed by many (Baldwin, 1962; Kunjufu, 1996; and Lincoln, 1961). As is also discussed above, racial issues in the U.S. played an instrumental part in the development of the Nation of Islam and the African American community.

The role that Christianity has played in the African American experience should also be considered in order to understand the rising appeal of the National of Islam. It was not uncommon for Islamic ministers to challenge the role that Christianity had played in America and the lives of black Americans, portraying it as "the white man's religion" that had been utilized to keep blacks under control and in a subservient position (Essien-Udom, 1962; Haley, 1964; and Muhammad, 1965). In these teachings, blacks were shown how Christianity was used to justify slavery and further oppress them. Drawing upon the negative aspects of Christianity, Islamic ministers were able to convince many blacks to reevaluate the role of Christianity in their lives. This reevaluation often caused confusion and doubt about Christianity. By casting such doubt upon Christianity, the Nation of Islam was able to portray itself as a religion that would uplift and empower its followers instead of oppressing them.

Elijah Muhammad's Nation of Islam continued to grow throughout the black community, and during the early 1940s, Elijah Muhammad's views and position regarding the treatment of blacks and their role in World War II thrust him further into national attention. Muhammad's open refusal to fight in World War II led him and many of his followers to be sent to prison. Once incarcerated, Muhammad discovered that the prison provided one of the most fertile grounds for Islamic recruitment (Butler, 1978). This fact was also noted by Lincoln (1961) when he concluded that a "good deal" of recruiting was done in jails and prisons amongst men and women whose resentment against society increased with each day of imprisonment. While incarcerated, Muhammad continued his teachings regarding the Nation of Islam and America's oppressive treatment towards blacks. Although the Nation of Islam's philosophy was present before Elijah Muhammad was incarcerated, his presence and direct teachings inside the prison were certainly instrumental in creating a catalyst for the prison Muslim movement.

The American government and many prison officials often felt that some of the Nation of Islam's teachings were not only controversial, but dangerous as well. One of the most controversial beliefs amongst these opponents to the Nation of Islam was its teaching of God. According to the Nation of Islam's theology, God was black. This particular religious ideology was combined with an additional teaching of the devil as white. Also, Islamic revelation of a "War of Armageddon," where blacks would conquer whites and regain control of the world created further concern (Haley, 1964; Lincoln, 1961; and Muhammad, 1965).

Racial issues emphasized in the teachings of the Nation of Islam were not the only concern for prison administrators. When Islam "in general" (i.e., traditional Islam) is compared to Christianity, there are some striking differences between the two religions. The Qur'an was used as a basis for written spirituality instead of the Bible. In addition, Muslims are required to perform five daily prayers at a specified time and manner. However, the most striking difference is the Islamic belief regarding Jesus Christ. According to Islamic belief, Jesus Christ was not the Son of God, but rather, that he was a prophet (El-Amin, 1991; Muhammad, 1965; Nu'Man, 1985). This belief regarding the identity of Jesus Christ itself was enough to cast scorn and impel retaliation against Muslim inmates.

As noted by Jacobs (1977), when considering any aspect of American corrections, focus must include the impact of broader social forces representing society. Bearing this in mind, one can argue convincingly that the treatment of blacks during the 1940s through the 1950s was certainly of an oppressive nature. Blacks were denied basic human rights by American courts, society, law enforcement, education, and prisons. Once incarcerated, African-American inmates reasonably saw their conditions during incarceration as an extension of the oppression they experienced in their local communities.

Many researchers have suggested that, given the teachings of the Nation of Islam and the climate of the prison environment, prison officials became concerned about the safety, security, and management of the prison (Dell'Olio, 1966; Jacobs, 1977; Murdy, 1961; and Yaker, 1962). Many correctional administrators believed that the teachings of Elijah Muhammad's Nation of Islam would compromise the security of the prison. Therefore, prison officials found it necessary to place a tight control on Islamic teachings behind prison walls. Acting upon this foreseen need, prison officials sought means to control the prison Muslim movement during its early stage of development. Prison officials implemented tactics against the Muslim inmates such as food deprivation, segregation from other inmates, denial of parole, and denial of religious practices, to name only a few (Atkins and Glick, 1972; and Mann, 1993).

Prison administrators were able to maintain these tactics and suppress Islamic practices without much controversy during this stage of Islamic development because of three basic reasons: (1) a hands-off doctrine of the courts, (2) a completely authoritarian structure in prisons, and (3) the overt racism against and social status of blacks during the 1940s and 1950s in the U.S. (Dix, 1997).

- *The Hands-Off Doctrine.* Prior to the 1960s, American courts practiced a "hands-off" doctrine concerning inmate matters (Palmer, 1991; and Shover and Einstadter, 1988). The *Ruffin v. Commonwealth* (1871) decision, which ruled that inmates were slaves of the state who had forfeited any rights as a consequence of their crime, is an extreme example of the hands-off doctrine (Shover and Einstadter, 1988). However, the ruling of *Stroud v. Swope* (1951) represents a more common perspective in that the court decided that judicial interference in inmate matters would only cause mischief and disruption in prison affairs (Shover and Einstadter, 1988). Given this non-interventionist approach, inmates had no viable means to address concerns relating to discrimination, harassment, or mistreatment from prison officials.
- *Completely Authoritarian Structure in Prisons.* Jacobs (1971) argued that prisons prior to the 1960s operated under completely authoritarian rule. Complete authoritarianism created a system

where no consideration was given to inmate concerns. The warden maintained complete control of the prison without much input from outside administrators or the general public. Prisons functioning under a complete authoritarian regime operated under an "out-of-sight, out-of-mind" reality (Jacobs, 1977). This type of system does not lend itself to overt public concern regarding inmate issues because the public is often unaware of the prison operations. This resulted in a lack of concern by the public regarding inmate issues up until the 1960s. Another contributing factor regarding the lack of correctional attention by the public is that there was a lack of major coverage of prison issues by the mass media during the authoritarian regime, especially when compared to today's coverage. A system that operates under this type of control lends itself to corruption and oppressive means to maintain order. The tactics of prison officials regarding Islamic practices (e.g., segregation, food deprivation, beatings, etc.) were not known to the public during this time because the general public was unaware of the daily routines of prison life. It was not until the late 1960s and the early 1970s that American citizens became commonly aware of prison conditions (Jacobs, 1977).

• *Overt Racism.* Jim Crow and racial oppression also were contributing factors in the suppression of Islam in its formative years in American prisons. Given the fact that blacks were overtly mistreated and regarded as second-class citizens during this stage of Islamic prison development, coupled with the fact that incarceration trends and practices reflect the views and practices of the dominant, majority population, prison administrators could easily suppress Islamic practices without much fear of retaliation from the inmates or the public. In addition, there was no major concern that criticisms would be raised by the black community regarding the prison treatment of Muslim inmates since blacks were routinely denied basic civil rights. Moreover, there would be no public outcry regarding the suppression of Islam since the majority of white Americans were against the black supremacy teachings of Elijah Muhammad. Overt racism that was practiced throughout America during this era certainly allowed prisons wide latitude in controlling Islamic practices.

In sum, during Islam's formative years in American prisons, legal barriers served as a bulwark for maintaining racism, oppression, and discriminatory economic, political, and societal inequalities for African

Americans. Considering the subordinated status of African Americans during this time, a religion that called for the elevation of African Americans and that was markedly different from American Christianity would be fervently opposed by prison administrators. However, although prisons tried to suppress Islamic practices, the religion prevailed. Why did Islam survive when prison administrators vehemently tried to oppress it? The following provides an explanation for the continuation and permanence of the prison Muslim movement in American prisons.

The Struggle for Legitimacy

Before the 1960s, American courts rarely intervened in correctional matters. Courts generally adhered to the hands-off doctrine which held that prison matters were not of legal concern for the court. However, with the changing climate of American society during the 1960s, courts found themselves addressing a plethora of issues, including the constitutionality of religious freedom behind prison walls. After suffering years of religious discrimination and harassment by prison officials, Muslim inmates sought legal intervention.

The end of the hands-off doctrine came partly as a result of the successful legal progress made by the inmates toward religious freedom (*Cooper v. Pate*, 1967). After the court ruled in *Fulwood v. Clemmer* (1962) and *Cooper v. Pate* (1967) that Islam, as practiced by members of the Nation of Islam, was indeed a religion, the right to practice the religion of one's choice was established in American prisons. Of greater importance, however, was the fact that now courts opened themselves to hear other issues brought forth by inmates. This initiated an era of incarceration that no longer resulted in an automatic loss of constitutional rights. This realization changed prison operations as well as inmate culture. Again, the efforts of Muslim inmates played an instrumental role in this major prison development.

Once the court established that Islam could be practiced behind prison walls, the next issue that the court had to address was to what extent Muslim inmates would be allowed to practice their religion. As mentioned above, there are some differences between Christianity and Islam, which initially caused obstacles in the daily routine of prison operations. Since prison officials and Islamic inmates faced difficulties in resolving these issues, the courts intervened. Among the various issues that courts found themselves addressing were name changes for Islamic inmates, the right to prayer, pork-free diets, the wearing of religious garments, the provision of the Qu'ran and other religious materials, visitations by imams, fasting during Ramadan, and correspondence with religious leaders. There have been numerous studies that have addressed the significance of the Muslim inmate legal battles and the courts' decisions and rationale regarding these issues (Palmer, 1991; Rigoli, 1990; Rudovsky et al., 1988; and Smith, 1993).

The significance of this particular era of historical development in the prison Muslim movement is twofold. First, Muslim inmates were able to successfully gain entry into an American social institution that had been traditionally deemed off limits for American prisoners. The additional importance of this legal success lies in the fact that it was accomplished by black inmates. Other inmates realized that if courts would rule in favor of black incarcerated defendants, who claimed that God was black and the devil was white, perhaps the courts would listen to their claims as well. This realization, that courts were now willing to intervene in inmate matters, changed the completely authoritarian regime of American prisons and thus the scope of corrections permanently.

Second, even though the Islamic struggle and legal controversy continues into the present, this era of Islamic development is the most important insofar as, through legal action, Islam was granted legitimacy in American prisons. This era of Islamic development represented a culminating point in the religion's existence in that the court established the permanence of Islam in American prisons. This era of Islamic development is also important as it relates to other non-traditional religions. Through the success of the Islamic lawsuits, American correctional institutions were faced with the reality that other religious groups would argue for their First Amendment rights within the legal arena. Some researchers have credited the legal battles of the Muslim inmates as the catalyst for creating recognized diversity within the inmate social system and changing the structure of the prison system (Dix, 1997; Flowers, 1988; and Jacobs 1977).

Islamic Diversity Recognized

Early researchers who attempted to explain inmate culture often considered it to be a homogenous group (Clemmer, 1940; Sykes, 1958; Wheeler 1961). Most early evaluations of the Islamic religion in American prisons used a similar approach in that the religion was often linked to the Nation of Islam. Although the Nation of Islam may have been dominant in early correctional history, Islamic diversity in American corrections has been noted for many decades (Acoli, 1995 and Cleaver,

1968). Divisiveness over Islam in African American communities is commonly viewed in connection to Malcolm X's acceptance of orthodox Islam and the death of Elijah Muhammad. However, religious diversity among inmates and within black communities existed years before either of these events (Acoli, 1995; Cleaver, 1968; Haley, 1964). Yet, these events represented culminating points as they projected the African American Muslim community into the public spotlight.

Malcolm X's decision to leave the Nation of Islam caused the American public to realize that not all African American Muslims were members of the Nation of Islam. This view was indeed reinforced when W. D. Mohammed succeeded his father as the leader of the Nation of Islam. Mohammed implemented changes (e.g., the belief surrounding God, the last prophet, and the structure of the organization, etc.) that were in complete opposition to the teachings of his father, Elijah Muhammad. Through his efforts, Mohammed tried to lead the Nation of Islam toward orthodox Islam. While many supported Mohammed's changes, there were those who still respected and found relevance in Elijah's teachings. Louis Farrakhan, for example, wanted to continue with the teachings of Elijah Muhammad. He therefore recreated the Nation of Islam in order that Elijah's original message could continue. Thus, the diversity of Islam in American prisons was emphasized again through this event.

The diversity of Islam in American prisons is not limited to these events and issues. There are various Islamic sects that exist within correctional institutions across America. Correctional administrators have been forced to recognize that Islam, as it exists behind prison walls, is not as uniform as once believed, and the diversity within this religious group could no longer be ignored.

Correctional administrators also soon discovered that in their interactions with these various groups they had to acknowledge each group's beliefs, traditions, values, etc. This heterogeneity created a more complex inmate culture because racial groups could no longer be considered as homogenous groups. Just as outside communities change, so, too, does prison culture. As Jacobs (1977) noted, prison culture does not occur in a vacuum. Broader social forces will often impact upon the prison community. Thus, over the years, the prison Islamic community has certainly changed for various reasons. Furthermore, the image of Islam has changed from the initially negative one that was once cast upon the group to a more positive image which has gained respect from some prison staff, governmental officials, and non-Islamic inmates as well (Butler, 1978; *Muslim Journal*, 1996).

Today's Prison Reality: Black Inmate Population Growth

The 1980s and the 1990s have been marked by an explosion in American incarceration rates (Irwin and Austin, 1994). Not only has the American prison population grown, but, as noted by Christianson, it has become "blacker" (1981). The increase in America's incarceration trend has been attributed to "get-tough" crime policies and the war on drugs (Irwin and Austin, 1994; and Lusane, 1991). The growth of black inmates has had an effect upon the inmate culture similar to that of the black political prisoner movement during the 1960s and 1970s. Despite that many black inmates find themselves incarcerated as a result of "get tough" crime policies or war on drug tactics, many of them perceive their incarceration as a reflection of racist and discriminatory crime control policies. If black inmates perceive their incarceration in this manner, a religion such as Islam, which addresses concerns relating to racial oppression, continues to have appeal.

In his 1961 study of the "Black Muslims," Lincoln stated:

> Apart from the public meetings and publications, a good deal of recruiting is done in jails and prisons, among men and women whose resentment against society increases with each day of imprisonment. Here their smoldering hatred against the white man builds up to the point of explosion. The black prisoner is reminded that he is in an institution administered by whites, guarded by whites, built by whites. Even the chaplains are white, "to continue to force upon you the poisonous doctrine that you are blessed by being persecuted." The judge who tried him, the jury who heard his case, the officers who arrested him–all were white. Can he, then, be justly imprisoned. (1961:113-114)

Many of the racial components presented above have changed since Lincoln's 1961 account. Yet, overall, there is still evidence of racial disparity in the practices and realities of criminal justice and corrections today. Thus, African Americans who find themselves under the control of correctional institutions may agree with this sentiment. It may seem illogical for black inmates to perceive their incarceration as a tool of racism and oppression implemented by society at large. However, several recent factors grant legitimacy to such a claim. Examples that support this claim include the racial disparity in arrest rates and prison admissions as noted by Donziger (1996). According to Donziger (1996), African Americans are incarcerated at a rate more than six times that of whites.

In addition, he reported in many cities that, one-third of all African American men aged eighteen to thirty-four are under the supervision of the criminal justice system. To illustrate further, at every stage in the criminal justice system (i.e., from arrest to incarceration), blacks are represented in numbers disproportionate to those of the general population (Tonry, 1995).

The Islamic movement within American prisons has found and continues to find a significant segment of the prison society that feels victimized, oppressed, and angry. Along with these aspects, deprivations and unique characteristics of the prison environment create a fertile ground for Islamic recruitment and conversion for the African American inmate. If the disparity in incarceration trends continues, it is foreseeable that Islam will continue to capture the attention and souls of African American inmates. According to Butler, "As a rule, for every one thousand black prisoners in an institution, at least two hundred will call themselves Muslims" (1978:56). McCloud (1995) estimates that there are approximately four thousand Muslims inmates within the federal prison system.

INTERSECTION OF RACE, RELIGION, AND THE INMATE CULTURE

How has Islam prevailed in American prisons over the last six decades? The sections above provided explanations of how Islam has evolved in American corrections over the past decades. The next question that must be answered is why it has evolved. In a 1997 study of Islam in American prisons, Dix considered the intersection of race, religion, and inmate culture in the existence of Islam in American prisons and concluded that Islam continues to exist behind prisons walls, in part, because it addresses the economic, social, and political inequalities leveled against African Americans. African American inmates often find themselves overly burdened with these inequalities. The prison experience has the tendency to increase these inequalities. However, it also has a way of causing inmates to focus on their plight regarding these issues. Despite the steps taken towards civil rights and racial equality in the past few decades, research and governmental policies suggest that race continues to be a major issue in contemporary society (Bell, 1992; Donziger, 1996; Hacker, 1992; Page, 1996; and West, 1993).

Race, religion, and inmate culture intersect with one another in a unique manner. They are intertwined so tightly at times that it is difficult to differentiate between them. Religion has played an instrumental role–sometimes forced, sometimes freely accepted–in the African American experience. Islam has been able to capture the imagination of the African American male inmate because it has the ability to draw upon this past and specifically address issues of immediate concern (e.g., as oppression, racism, spirituality, manhood, self-empowerment, etc.). The appeal of Islam to young black men has been so apparent that black churches and religious scholars have begun to discuss, debate, and research this issue (Kunjufu, 1994; and Lincoln and Mamiya, 1990).

When considering why Islam has maintained its presence within prisons, we must not ignore issues pertaining to inmate culture. Early researchers tried to explain inmate culture in terms of deprivation or importation (Clemmer, 1942; Sykes, 1958; and Irwin and Cressey, 1962). The deprivation model assumed that inmates learned a particular code of conduct while incarcerated, whereas the importation model assumed that inmate behavior represented the values that were portrayed prior to incarceration. The deprivation model also assumes that inmates have suffered the pains of imprisonment and certain deprivations due to incarceration (Sykes, 1958). It has been suggested that Islam plays a unique role in alleviating some of these deprivations, such as the loss of autonomy and security. For example, Islamic inmates can regain some of their individuality by practicing a religion that often dictates a lifestyle and rituals that are different from traditional religious and correctional expectations (Dix, 1997). Also, it has been suggested that Islam has the tendency to serve as a means of protection for those who convert. However, Muslim inmates do not generally seem to consider this to be a major reason for converting to the religion (Dix, 1997).

Another interesting area regarding inmate culture is the racial component of the prison. African American inmates realize that when they are incarcerated, they no longer represent a minority, but rather, in prison, they constitute the majority population. The reality of the overrepresentation of the African American inmate population behind prison walls certainly leads to questions regarding the purpose of incarceration.

Due to the fact that the courts have acknowledged that inmates have the right to practice the religion of choice, Islam has become a legitimate means of addressing the unique issues regarding race, prison administration, and prison deprivations. Through the intersection of race, religion, and the unique circumstances surrounding the inmate culture, Islam has found its place within American corrections.

THE REFORMING POSSIBILITIES OF ISLAM

Inmate reformation through religious interaction has been a major emphasis of American prisons from the beginning. During the early stages of penal development, prisons were often referred to as penitentiaries and reformatories. Not only were inmates expected to repent, they were also expected to reform their behavior. A major means of achieving these goals was religious interaction. However, Christianity was virtually the only religion through which repentance and reformation was sought. Now that Islam has become an accepted reality of the prison religious foundation, one must ask, can Islam have a reforming impact upon the African American male inmate? In order to answer this question one must consider what is meant by reform. When one's behavior is reformed, it is assumed that an individual has altered his or her behavior to reflect positive attitudes and values that were not once held. Thus, the question "does Islam have the ability to reform the individual" becomes, "can it create positive conforming attitudes in those who convert?"

It is obvious that Islam certainly has had the capability of creating a positive impact upon many African American male inmates who convert. The positive impact of Islam upon young black males has been well documented in sources ranging from personal testimony, literary accounts, television documentaries, to social research (Atkins, 1972; Baldwin, 1962; Brown, 1965; Farrakhan, 1993; Haley, 1965; Kunjufu, 1996; Lincoln, 1961, 1984). One of the most noted examples of the reforming ability of Islam can be found in the life of El-Hajj Malik El-Shabazz (Malcolm X). In his autobiography, he shows how Islam transformed a common convict into one of America's most powerful and controversial men. His transformation was so dramatic that volumes of books, articles, and documentaries have continued to be written long after his death.

Several prominent African American literary authors during the 1960s discussed the significant impact that Elijah Muhammad and his followers had upon inmates and the Black community. In his book, *Manchild in the Promised Land*, Brown (1965) considered the fact that many young men from the Harlem community were converting to Islam while incarcerated. Not only did he note that they were converting, he noticed that these new Islamic converts were changing their behavior as well. For example, Sonny, the protagonist of the novel, noted that there was a change in the behavior of those who become Muslims. He notices that his friends who have adopted this new religion no longer drink alcohol, use drugs, or commit crimes. Likewise, in *The Fire Next Time*, Baldwin acknowledged the positive impact of Islam. According to Baldwin, Elijah Muhammad has been able to do what generations of welfare workers and communities and resolutions and reports and housing projects and playgrounds have failed to do: to heal and redeem drunkards and junkies, to convert people who have come out of prison and to keep them out, to make men chaste and women virtuous, and to invest both the male and female with a pride and a serenity that hang about them like an unfailing light (1962:50-51).

Social researchers also studied aspects of Islam as it relates to inmates. Research regarding Islam within the prison system generally concluded that Islam promotes morality, conformity, self-esteem, responsibility, productivity and a desire for spiritual and intellectual growth (Atkins and Glick, 1972; Dannin, 1992; and Sharif, 1981).

The Islamic influence upon the inmate has also been noted by the media. In 1991 "The World Monitor," a television news show on the "Discovery" channel, presented a segment highlighting the lives of ex-inmates who had converted to Sunni Islam while incarcerated. This documentary considered whether Islam had any impact upon the inmate after release from prison and found, through interviews with the inmates, that Islam continued to positively impact upon their lives. For example, an inmate who had difficulty gaining employment upon release established his own lawn care business. He hired other ex-inmates who accepted Islam while they were incarcerated. With their profits, they purchased an old crack house and converted it into a community center (*World Monitor*, 1991).

Some Islamic leaders are also cognizant of Islam's reforming abilities. Convinced that his Nation of Islam is best equipped to reform African American inmates, Minister Louis Farrakhan created a proposal requesting that the government give the Nation of Islam control over the inmates. Farrakhan presented his rationale by stating:

> Since so many of the inmates are our people, why not let us reform them and help to save some of the taxpayer's money. Why not let us handle the inmates and lessen the taxpayer's burden. We can handle the inmates for less than what America is paying now. And better, we can reform our people and make them productive members of society. (1993:115)

These examples serve as evidence that Islam, whether it is the Nation of Islam or Sunni Islam, can have a positive impact upon those who convert while incarcerated. However, more research in this area is certainly needed to answer the complex array of questions that pertain to religious reformation. The purpose of this section was not only to demonstrate that reform through Islamic efforts is possible, but to show that this issue has captured a large audience, including novelists, researchers, reporters, and religious leaders.

CONCLUSION

Over the past decades, Islam has found permanence in American corrections. Its ability to sustain itself can be attributed to many factors. Broad social forces such as court intervention, the reality and impact of race in America, the role of religion in the African American experience, and the unique characteristics of the inmate culture have all been instrumental in the prison Muslim movement. As these forces continue, the Prison Muslim movement will continue to grow and develop within American corrections.

REFERENCES

Acoli, Sundiata (1995). A Brief History of the New Afrikan Prison Struggle. (In a special issue: Network of Black Organizers: Black Prison Movements, USA.) *Journal of African American Dialogue*, 11 (1), 1-26.

Alexander, Amy (1998). *The Farrakhan Factor: African-American Writers on Leadership, Nationhood, and Minister Louis Farrakhan*. New York: Grove Press.

Atkins, Burton M., and Henry R. Glick (1972). *Prisons, Protest, and Politics*. Englewood Cliffs, NJ: Prentice-Hall.

Baldwin, James (1962). *The Fire Next Time*. New York: Dell.

Bell, Derrick (1992). *Faces at the Bottom of the Well: The Permanence of Racism*. New York: Basic Books.

Brown, Claude (1965). *Manchild in the Promised Land*. New York: Signet.

Brown, Lee P. (1965). Black Muslims and the Police. *Journal of Criminal Law, Criminology, and Police Science*, 56 (1), 119-126.

Butler, Keith (1978). The Muslims Are No Longer an Unknown Quantity. *Corrections*, 4, 55-63.

Christianson, Scott (1980). Corrections Law Developments: Legal Implications of Racially Disproportionate Incarceration Rates. *Criminal Law Bulletin*, 16(1):58-63.

Christianson, Scott (1980). Corrections Law Developments: Racial Discrimination and Prison Confinement: A Follow-up. *Criminal Law Bulletin*, 16(6):616-621.

Churchill, Ward, and Jim Vander Wall (1990). *The Cointelpro Papers: Documents from the FBI's Secret War Against Dissent in the United States*. Boston: South End Press.

Clear, Todd, and George Cole (2000). *American Corrections*, Fifth ed. Belmont, CA: Wadsworth.

Clear, Todd, Bruce Stout, Harry Dammer, Linda Kelly, Patricia Hardyman, and Carol Shapiro (1992). *Prisoners, Prisons, and Religion.* Unpublished report, School of Criminal Justice, Rutgers University, Newark, NJ.

Cleaver, Eldridge (1968). *Soul on Ice.* New York: Dell.

Clemmer, Donald (1940). *The Prison Community.* New York: Holt, Rinehart.

Close, Billy R. (1997). Towards a Resolution of the Discrimination/No Discrimination Debate in Criminology and Criminal Justice: Revisiting Black Criminality and Institutional Racism. Unpublished dissertation, Florida State University.

Cooper v. Pate, 378 U.S. 546, 12 L.Ed. 2d, 1030, 84 S.Ct. 1733 (1967).

Dannin, Robert (1992). Island in a Sea of Ignorance. At www.nyu.edu/classes/crisis/prison.html.

Dix, Felecia A. (1997). Race, Religion, and the Inmate Culture: An Interpretation of Islam in American Prisons. Unpublished dissertation, Florida State University.

Donzinger, Steven (1996). *The Real War on Crime: The Report of the National Criminal Justice Commission.* New York: HarperCollins.

Drake, St. Clair, and Horace Cayton (1993). *Black Metropolis: A Study of Negro Life in a Northern City.* Chicago: University of Chicago Press.

El-Amin, Mustafa (1990). Al-Islam, Christianity and Freemasonry. Jersey City: New Mind Productions.

Essien-Udom, E. U. (1962). *Black Nationalism: A Search for an Identity in America.* Chicago: University of Chicago Press.

Farrakhan, Louis (1993). *A Torchlight for America.* Chicago: FCN Publishing.

Flowers, Ronald (1990). *Minorities and Criminality.* New York: Praeger.

Frankel, Geoffrey (1991). Untangling First Amendment Values: The Prisoners' Dilemma. *George Washington University Law Review*, 59:1614-1646.

Franklin, John Hope, and Alfred A. Moss, Jr. (1994). *From Slavery to Freedom: A History of African Americans.* New York: McGraw-Hill.

Fulwood v. Clemmer, 209 F.Supp. 370 (1962).

Gardell, Mattias (1996). *In the Name of Elijah Muhammad: Louis Farrakhan and the Nation of Islam.* Durham, NC: Duke University Press.

Gomez, Michael (1994). Muslims in Early America. *Journal of Southern History*, 60, 671-710.

Hacker, Andrew (1992). *Two Nations: Black and White, Separate, Hostile, Unequal.* New York: Ballantine Books.

Haley, Alex (1964). *The Autobiography of Malcolm X.* New York: Ballantine.

Hooks, Bell (1995). *Killling Rage: Ending Racism.* New York: Holt.

Irwin, John (1980). *Prisons in Turmoil.* Boston: Little, Brown.

Irwin, John, and Donald Cressey (1962). Thieves, Convicts, and the Inmate Culture. *Social Problems*, 10(2):142-155.

Irwin, John, and James Austin (1994). *It's About Time: America's Imprisonment Binge.* Belmont, CA: Wadsworth.

Jacobs, James B. (1977). *Stateville: The Penitentiary in Mass Society.* Chicago: University of Chicago Press.

Jones, Oliver (1983). The Black Muslim Movement and the American Constitutional System. *Journal of Black Studies*, 13(4):417-437.

Kunjufu, Jawanza (1994). *Adam, Where Are You?–Why Most Black Men Don't Go to Church*. Chicago: African American Images.

Lee, Martha F. (1996). *The Nation of Islam: An American Millenarian Movement*. Syracuse, NY: Syracuse University Press.

Lincoln, C. Eric (1961). *The Black Muslims in America*. Boston: Beacon Press.

Lincoln, C. Eric (1984). *Race, Religion and the Continuing American Dilemma*. New York: Hill and Wang.

Lincoln, C. Eric, and Lawrence H. Mamiya (1990). *The Black Church in the African American Experience*. Durham, NC: Duke University Press.

Lusane, Clarence (1991). *Pipe Dream Blues: Racism and the War on Drugs*. Boston: South End Press.

Mann, Coramae Richey (1993). *Unequal Justice: A Question of Color*. Bloomington, IN: Indiana University Press.

Muhammad, Elijah (1965). *Message to the Blackman in America*. Newport News: United Brothers Communications Systems.

Murdy, Ralph G. (1961). Islam Incarcerated. *American Journal of Corrections*, 23, (January-February), 23 (1), 18-21.

Nu'Man, Muhammad A. (1985). *What Every American Should Know About Islam and the Muslims*. Jersey City, NJ: New Mind Productions.

Page, Clarence (1996). *Showing My Color: Impolite Essays on Race and Identity*. New York: HarperCollins.

Palmer, John W. (1991). *Constitutional Rights of Prisoners*. Cincinnati: Anderson.

Pass, Michael G. (1999). Religious Orientation and Self-Reported Rule Violations in a Maximum Security Prison. *Journal of Offender Rehabilitation*, 28 (3/4), 119-134.

Rigoli, Lisa (1990). Power Exercised in the Shadows: *O'Lone v. Shabazz* as a Signal of the Court's Return to Interpretivism in Institutional Reform Litigation. *New England Journal of Criminal and Civil Confinement*, 16(1):141-170.

Robbins, Ira P. (1980). The Cry of Wolfish in the Federal Courts: The Future of Federal Intervention in Prison Administration. *Journal of Criminal Law and Criminology*, 71(3):211-225.

Rudovsky, David, Alvin J. Bronstein, Edward I. Koren, and Julia Cade (1988). *The Rights of Prisoners: A Comprehensive Guide to the Legal Rights of Prisoners Under Current Law*. Carbondale, IL: Southern Illinois University Press.

Ruffin v. Commonwealth, 62 Va. 790 (1871).

Sharif, Sidney R. (1981). *Crime and Corrections: An Al-Islamic Perspective*. Chicago: Kazi Publications.

Shover, Neal, and Werner Einstadter (1988). *Analyzing American Corrections*. Belmont, CA: Wadsworth.

Smith, Christopher (1993). Black Muslims and the Development of Prisoner's Rights. *Journal of Black Studies*, 24(2): 131-146.

Sykes, Gresham (1958). *The Society of Captives: A Study of a Maximum Security Prison*. Princeton, NJ: Princeton University Press.

Tonry, Michael (1995). *Malign Neglect: Race, Crime, and Punishment in America*. New York: Oxford University Press.

Van Sertima, Ivan (1992). *African Presence in Early America*. New Brunswick, NJ: Transaction Books.

West, Cornell (1993). *Race Matters*. New York: Vintage Books.

Wheeler, Stanton (1961). Socialization in Correctional Communities. *American Sociological Review*, 26(1):697-712.

Yaker, Henri M. (1962). The Black Muslims in the Correctional Institution. *Welfare Reporter*, October: 158-165.

AUTHORS' NOTES

Felecia Dix-Richardson, PhD, is an assistant professor in the Department of Sociology and Criminal Justice at Florida A&M University.

Billy R. Close, PhD, is an assistant professor in the School of Criminology at the Florida State University.

This paper is based on *Race, Religion, and the Inmate Culture: An Interpretation of the Development of Islam in American Prisons*, an unpublished dissertation by the first author. The authors thank Tom O'Connor for all of his assistance and suggestions on previous drafts of the manuscript.

Address correspondence to Felecia Dix-Richardson, PhD, Florida A&M University, Department of Sociology and Criminal Justice, Perry-Paige 403, Tallahassee, FL 32307.

Religion, the Community, and the Rehabilitation of Criminal Offenders. Pp. 109-126.

Resistance to Conversion to Islam Among African American Women Inmates

FELECIA DIX-RICHARDSON

Florida A&M University

SUMMARY While the tendency to convert to Islam is common among African American male inmates, Islamic conversion among African American female inmates does not commonly occur. Educated estimates and telephone interviews with chaplains of major female correctional institutions in Florida and Alabama, indicate that Islamic conversion among African American female inmates is extremely low. Why is there such a stark contrast between the religious practice of incarcerated African American men and women? This research takes a social context approach to explore several reasons why African American women do not convert to Islam to the same degree as African American men while incarcerated. The paper gains insight into this disparity through considering several factors: (1) Lack of familiarity/comfort; (2) Social support and church involvement; (3) Female inmate social system; and (4) Islamic prison ministry. *[Article copies available for a fee from The Haworth Document Delivery Service: 1-800-HAWORTH. E-mail address: <getinfo@ haworthpressinc.com> Website: <http://www.HaworthPress.com> © 2002 by The Haworth Press, Inc. All rights reserved.]*

KEYWORDS Conversion, prison, inmate, women, Islam, race, social support, religion

According to one commentator, there were fewer than 500,000 Muslims in the U.S. That number today is over six million, of whom approximately 40% are African American. Smith (1999) estimates that over 300,000 prisoners are converts to Islam with the yearly number of prison converts being 30,000. For over 60 years, incarcerated African American men have been discovering and converting to Islam as part of their prison experience; however, while the tendency to convert to Islam is common among African American male inmates, Islamic conversion among African American female inmates does not seem to be as common. Recent surveys conducted with chaplains of some of Florida's major female institutions indicated that there are less than 30 known practicing African American female Islamic inmates in Florida's state prison system.

At Julia Tutwiler prison for women, the only major female institution in the state of Alabama, there are no known inmates who are practicing Islam within the institution. Yet, when one observes male institutions, there is a high presence of inmates who practice Islam.

To illustrate, in his descriptive study of Islamic practices in a major male institution, Butler (1978) estimated that as a rule, for every 1,000 black prisoners in an institution, at least 200 will call themselves Muslims. In 1995 McCloud estimated that there are approximately 4,000 Muslim inmates within the federal prison system (McCloud, 1991). According to the Chaplain Administrator of the Federal Bureau of Prisons, McCloud's estimates were correct but they did not include Nation of Islam inmates. If one includes Nation of Islam in the 1995 Federal figures there were 5,574 inmates (4,503 Muslim and 1,071 Nation of Islam) who identified in some way with the Muslim faith representing 6.1% of the total population of 90,323. In 1995 males were 6.4% of the total male population of 84,027 (4,342 Muslim and 1,059 Nation of Islam) whereas females (161 Muslim and 12 Nation of Islam) were only 2.7% of the total female population of 6,296.

By 2001 there were 10,362 prisoners (or 7.8% of the total federal inmate population) who self-identify as Muslim (7,221) or Nation of Islam (3,141). Males were 8.1% of the total male population of 123,156 (6,953 Muslim and 3,122 Nation of Islam) whereas females (268 Muslim and 19 Nation of Islam) were only 3.2% of the total female population of 8,887 (Van Baalen, 2001).

Why is there such a prevailing difference between the religious practice of incarcerated African American men and women? This paper explores some possible explanations for the difference using a social context approach that addresses several issues that may be impacting upon the lack of Islamic participation by African American female inmates. The paper explores the following topics: (1) lack of familiarity; (2) social support and church involvement; (3) female inmate social system; and (4) Islamic prison ministry.

Given the exploratory nature of this research and the contextual approach sought, I first review the literature pertaining to the issues listed previously, and then I gather descriptive data regarding Islamic inmate characteristics from telephone interviews with prison chaplains from institutions in Alabama and Florida. The use of more than one research method provides a more complete answer to the research question (Maxfield and Babbie, 1998).

LACK OF FAMILIARITY WITH ISLAM

The most logical place to search for an answer to the disparity of Islamic conversion between incarcerated African American men and women is to consider the African American woman's familiarity with Islam and her perceptions towards the religion. What one perceives to be reality, whether it is true or not, will shape attitudes and beliefs. If a particular group holds a similar perception, they will eventually manifest it into reality. It is important to understand the beliefs of women prior to imprisonment because incarceration does not automatically change prior views or values. As the inmate literature on adjustment and the inmate social system has shown, the beliefs, values, and everyday experiences of inmates are often imported into the daily lifestyle of incarcerated individuals (Goodstein and McKenzie, 1984; Irwin and Cressey, 1962; Thomas, 1975). Thus, within the following discussion, consideration will be given to a possible perception of Islam that may be held in general by many African American women. That perception is the belief that Islam may have negative implications for African American women.

It is not uncommon for the unfamiliar to be regarded with skepticism. This certainly applies to religion, especially those religions that may be deemed as unfamiliar through personal experience. In a society where Christianity is the dominant religion, any religion that presents opposite views, rituals, and traditions will be approached with caution. Any religion, given the complex nature of most religions, challenges one to search for its meaning and his/her role within that religion. When the role that one will play in a particular religion is unclear, contradictory to the reality of daily life, or in possible contrast to past religious practices, the exploration of that religion will probably be done carefully and cautiously. This may certainly be the case for African American women who are exposed to Islam.

If African American women foresee Islam as an unfamiliar or unappealing religion, the question that must be asked is why, considering the fact that Islam has had an extensive presence in the African American community. Islam has been a part of the African American experience from the beginning, as many Africans who came to America during its formative years were Muslims (Gomez, 1994). In addition, the Nation of Islam has maintained a constant presence in America for over 60 years. However, even though Islam, with its many diverse sects, has maintained a visual presence in the African American community for quite some time, various aspects of the religion have been questioned by those who have had the opportunity to observe it. Not only has the role of Islam in the African American community been questioned, it has been met with confusion.

Even though Islam may have been present from the very beginning of the African American experience, Christianity is the religion that has maintained a strong force in the lives and experiences of most African Americans, especially African American women. African American women have traditionally represented the majority of the black church membership and this fact may account for the African American woman's lack of familiarity and interest in Islam. As noted by Lincoln and Mamiya (1990), even though many mainline black denominations maintain a mostly male leadership, the major programs of the black church regarding politics, economics, and music depend heavily on women for their promotion and success. Thus, black churches could scarcely have survived without the active support of black women (Lincoln and Mamiya, 1990). Due to their central role and active participation in this Christian religious environment, black women might find more comfort in the black church than in the Islamic religion.

Even though there are similarities in the teachings of Islam and Christianity, the differences are often what are noticed. When one considers the contrast in ideologies between Islam and Christianity (e.g., the relevance of Jesus Christ), it can be easily understood that friction will probably arise between family, friends, the community, etc., and those who consider converting to Islam. A foreseen negative reaction from significant others can create questions and confusion regarding an Islamic lifestyle. Thus, for the African American women in general Islam may not necessarily be unfamiliar. Instead, Islam with regard to traditions, rituals, beliefs, and values may create a sense of uneasiness or lack of comfort for the African American woman.

The uncertainty that arises from the questions and confusion can often lead to negative feelings and interpretations. Considering the fact that Islam is not a new phenomenon in the African American community, what has caused this negative perception regarding the role of women in Islam? It has been suggested by some researchers and religious scholars that a negative view of Islam has possibly stemmed from such factors as the lack of knowledge of the role and treatment of women in Islam, misinterpretation of the religion, media portrayal, and the attire of the Islamic woman (McCloud, 1991; Shah and Diamond, 1995; and Wadud-Muhsin, 1992).

Role and Treatment of Women in Islam

As mentioned earlier, the unknown or unfamiliar is often guarded with skepticism. Skepticism can easily transform itself into negativism if doubts and concerns are not countered with accurate information. It is not uncommon for an African American woman, or other women from various ethnic/racial groups, who encounter Islam as a mere observer, to find the religion to be sexist, patriarchal, oppressive and domineering towards women. Acknowledging that this is the belief of some women, religious scholars, as well as Islamic women in general, have tried to diminish this view by pointing to contributing factors of this negative belief and by trying to describe a more accurate picture of the role of women in Islam. If women obtained an accurate view of Islam instead of a distorted image, Islam might not continue to be viewed as an oppressive religion towards women (Nu'Man, 1985; and Wadus-Muhsin, 1992).

For example, negative views and misinterpretation of Islam and the role of women often stem from the misinterpretation of the Qur'an. According to Wadus-Muhsin, "It was not the text which restricted women, but the interpretations of that text which have come to be held in greater importance than the text itself" (1992:vi). Then, Wadus-Muhsin (1992) suggests that the Qur'an must be continually reinterpreted and that Muslim women must read the text of the Qur'an unconstrained by exclusive and restrictive interpretations in order to gain an undeniable liberation. In addition, as noted by Nu'Man, Islamic tradition emphasizes kindness and equity toward women. If women are subjugated it is a problem created by people, not the Qur'an (Nu'Man 1985).

Another issue regarding Islam is that some African American women hold the assumption that Islamic women must behave submissively towards the men in their families. Additionally, Islamic women often are assumed to be denied basic human rights. Media accounts of extreme laws such as the Taliban and its enforcement in countries such as

Afghanistan (Herbert, 1998) or polygamy practices in some Muslim communities tend to reinforce and confirm these beliefs. Also, images of gender separation during religious services create additional concerns. If these beliefs and assumptions represent the views of many black women, it can easily be understood why this religion would not appeal to those who are incarcerated especially given the fact that such beliefs do not automatically diminish upon incarceration.

Yet another issue that might present an obstacle for Islamic conversion by African American women is the historical reality that these women have encountered. When one considers the historical reality of the African American female experience, a story of mistreatment, exploitation, and a struggle for survival unfolds. The historical reality of African American women may cause many of them to question whether an Islamic lifestyle can adequately enhance their well-being or only add to the contradiction of their experience and existence.

To illustrate, since the beginning of the African American experience, African American women were not treated or viewed very differently than her male counterparts. African American women were expected to provide manual labor as slaves and as an inmates under the concept of convict leasing (Davis, 1983). In many instances, they were forced into situations where they became the head of the household. African American women realized early on that the lives and roles they played in American society were contradictory to the ideology of womanhood. As noted by Collins, "If women are allegedly passive and fragile, then why are Black women treated as 'mules' and assigned heavy cleaning chores?" (1991:12).

The contradictory lifestyle of African American women and the concept of woman was documented nearly 150 years ago by Sojourner Truth when she delivered her famous "Ain't I a Woman?" speech at the women's convention in Akron, Ohio in 1851 (Davis, 1983). In her speech, Sojourner Truth illustrated the duality and contradictory lifestyle of the African American female slave. Considering the contradictory reality of the meaning of African American womanhood, a religion that appears to elevate the position of men and emphasizes the protection of women may breed resentment since many African American women may harbor the belief that they have lived in a society where they have been unprotected and exploited. However, while they were experiencing the maltreatment of society, they were simultaneously able to play an instrumental role in supporting the emotional and economic needs of their families. In a society where the differences of men and women are often emphasized, African American women realize that they are often treated similarly to men in many situations. Thus, if they interpret Islam as a religion that subjugates women, conversion is less likely. The argument can be made that in many instances Christianity can be interpreted as a religion that practices the subjugation of women also; therefore, African American women should harbor the same type of skepticism toward Christianity. For this reason, many African American women do critically object to Christianity and its treatment of women; however, it must be understood that Christianity may not face the same scrutiny because Christianity has been incorporated into the lives of many African Americans since the inception of American slavery.

If Islam is viewed skeptically by non-Muslim women, criticism of the religion by those who once were members only strengthens this skepticism. An example of this can be illustrated in the works of Sonsyrea Tate. In her book, *Little X: Growing Up in the Nation of Islam*, Sonsyrea Tate (1997) provides a detailed description of life for a young female growing up in the Nation of Islam and Sunni Islam religions. Her emotions regarding Islam range from a complete love, respect, and devotion to an uncertainty and ambivalence toward the religion. Her uncertainty and ambivalence stemmed from reactions of the community, friends, non-Muslim family members, expectations and demands of the religion, and an apparent contrast between lessons taught and the realities of daily life.

In sum, when one chooses to convert to a religion there is the belief that the new religion will have a meaningful and positive impact upon one's life. Often there is the hope that the new religion will change one's life, create comfort, provide strength and encouragement, etc. African American women may believe that an Islamic lifestyle will create negative consequences and a lifestyle that is contradictory to the expectations and reality of their daily lives.

The Attire of Islamic Women

As stated earlier, African American female perspectives regarding Islam may be a possible reason why some women might not view this religion as a plausible religious option. Why do non-Muslim African American women have the tendency to cast a negative stereotypical view on the role of women in Islam? Another obvious answer lies within issues relating to the attire of many Islamic women. Those who embrace the religion of Islam believe that many non-Muslim women often misunderstand the religion due to Islamic dress traditions as they relate to Muslim women (McCloud, 1991; and Shah and Diamond, 1995). Often, the words "Muslim woman" conjures up images of women who cover everything except for their face and hands. Though this image certainly does not depict the attire of all Muslim women, even the slightest modification in clothing to conform to religious practices can draw attention from the non-Muslim general public.

To illustrate this problem, in her autobiography, Tate (1997) vividly recalls her feeling towards her dress restrictions as a little girl growing up in the Nation of Islam. Not only did she recall how her classmates and others taunted her clothing, she remembered how special accommodations had to be made for her during physical education classes. After Elijah Muhammad died leaving his son W. D. Mohammed in charge, the Nation of Islam began a phase of transformation. This transformation relaxed the dress code for female Muslims. Tate remembered how excited she was to finally be allowed to go shopping at department stores for school clothes. In a society where clothing appears to be highly important to the self-image of women, it can easily be seen how a restrictive code regarding the attire of women may be viewed negatively by women who may be already struggling to gain the respect and recognition of society.

To further illustrate the impact of the attire of Muslim women, McCloud (1991) conducted a study where she collected oral histories of African American women residing in Philadelphia who had converted to Islam. Some of the women discussed how the attire of a Muslim woman can draw negative attention, and even jeopardize her livelihood if worn in a country where Islam is not the dominant religion.

A somewhat contrasting view of Islamic attire can be shown in Shah and Diamond's 1995 study of women who enjoyed wearing khemars (i.e., headcovering). The women in their study indicated that khemars gave women a powerful sense of identity. The women in the study did not see khemars as oppressive. Rather, they saw them as a source of identification with other Muslim women and a source of empowerment.

Acknowledging the fact that Muslim women are often misunderstood with regard to their attire, image, and role within the Nation of Islam, *Essence* magazine, which is devoted to issues surrounding African American women, published an article in its July 1996 edition that attempted to diminish myths regarding these women. The article highlighted the fact that Muslim women did play a leading role in the Nation of Islam. It also showed that women in the Nation could be successful lawyers, entrepreneurs, and pointed out that Islamic attire could be extremely attractive and stylish (Chance, 1996).

This issue of attire may intensify when the dress code of the prison is taken into consideration. In an environment where clothing restrictions may often be the norm, some incarcerated women may feel that prison makes it too difficult to abide by the dress guidelines of the Islamic religion. Also, if non-incarcerated women have the tendency to feel somewhat isolated and ridiculed from society when they dress differently due to religious reasons, incarcerated women may feel even more isolated and ridiculed given the small community in which they live.

SOCIAL SUPPORT AND CHURCH INVOLVEMENT

In order to understand any prison phenomenon, one must consider factors occurring prior to incarceration. Religious conversion in prison is no exception. The fundamental question that must be asked is, "Does the pre-prison experience of African American men and women differ?" I suggest it does in a number of areas; however, in many ways they are the same: Among the experiences compared are: family roles, social roles, and religious affiliation prior to incarceration.

The contradictory roles that African American women have historically held in their families and society have already been discussed in the section above. In this section of the report I will consider how comparable are women's roles to men's roles when the background of incarcerated African American men and women is taken into account. The majority of incarcerated African American men and women are single and young. In Islam, the image of the man/father as the head of the household is the view that is often projected. For many incarcerated African American women, this image does not reflect the reality of their experience. It has been found that approximately 75% of incarcerated women are mothers who mostly had custody of their children before incarceration.

If this is a part of their reality, an Islamic lifestyle may seem contradictory to their lives prior to incarceration as well. Also, many women who are currently incarcerated have been sentenced under mandatory minimum laws (Newsome, 2000). When a 24-year-old woman is given a 24-year sentence without the possibility of parole, an Islamic lifestyle that reflects family unity with the husband as provider and protector of his family may not be seen as a viable option.

Incarcerated African American men and women share many of the same characterizations: both are disproportionately represented in the prison population, both are young, most have not completed high school, and both have the tendency to be economically deprived (U.S. Department of Justice, 1994). Considering the similarities of these characteristics, it should be asked if African American women respond in the same way to these similar states? Even though the fight for gender equality is gaining attention in American society, black women still find themselves in a unique struggle for survival and against the criminal justice system (e.g., competitive wages, education, discriminatory laws, etc.). Even though African American men and women have both experienced the negative effects of society, will their responses to them, societal and family roles, and the conditions of incarceration impact the decision to embrace Islam?

Incarcerated African American men and women tend to have experienced similar social issues (e.g., racism, discrimination, under and unemployment, poverty, lack of education, etc.); however, African American women compared to African American men may tend to focus more on other issues (e.g., the well-being of their children) instead of the social problems they may have experienced and their status in society.

Another issue to consider regarding pre-prison experiences is religious affiliation prior to incarceration. Research on the black church and the African American community has found that African American women often constitute the majority of the Christian church membership (Lincoln and Mamiya, 1990).

Noting this disparity, Kunjufu (1994) wrote an entire book, *Adam! Where Are You?: Why Most Black Men Do Not Go to Church*, devoted to uncovering reasons why young black men are not actively participating in the Christian church. In many African American communities girls are expected and forced to attend church; whereas, the attendance expectation is relaxed for male members of the family. Not only do women represent the majority in the black church, but the active participation of African American women has sustained the black church.

Even though women have been historically denied leadership roles (i.e., ministers, bishops, presiding elders, deacons, etc.) in many mainline black denominations, black women have been given honorable titles such as "mothers of the church" (Note 1). According to Lincoln and Mamiya (1990), "mothers of the church" is an honorific title usually reserved for the wife of the founder or the oldest and most respected female members of the church. The "mother of the church" has great influence because the pastor of the church will often consult with her before making important church decisions. It is interesting to note that there is no parallel of the "church mother" in white churches. Furthermore, even though women have been denied formal leadership roles in many mainline black denominations, this has not kept black women from establishing their own churches. To avoid the strictures of the traditional black church, black women preachers established independent storefront churches. In fact there probably have been more black women preachers historically in proportion to their numbers in the total population than white women preachers (Lincoln and Mamiya, 1990). When the issues presented above are considered, it appears that the black Christian church, whether it is mainline or independent, has a significant and meaningful role to offer black women. The black church could not survive without the support of black women; however, the same conclusions cannot be drawn for the role of women in the mosque and Islam where women are not generally given spiritual leadership roles.

FEMALE INMATE SOCIAL SYSTEM

Some researchers state that there are major differences between male and female inmates, prisons, and the prison social systems (Pollock-Byrne, 1990). To illustrate, approximately one third of females are serving time for violent offenses; whereas, nearly half of male inmates are serving time for violent offenses. Of the women who are serving time for violent crimes, many of them were convicted for defending themselves or their children. The majority of women are in prison for economic crimes.

There is less violence in female institutions than in male institutions. When compared to men, women tend to show greater responsiveness to prison programs. Regarding prison structure, male populations are divided by security levels; whereas, female inmates generally serve their time in a setting where the entire population is mixed. Female inmates spend more time, on average, in their cells than men. Men spend more time outside for exercise than women. When race is considered, men tend to segregate themselves by race; however, this is less true for women. Also, female inmates tend to share aspects of their lives with correctional officers; whereas, male inmates generally do not (Belknap, 1996; Clear and Cole, 2000).

These factors seem to illustrate that there are some major differences between incarcerated men and women, but how these differences may impact upon the low representation of African American women who choose Islam while incarcerated is yet to be understood. Differences in male and female habits during incarceration may become significant.

For example, women form pseudofamilies while incarcerated. These makeshift families enable the female inmate to adjust more easily to prison life and serve as a center in the social organization of women's prisons (Giallombardo, 1966; and Pollock-Byrne, 1990) If these pseudofamilies provide comfort and friendship for the female inmate, Islamic conversion based upon prison comfort would certainly not be as popular within male institutions since male inmates tend not to form these types of prison families.

Islam, within the prison setting, has the tendency to address issues that relate to unequal treatment of relegated members of society by those who are in control of societal institutions and laws (Note 2). This unequal treatment is often intertwined with issues of race. America has had a long past of racial injustice towards African Americans. This racial injustice has been argued to be a contributing factor to the disproportionate incarceration rate between blacks and whites (Tonry, 1995; and Walker et al., 1999). If an appealing aspect of Islam is the power of its message regarding racial injustice, one should consider whether this message is appealing to both incarcerated African American men and women. In order for this consideration to be given, it must be determined if incarcerated African American men and women experience similar acts of racial injustice.

When the historical reality of incarceration trends of African American men and women are evaluated, it is clear that both have experienced institutionalized racism resulting in unfair treatment by law enforcement, courts, and corrections (Davis, 1981; Flowers, 1988; and Mann, 1993). Based upon this assertion, it would seem that incarcerated African American women would be just as eager to accept Islam; however, this does not appear to be the reality for African American female inmates. Thus, racial injustice alone does not seem to create a strong desire for Islamic acceptance among African American incarcerated women.

Another dimension of race that has to be considered is the impact that it has upon the inmate social system. Some research indicates that race is an intricate component of the male inmate social system (Irwin, 1980). Irwin (1980) indicated that male inmates had the tendency to divide along racial lines. Only in certain situations would male inmates form relationships with inmates from other racial groups (Irwin, 1980). However, research on race in female institutions has found just the opposite (Pollock-Byrne, 1990). According to Pollock-Byrne (1990), racial problems usually do not exist in prisons for women. Integration tends to be the norm rather than the exception. To illustrate this point further, Kruttshnitt (1983) found that 75% of black women had one or more close ties with white women. Therefore, if race does not play the same role in female institutions as it does in male institutions, the need to accept Islam to address and combat racial issues within the female institution lacks necessity.

CHAPLAIN INTERVIEWS ON ISLAMIC PRISON MINISTRY

Another area of concern is Islamic prison ministry. If African American female inmates are unfamiliar with Islam in the prison setting, one must ask why? To what degree are women, as opposed to men, exposed to Islam while incarcerated? Even though Islam has maintained a visible presence in the African American community for quite some time, many male inmates who convert to Islam indicate that while they might have heard of Islam prior to incarceration, they were personally exposed to Islam within the prison system (Dix, 1990). Are incarcerated African American women and men equally exposed to Islam? Islamic prison ministry has been relatively active in male institutions for several decades. Muslim inmates have even sought redress in the courts to ensure their right to freely practice their faith. However, it is yet to be seen if Islamic prison ministries devote the same amount of attention to male and female institutions.

To help answer this question, telephone interviews/inquiries were conducted with chaplains of five female institutions in Alabama and Florida. Three out of five state institutions from Florida and the only female institution in Alabama were included in the sample.

The telephone interviews were unstructured and open-ended. This approach yields the richest information because respondents are allowed to answer questions in their own words as fully as possible (Maxfield and Babbie, 1998). The purpose of this approach was to allow chaplains to provide administrative insight regarding the role of Islamic prison ministry within the prison. Also, chaplains would be in a better position to answer questions pertaining to the number of women who are practicing Islam within the institution since it would be their duty to assist these women in obtaining religious services and guidance from the outside community.

Five institutions were included within this study. The institutions included were Julia Tutwiler, an Alabama state facility, Lowell and Broward state correctional centers, Gadsen correctional center, a private facility, and the Federal correctional Institution, located in Tallahassee, Florida.

Julia Tutwiler Prison for Women, located in Wetumpka, Alabama, is the only major female institution in the state of Alabama. This facility is equipped to house 800 to 900 inmates. Lowell Correctional Institution–Women's Unit is located in Marion County. This Region III facility represents the central portion of Florida. Lowell's total capacity is 765. Its custody grade is close, medium, and minimum. This is a youth-populated facility housing 14-18 and 19-24 age groups. Broward Correctional Institution is located in Broward County. This Region IV facility represents southern Florida. Broward's total capacity is 532. This institution, which houses death row inmates, maintains maximum, close, medium, and minimum custody grades. Gadsen Correctional Facility, which is located in Gadsen County (North Florida), is a privately owned facility that is under contract with Florida Department of Corrections. The total capacity at Gadsen is 800. The custody grade of this facility is medium and minimum.

The chaplain at Gadsen Correctional Facility indicated that there was only one inmate who expressed an interest in Islam (i.e., the inmate had requested Islamic literature). This inmate was not a devout Muslim in the sense of observing religious tenets and rituals. During the chaplain's six-year employment at Gadsen, she indicated that she had only encountered six Islamic inmates. These encounters did not occur at the same time. There were no more than two or three inmates practicing the Islamic faith at any given time. The Gadsen chaplain also said that, on the whole, Islamic prison ministry does not normally run programs in the facility but they do send some literature and videos to the facility. Another important issue that surfaced in the interview was the fact that proselytizing is not allowed in Florida correctional institutions. The implications of this issue will be discussed in the next section.

At Lowell Correctional Institution, there were seven Islamic inmates. When asked about Islamic prison ministry from the community, the chaplain indicated that when they tried to contact an Islamic ministry service from Gainesville, they received no response. Currently an Imam and his wife from Ft. Myers are volunteering their services for the Muslim inmates at Lowell. When asked his opinion regarding Islamic practices by African American female inmates, the chaplain stated that if a significant male (e.g., a husband, boyfriend, or close relative) was involved in Islam, it might have an impact upon the female converting to Islam.

At Broward Correctional Institution, there were two Muslim inmates. One was affiliated with the Nation of Islam and the other one was identified as Sunni. The Nation of Islam inmate converted prior to incarceration, while the Sunni converted while incarcerated. Like the other institutions, there has not been much involvement from the free-world prison ministry. Currently, they have a female volunteer who meets with the women. When asked about the low number of women who convert to Islam, the chaplain indicated that the nesting (pseudofamilies) aspect of the female social system probably plays a significant role in the low Islamic conversion rate of female inmates.

Julia Tutwiler Prison for Women, located in Wetumpka, is the only major female institution in Alabama. An interview with its chaplain concluded with information that there were no known Muslims at Tutwiler. It is interesting to note that within a 20-mile radius of Tutwiler there are three male institutions, Draper Correctional Center, Elmore Correctional Center, and Thomas F. Staton Correctional Center. All of these institutions maintain a visible Islamic population. Given the close proximity of these institutions it would seem that gender differences are certainly a contributing factor in this religious disparity.

DISCUSSION

Interviews with chaplains in the institutions included in this study and a review of existing relevant literature suggest several issues that may lend themselves as plausible explanations regarding the scarce Islamic presence in female institutions. Possible institutional factors include: race relations in female institutions, the inmate social system, and Islamic prison ministry.

It has often been thought that Islamic conversion by African American male inmates may be linked to racial issues. Research indicates that racial issues are not that problematic among female inmates. If race is not a major concern for the African American female inmate, Islam would not be sought as a possible source of redress to combat racial issues.

As discussed earlier, there are vast differences between male and female social systems. If women have the tendency to find comfort and unity with one another, the need to reach out to an unfamiliar religion would certainly become more unlikely than it is for men.

The chaplain interviews suggest that Islamic prison ministry is not very strong in female institutions. If this is coupled with the fact that proselytizing is not allowed in Florida prisons, it is obvious that African American women may not become exposed to Islam while incarcerated. If this is the reality of their prison experience, it is likely that Islamic conversion by African American female inmates will continue as an uncommon trend.

Another issue that was not mentioned by the chaplains but may have merit is the level of violence in female institutions. It has often been viewed that Islam can serve as a means of protection from violence for its members. If this assertion is true and if violent encounters in female institutions are not as problematic for female inmates as they are for male inmates, then the need to join an Islamic group as a means of protection would not become necessary.

Not only are there institutional factors that seem to impact upon the low conversion rate of African American female inmates, pre-prison/external factors seem to be influential as well. Pre-prison factors include: prior religious affiliation/expectation, commonly held views regarding Islam by African American women, and the African American female role in the family and society. As noted earlier, the black Christian church has had the tendency of maintaining a female majority. Even though African American women have traditionally been excluded from formal leadership roles in the black church, they often represent the backbone of its existence. Thus, if African American women view Christianity and the black church as a source of solace, conversion to Islam may not represent a viable religious choice.

If African American women view Islam as a religion that subjugates women, Islamic conversion may not occur considering the role that African American women have traditionally held in society and their families. The reality of the African American female experience has often created a contradictory lifestyle for African American females abiding under the protected elements of womanhood. For example, many African American women have been thrust into various situations that did not allow for protection or submissiveness (e.g., slavery, convict leasing, heads of households, etc.). For these reasons, many may find that they cannot fully integrate Islam into the daily reality of their lives.

Religion has traditionally been viewed as a means of offender rehabilitation. Much has been written regarding the impact of religion upon those who are incarcerated. Christianity and Islam may both play an instrumental role in offender rehabilitation and the inmate culture; however, when the religious experience of women and more specifically African American women is considered, a different reality emerges. Unlike their incarcerated male counterparts, African American women are not incorporating Islam into their prison experience to the same degree as their male counterparts. This study serves only as an inquiry to this religious disparity. More research is needed to gain a better perspective on why Islam has not become a major reality of the African American female inmate experience. As a next step, actual interviews with or questionnaires completed by incarcerated African American women would certainly add another dimension to this area of study. In addition, interviews/questionnaires with those women who have accepted Islam while incarcerated would provide further rich and invaluable insight into the issues surrounding Islam and African American incarcerated women, which we have begun to articulate in this paper.

NOTES

1. The African Methodist Episcopal Church allows female ministers. In July 2000 it elected its first female bishop.
2. There are various sects of Islam within prisons across America. While some sects, such as the Nation of Islam, may have the tendency to specifically address immediate concerns of the African American community, other sects, such as the Sunni, do address societal issues relating to oppression, poverty, education, etc., as well.

REFERENCES

Belknap, Joanne (1996). *The Invisible Woman: Gender, Crime, and Justice.* New York: Wadsworth.

Butler, Keith (1978). The Muslims Are No Longer an Unknown Quantity. *Corrections*, 4(2), 55-63.

Chance, Julia (1996). Lifting the Veil. *Essence*, July: 86-91.

Clear, Todd, and George Cole (2000). *American Corrections*, 5th edition. Belmont, CA: Wadsworth.

Collins, Patricia H. (1991). *Black Feminist Thought: Knowledge, Consciousness, and the Politics of Empowerment.* New York: Routledge.

Davis, Angela (1983). *Women, Race, and Class.* New York: Vintage.

Dix, Felecia (1990). Islamic Coversion Among African American Males at Draper Correctional Institution. Unpublished thesis, Florida State University.

Flowers, Ronald B. (1988). *Minorities and Criminality.* New York: Praeger.

Giallombardo, Rose (1966). *Society of Women: A Study of a Women's Prison.* New York: Wiley.

Goodstein, Lynn, and MacKenzie, Doris (1984). Racial Differences in Adjustment Patterns of Prison Inmates: Prisonization, Conflict, Stress and Control. In Daniel E. Georges-Abeyie (Ed.), *The Criminal Justice System and Blacks.* New York: Clark Boardman.

Haddad, Yvonne Y. (1991). *The Muslims of America.* New York: Oxford University Press.

Herbert, Bob (1998). Leno's Wife Joins Afghan Women's War. *Tallahassee Democrat.* October 7: 11A.

Irwin, John (1980). *Prisons in Turmoil*. Boston: Little, Brown.

Irwin, John, and Donald Cressey (1962). Thieves, Convicts, and the Inmate Culture. *Social Problems*, 10, 2: 142-155.

Kunjufu, Jawanza (1994). *Adam! Where Are You? Why Most Black Men Don't Go to Church*. United States: African American Images. Chicago: African American Images.

Lincoln, C. Eric, and Lawrence Mamiya (1990). *The Black Church in the African American Experience*. Durham: Duke University Press.

Mann, Coramae (1993). *Unequal Justice: A Question of Color*. Bloomington, IN: Indiana University Press.

Maxfield, Michael G., and Earl Babbie (1998). *Research Methods for Criminal Justice and Criminology*. Belmont, CA: West/Wadsworth.

McCloud, Aminah B. (1995). *African American Islam*. New York: Routledge.

McCloud, Beverly T. (1991). African-American Muslim Women. In Yvonne Haddad (Ed.), *The Muslims of America*. New York: Oxford.

Newsome, Melba (2000). Hard Time. *Essence*. September: 146-150 & 210, 213-214, & 218.

Nu'Man, Muhammad (1985). *What Every American Should Know About Islam and the Muslims*. Jersey City, NJ: New Mind.

Pollock-Byrne, Joycelyn M. (1990). *Women, Prison, and Crime*. Belmont, CA: Wadsworth.

Shah, Tabassam, and Jeffrey Diamond (1995). A Research Paper on the Sunni Muslim Community of West Philadelphia. Unpublished paper, Department of History, University of Pennsylvania.

Smith, Jane. (1999). *Islam in America*. New York: Columbia University Press.

Tate, Sonsyrea (1997). *Little X: Growing Up in the Nation of Islam*. New York: Harper-Collins.

Thomas, Charles (1975). Prisonization or Resocialization: A Study of External Factors Associated with the Impact of Imprisonment. *Journal of Research in Crime and Delinquency*, 10(1): 13-21.

Tonry, Michael (1995). *Malign Neglect: Race, Crime, and Punishment in America*. New York: Oxford University Press.

U.S. Department of Justice, Bureau of Justice Statistics (1994). *Special Report*. Washington, DC: U.S. Government Printing Office.

Van Baalen, Susan (March, 2001). Telephone conversation with the Chaplain Administrator, Federal Bureau of Prisoners, Washington DC [Date not retrievable.]

Wadud-Muhsin, Amina (1992). *Qur'an and Woman*. Kuala Lumpur, Malaysia: Penerbit Fajar Bakti Sdn. Bhd.

Walker, Samuel, Cassia Spohn, and Miriam DeLeon (1999). *The Color of Justice: Race, Ethnicity, and Crime in America*. Belmont CA: Wadsworth.

AUTHOR'S NOTE

Felecia Dix-Richardson, PhD, is an assistant professor in the Department of Sociology and Criminal Justice at Florida A&M University.

Address correspondence to Felecia Dix-Richardson, PhD, Florida A&M University, Department of Sociology and Criminal Justice, Perry-Paige 403, Tallahassee, FL 32307.

Religion, the Community, and the Rehabilitation of Criminal Offenders. Pp. 127-159.

Prisoners, Prison, and Religion:
Religion and Adjustment to Prison

TODD R. CLEAR

John Jay College, City University of New York

MELVINA T. SUMTER

Old Dominion University

SUMMARY During the twentieth century there has been much speculation by scholars in the United States about the relationship between religion and prisoners. In spite of the fact that both religion and the prison have been subjected to considerable study, we know little about religion in prison, particularly as it relates to the psychological adjustment of offenders to the prison environment and reduction in problematic behaviors such as disciplinary infractions. Applying a survey methodology which incorporates a recently developed scale of religiousness (the first to be developed with the assistance of inmates specifically for use with inmates) and a previously developed scale of inmate adjustment to prison, this study explores the relationship between inmate religiousness and adjustment to prison and the number of disciplinary confinements they receive. A self-report questionnaire was administered to a non-random sample of 769 inmates in 20 prisons from 12 states in order to determine if an inmate's religiousness was related to prison adjustment and the number of disciplinary infractions they received. The findings from the study indicate that a significant relationship exists between inmate religiousness and multiple measures of inmate adjustment to the prison environment. More specifically, increasing levels of religiousness, as measured by a self-report questionnaire, are associated with higher levels of in-prison adjustment, as measured by the Wright prison adjustment questionnaire. Similarly, inmate religiousness (as measured by the same self-report questionnaire) is also significantly related to the number of times inmates report being placed in disciplinary confinement for violation of prison rules. Thus, higher levels of inmate religiousness are associated with better psychological adjustment to the prison environment and fewer self-reported disciplinary confinements. *[Article copies available for a fee from The Haworth Document Delivery Service: 1-800-HAWORTH. E-mail address: <getinfo@haworthpressinc.com> Website: <http://www.HaworthPress. com> © 2002 by The Haworth Press, Inc. All rights reserved.]*

KEYWORDS Prison, religion, inmate, adjustment, infractions

The historical development of the penal system in the United States is strongly influenced by religious views. Ever since the first penitentiary was built, religion has played a principal role in the efforts of correctional professionals to reform offenders. In fact, the word "penitentiary" is itself derived from "penitence," meaning "regret for wrongdoing or sinning." Thus, penitentiaries were originally seen by some as places where offenders could go and atone for their sins. Throughout penal history, religion continued to play an important role, and has possibly been employed more frequently than any other type of correctional intervention. Yet, despite the fact that prisons (as we now more commonly call penitentiaries) and religion are inexorably intertwined, we know little about the role religion plays in prisons.

During the twentieth century there has been much speculation by scholars about the relationship between religion and prisoners. Despite this interest, few studies have examined the effect of religious participation on institutional adjustment and the commitment of infractions. This study focuses on a particular aspect of prisons, inmate adjustment to the prison environment. Applying a survey methodology which incorporates a recently developed scale of religiousness (the first to be developed with the assistance of inmates specifically for use with inmates) and a previously developed scale of inmate adjustment to prison, this study explores the relationship between inmate religiousness and adjustment to prison.

RELATED STUDIES

Prisons are notoriously harsh and painful environments. The most basic challenge of being in prison is coping with the deprivation of loss of freedom. The literature abounds with information describing the "inmate culture" as an adaptation to the prison setting which facilitates coping in the prison community. For some inmates religion is one of their methods of coping because it offers them a variety of ways to help endure the stressors often associated with the prison environment. To the extent that it is successful, religiousness should be associated with an improved adjustment to prison. However, religious values often conflict with the values of the traditional inmate code. To this extent, being religious in prison may complicate prison adjustment.

Three bodies of literature can be drawn upon to direct this research.

- First, a considerable amount of research has focused on the impact of religion on deviance in the general population. While the generalizability of this research to a population of prisoners is unknown, the work in this area provides a basic understanding of the role religion plays in people's lives and how religion enhances psychological adjustment and well-being.
- Second, while limited in numbers, there are a few studies which describe the relationship between religion and prisoner adjustment. To date, only three studies have examined this relationship.
- Third, there is a vast amount of literature describing inmate adjustment to prison life which can inform us of other factors, apart from religion, which may influence adjustment in a prison environment.

Religion and Deviance in General Population

Speculation about the role religion has played in different societies as a means of social control has a rich history with roots deeply imbedded in the functionalist perspective. That model assumes that the stability of society is assured by teaching and reinforcing an approved set of values, beliefs, and norms for all citizens. The modern sociological version of this model derives from Emile Durkheim, who viewed religion as a crucial, integrative mechanism for maintaining social order and fostering a common set of values and beliefs. Functionalists have argued that religion promotes social cohesion by uniting members of society with shared values and norms. Hence, religious beliefs are viewed as providing the foundation for moral behavior (Chadwick, 1993). It follows that the more religious a person is, the less likely it is that he will deviate from societal norms; conversely, as Pettersson (1991, p. 279) stated, "for centuries criminal behavior has been explained by the erosion of religion."

The postulate that religion inhibits deviance also has an extensive history in the United States, dating back to the early 1900s, grounded in theoretical perspectives such as anomie, social disorganization, differential association and social control explanations of deviance. Despite this legacy of belief in religion as a social control mechanism, many scholars remain skeptical about the potential of religion to inhibit deviant behavior.

Their critical views received support from the landmark study by Hirschi and Stark (1969), which questioned the efficacy of religion as a social control mechanism. Hirschi and Stark (1969) administered a self-report survey to 4,077 adolescents in Western Contra Costa County, California. These researchers found that children who attend church were as likely as non-attendees to report involvement in deviant and criminal acts. They also found that "children who attend church are no more likely than non-attenders to accept ethical principles, and they are only slightly more likely than non-attenders to respect conventional authority" (Hirschi and Stark, 1969, p. 202). Based on these findings, Hirschi and Stark concluded that religion was not an inhibitor of deviance. These findings pleased many critical social scientists and stunned others, but eventually they "became, for many observers, the accepted conclusion to a long debated issue in the literature" (Benda, 1995, p. 446).

Despite the scholarly consensus spawned by Hirschi and Stark (1969), subsequent empirical research examining religion as a preventative of deviance consistently provided evidence of a significant, inverse relationship between religion and deviance, although the strength of this relationship was typically modest or weak (Akers et al., 1994; Cochran, 1988; Cochran, 1989; Ellis, 1985; Johnson, 1984; Tittle and Welch, 1983). In 1983, Tittle and Welch examined 65 previously published studies that reported evidence concerning the nature of the relationship between religion and deviance. Out of the 65 studies, only 10 (15%) had failed to report a significant negative relationship between religion and deviance. In 1985, a review of 31 studies that had investigated the link between religion and deviance concluded that "people who attend church most frequently were significantly less involved in crime than those who attended less often" (Ellis, 1995, p. 26).

The evidence of an inverse relationship among studies was so consistent that in 1988 Cochran (p. 294) said that "virtually every research effort subsequent to the Hirschi and Stark (1969) study has consistently found evidence of a statistically inverse relationship between some measures of religion and various indicators of deviance." Recently, Cochran et al. (1994) stated that with the exception of the Elifson, Peterson, and Hadaway study in 1983, every published work since Tittle and Welch's (1983) review of the literature also reported that religion has a statistically significant and inverse association to deviance. In essence, since the 1970s, empirical results have consistently demonstrated a significant inverse association between religion and deviance. A more recent review (Sumter and Clear, 1998) of the research published since 1985 found that 18 of 23 studies produced evidence of a statistically significant inverse relationship between some measures of religion and various indicators of deviance.

Religion and Prisoners

Since 1984 researchers have cited the virtual neglect of the religion variable when investigating prison and post-release adjustment. Despite this concern, to date, only a few studies have examined religious participation as an important indicator of either prison adjustment (Clear et al., 1992; Johnson, 1984; Johnson et al., 1997) or of post release adjustment (Clear et al., 1992; Johnson et al., 1997). Among these, two produced evidence of a statistically significant inverse association between religion and deviance (Clear et al., 1992; Johnson et al., 1997), and one did not (Johnson, 1984).

In the first study examining the relationship between religion and prisoners, Johnson (1984) collected data on 782 inmates released from Apalachee Correctional Institution in Chattahoochee, Florida, during the period 1978-1982 to determine if: (1) a greater degree of religiosity was likely to reduce the amount of disciplinary confinement; (2) if an inmate's religiosity lowers the likelihood that he would receive disciplinary confinement; and (3) if the frequency of attendance at institutional church services and related activities is related to the likelihood of disciplinary confinement. The study found no differences in disciplinary confinement for religious and non-religious inmates on all these measures.

A later study by Johnson et al. (1997) investigated a non-random sample of two matched groups of inmates released from four adult male prisons in New York to determine the impact of religious programs on institutional adjustment and recidivism rates. One group had participated in Prison Fellowship programs and the other group had not. The two groups were matched on key characteristics such as age, race, religious denomination, county of residence, military discharge, minimum sentence, and initial security classification. While there were no overall differences between the Prison Fellowship inmates and the other inmates on measures of institutional adjustment or recidivism, the level of participation in Prison Fellowship did influence institutional adjustment or recidivism: high participation prison fellowship inmates were less likely to commit infractions than either low or medium participants, and less likely than non-religious inmates to commit serious infractions. High participants also received more serious infractions than their low participant counterparts, but were significantly less likely than their matches to be arrested during the follow-up period.

Clear et al. (1992) administered a self-report questionnaire to a non-random sample of 769 inmates in 20 prisons from 12 states in order to determine if an inmate's religiousness was related to prison adjustment and the number of disciplinary infractions they received. This paper elaborates on the results originally reported by Clear et al.

Inmate Adjustment to Prison: Prisonization

Prisonization, a term first used by Clemmer (1958) to mean the "taking on in greater or lesser degree of the folkways, mores, customs, and the general culture of the penitentiary," occurs when inmates integrate the values they find in the penitentiary into their way of life in prison (Clemmer, 1958, p. 299). According to Slosar (1978), the inmate code (the norms and values of the prison culture) requires an unqualified loyalty to fellow inmates and prohibits cooperation with prison staff. Slosar (1978) further states that according to Clemmer's proposition, the more exposure one has to the prison culture the more prisonized one is likely to become.

Sykes and Messinger criticized the work of Clemmer for failing to explain the existence of the prison culture (Sykes and Messinger, 1960). They argue that the concept of prisonization explains how the inmates are socialized in prison and how the inmate culture is maintained but "there has been little concerted effort to account for the structure and functioning of the system into which the individual becomes socialized" (Sykes and Messinger, 1960, p. 12). Since Clemmer's initial work, a considerable amount of research has attempted to account for the existence of the prison culture. Two alternative ways of explaining the existence of the inmate culture and value system are the deprivation and importation models.

The deprivation model was initially proposed by Sykes to explain the inmate's response to the pains of imprisonment (Sykes, 1958). Under this model, inmates are seen as being deprived of five basic needs: personal security, heterosexual relationships, material possessions, autonomy, and social acceptance (Sykes, 1958; Sykes and Messinger, 1960). Proponents of the model argue that in order to cope with these hardships inmates create a culture of their own with its own normative values or "inmate code" of behavior (Goodstein and Wright, 1989; Parisi, 1982; Slosar, 1978). The inmate code is generally in opposition to prison authority and institutional rules (Goodstein and Wright, 1989). It prohibits establishing relationships with guards and staff, reporting inmate infractions, and assisting authorities in maintaining order. Above all else, the code stresses loyalty to the inmate community (Goodstein and Wright, 1989; Heffernan, 1972; Johnson, 1976; Parisi, 1982). The inmate subculture emerges out of collective adherence to the inmate code. Participation in the inmate subculture and following the inmate code allows the prisoner to mitigate some of the deprivations caused by his confinement (Goodstein and Wright, 1989; Sykes, 1958).

In contrast, advocates of the importation model argue that an inmate subculture is a manifestation of attitudes and behaviors held prior to commitment (Slosar, 1978). Inmates bring with them values and norms which they subscribed to in the free world. These are values which are in opposition to the values of the dominant culture outside of prison. Irwin and Cressey (1962, p. 144) argue that "the 'prison code'–don't inform on or exploit another inmate, don't lose your head, be weak or be a sucker, etc.–is also part of a criminal code, existing outside prisons." The beliefs and values the inmate held prior to incarceration are thought to influence patterns of behavior inside the institution. Thus adherence to the prison code is not merely a reaction to the pains of imprisonment, it is a reflection of pre-prison characteristics and experiences (Goodstein and Wright, 1989; Slosar, 1978).

Supporters of this interpretation criticize the deprivation model as being overly simplistic because it assumes that the prison community is a unified social organization with widespread inmate solidarity (Carroll, 1974; Jacobs, 1976). In actuality, detractors argue, the prison culture may be comprised of any number of inmate groups which adhere to different and often competing sets of norms (Goodstein and Wright, 1989, p. 234). These groups may resemble gangs which exist on the outside and rival each other for power and status in the prison (Jacobs, 1976).

Parisi (1982) has argued that both models have merit and that both internal and external stimuli affect adjustment to prison. Similarly, Thomas et al. (1978) argue that prisonization is associated with factors related to the prison and "extra-prison" variables which include pre-prison characteristics and experiences, relationships with people outside of the prison while incarcerated, and perception of post-release life chances. They advocate shifting the focus of research toward determining which factors related to these models best explain adjustment and merging them into a single theoretical framework (Thomas et al., 1978, pp. 390-391).

Although these models provide some understanding of how inmates adapt to prison life, they have been subjected to a number of criticisms in recent years. Goodstein and MacKenzie (1989) highlight the weaknesses of the prisonization construct. A number of researchers have developed instruments to measure the degree of individual prisonization. However, simply knowing the extent to which an inmate subscribes to the inmate code according to these measures, is not a good predictor of how that person will behave in confinement. As Goodstein and Mac-Kenzie (1989, p. 239) point out, "it is likely that equally prisonized inmates differ from one another on other behavioral factors that are at least as important as prisonization in developing an understanding of adaptive functioning."

Furthermore, the prisonization construct assumes a similar value system for all inmate groups which opposes the value system of prison staff and authority (Goodstein and MacKenzie, 1989). Recent research indicates that staff and inmates are not constantly in opposition to one another. Ramirez (1983) found considerable agreement between inmates and staff regarding the proper code of inmate conduct. Although most inmates were in agreement about the proper code of conduct, some inmate groups expressed a greater degree of consensus with staff than with other inmates. Likewise, Garofalo and Clark (1985) found a wide range of disagreement among inmates on a measure of prisonization.

Given the problems associated with the prisonization construct and the waning support for the two models of adaptation (deprivation and importation), researchers have begun to explore new approaches to investigating inmate adjustment to the prison environment. Rather than focusing on inmate conformance to the code of conduct of an inmate subculture, researchers are using different measures of adjustment to prison such as disciplinary record, psychological measures including scales of depression, anxiety, self-esteem, measures of fear of victimization, and others. Based on the premise that prison adjustment is likely to be a function of a set of complex interactions between a number of factors including characteristics of the individual, the prison setting, and other inmates and staff, the research has focused on identifying those factors associated with these alternative measures of adjustment.

One such alternative is problem solving and coping in prison. In recent years some researchers have begun to examine how individuals cope with incarceration, rather than focusing on the frequency and severity of the problems experienced by inmates. Zamble and Porporino (1984, 1988) hypothesized that adjustment to prison may be a function of individual coping skills, perceptions of the prison environment and incarceration experience. The authors found that inmates who relied on poor coping mechanisms prior to incarceration also had poor coping skills in the prison setting. Although most inmates in the study attempted to solve their problems in some manner, the methods utilized tended to be short-sighted and not well planned. Many inmates relied on coping mechanisms, such as avoiding a situation or refusing to think about one's problem, which would alleviate a problem in the short-run but do nothing to eliminate the problem in the long-run (Zamble and Porporino, 1984, 1988).

Zamble and Porporino (1984, 1988) found that coping behaviors were more powerful predictors of inmate adjustment than background characteristics. Coping mechanisms which were geared towards eliminating or minimizing problems without negative consequences were indicative of lower rates of disciplinary infractions and fewer medical complaints and problems. Zamble and Porporino (1984, 1988) also found that inmates' cognitive appraisals of their situations, measured in terms of problems experienced in prison, inmates' perceptions of the amount of control they have over what happens to them, and how often inmates felt bored, were predictive of their emotional adjustment (as measured by scales of depression, anxiety, and anger).

DATA AND METHODS

The data for this study comes from a larger project designed to study the relationship between an inmate's religiousness and prison adjustment. The study was carried out by: (1) conducting group interviews of inmates who were later classified as "religious" and "non-religious"; (2) interviewing chaplains, correctional officers, and others associated with institutional programming (administrators, counselors, etc.); (3) conducting group administrations of the Wright "institutional climate" questionnaire to inmates and to staff; and (4) compiling data about the facility, its population, and its staff. Lasting more than three years, the study represents prisons from each region of the country which differ in terms of security levels and classification of inmates.

Twenty prisons in 12 states were purposely selected for participation in this study in an attempt to increase the probability that our findings would be generalizable to a broader range of prisons than if the sample was limited to a particular region or a particular type of prison. Also, the prisons were chosen because they had active religious programs in the institution and because the states' department of corrections expressed willingness to participate and provide staff support for the project.

The data for this study were collected by administering anonymous, confidential questionnaires to a non-random sample of 769 male inmates who volunteered to participate in the study. We must emphasize, then, that our subjects are an opportunity sample which consists of a non-representative sample of volunteer participants from a purposively selected set of prisons around the country. The prisoners were administered a "Prisoner Values Survey," a multifaceted religiousness instrument to determine their level of religiousness. (The inmate religiousness instrument, a modified and expanded version of the King-Hunt religious belief and practice questions, was developed in conjunction with inmates as a part of previous research conducted by Clear et al. A full discussion of the development and validation of that instrument can be found in the final report from that research: Clear et al., *Prisons, Prisoners, and Religion*, Newark, NJ: Rutgers University, 1992.) In some of the analyses, in order to be considered devout, prisoners had to have scored in the top 20th percentile of the self-report questionnaire.

The Questionnaire

The study questionnaire was divided into four sections. The first included 12 prison situations which focus groups conducted with the inmates indicated would help distinguish sincerely devout prisoners from those with less than sincere religious beliefs. The second section of the questionnaire included the adaptation of self-report religiousness scale. The religiousness scale was developed by Richard King and Morton Hunt in 1975. Together, the questions in these two sections provided a measure of the inmates' overall religious beliefs and practices. (A complete discussion of the development and validation of these sections of the questionnaire can be obtained by contacting the senior author at John Jay College of Criminal Justice, City University of New York, at the address given at the end of this paper.)

Section three of the questionnaire consisted of a measure of inmate adjustment to prison. (The prison adjustment instrument was developed by Kevin Wright.) This measure served as the principal dependent variable in the analyses. It is a series of 20 questions about problems commonly confronted by prisoners in a prison setting, including: (1) the extent to which they feel uncomfortable with other inmates and prison staff; (2) how often they are angry, afraid, sick, injured or taken advantage of; and (3) how often they get into physical fights or arguments or have difficulty sleeping. The questions assess the inmate's perception of adjustment to the prison environment and attempt to identify the extent to which problems have been exacerbated by incarceration. Responses to the questions are summed, resulting in a prison adjustment scale score with a range from 0 to 44, with 44 indicating the best-adjusted and 0 the least well-adjusted.

Section four of the questionnaire consisted of an assortment of questions: measures of depression, self-esteem and self-mastery as well as a variety of questions about the individual's background and current incarceration. Depression, self-esteem and self-mastery were measured using truncated versions of previously validated instruments. The self-esteem scale, developed by Rosenburg, refers to an individual's sense of his own self-worth. (For a discussion of the validity of the Rosenberg self-esteem scale see Ruth C. Wylie's *Measures of Self-Concept*, published by the University of Nebraska Press in 1989, or the chapter "Assessment of Habit Disorders: A Tripartite Perspective in Measuring Change" by M. G. Eppinger and M. J. Lambert in *The Assessment of Psychotherapy Outcome* edited by Lambert, Christen, and DeJulio and published by John Wiley in 1983.) The self-mastery scale, is concerned with the individual's perception of the degree of control he has over the important factors in his life. (The self-mastery scale was developed by Pearlin et al., 1981.) Each scale asks respondents to indicate how strongly they agree or disagree with a series of statements about themselves, and is scored additively resulting in scores ranging from 6 to 30. The higher the score, the greater the self-esteem or self-mastery.

The depression scale used in this study was the shortened version of the Center for Epidemiological Studies Depression Scale. (The depression scale used in this study is the shortened version of the CESD Depression Scale modified by Radloff in 1977.) The scale is a measure of the major elements of depressive symptomatology. This scale consists of 13 items covering various depressive symptoms including loss of appetite or sleep, feelings of guilt, helplessness, hopelessness and others. Respondents were presented with a series of statements and were asked to indicate how often they felt this way during the past week. An overall score for depression was calculated by summing the responses. Possible scores ranged from 13 to 39, with a high score indicating a low level of depression.

Data were also collected on certain background characteristics including race, age, marital status, education, prior substance abuse problems, prior criminal record, and the number of prior incarcerations. Questions related to the inmate's current incarceration included length of sentence, amount of time served, commitment offense, and types of prison programs (i.e., counseling, educational, etc.) participated in. Each respondent was also asked to report how many times he had been convicted of a variety of specified offenses and the number of times he had been convicted of a felony offense(s). For each inmate, the proportion of the sentence served was calculated by dividing the amount of time served by the length of the individual's sentence.

Finally, section four of the questionnaire included questions which asked the inmates to report the number of times they were written up for 11 different prison rule infractions. In addition to rule infractions, respondents were asked to report the total number of times they were placed in segregation for a violation of the rules and to indicate the type of infraction they were placed in confinement for. These self-report measures of institutional rule adherence provided alternative measures of adjustment to the prison environment.

Measures of Religiousness

Neither criminologists nor other social scientists have been able to agree on what religion is, much less operationalize the concept of religion (Comstock, 1995; Cunningham et al., 1995: Glock, 1973; James, 1936; Stark, 1984). As a result, they have not been able to develop a construct to measure what it means to be religious. Therefore, no one knows with complete assurance how "religious" a person is. This is because religiosity is a complex construct that includes belief and behaviors that are often internal and oftentimes independent of a person's external religious practices, such as church attendance and participation in various religious activities. What goes on inside a person when it comes to religion may not be well-indicated by what they say. Although a religious construct may be poorly represented by self-reports, at this point we have no other means to assess "religiosity" other than reference to what people themselves say.

The degree of "religiousness" in our study is represented by RELIG, which is the total score inmates received from the "Prisoner Values Survey," a multidimensional religious measurement instrument, which is a series of situations in the prison designed to test an inmate's religious sincerity. For some of the analyses in this study, the top 20% of these scores is treated as a separate group, called Devout.

Measures of Adjustment

In this study of religion and adjustment, we used two measures of adjustment. The first is Wright's prison adjustment scale; the second is self-reported rates of disciplinary infractions. The total score on the Wright prison adjustment questionnaire is called ADJUST, and the total number of self-reported infractions is called INFRACS.

Wright's adjustment scale is a series of items designed to test the degree to which first, an inmate is feeling threats to his personal and psychological equilibrium in prison that are *greater than* those he normally feels on the streets; and second, how strongly he feels those threats. The instrument is a direct test of an inmate's self-reported "coping." We note that this instrument tests almost exclusively the environmental adjustment that we would associate with "extrinsic" orientations toward religious activity.

The total number of self-reported infractions is an indirect measure of adjustment, for the relationship between infractions and adjustment is itself unclear. Certainly, a person who has low levels of infractions may be so deeply immersed in the prison culture that he is "prisonized"–he knows well and practices routinely the "games" needed to placate corrections officers and get along without trouble. In contrast, a prisoner who is coping well with prison precisely because he has resisted prisonization might, as a result, have occasional conflicts with corrections officers or other prisoners leading to infractions.

Co-Variate Measures

Co-variate measures fall into two categories. Three of these measures were psychological: "self-esteem," "depression" and "mastery" (collapsed versions of standard scales). The remaining measures were demographic: age, ethnicity, sentence information, prior record, drug and alcohol history, program participation in prison, classification data, etc.

RESULTS

Our analysis proceeds in a logical sequence. It is designed to first explore the basic patterns within the data, then to elucidate some of the more interesting patterns, and draw out their theoretical significance. Our basic question is, "Is religiousness related to adjustment in prison, and, if so, in what ways?"

Table 1 displays the correlation matrix of significant correlated variables with adjustment and infractions. The table shows a number of basic patterns:

☐ **Table 1: Correlation Matrix–Dependent vs. Independent Variables**

	ADJUST	INFRACS	RELIG	INTRINS	EXTRINS
ADJUST		.04	.11	.12	.00
INFRACS	.04		−.24	−.19	−.12
RELIG	.11	−.24		--	--
AGE	.19	−.07	.16	.09	−.01
AGERELIG	.18	−.18	.59	.39	.06
ETHNICITY	−.09	−.05	−.20	−.22	−.32
ESTEEM	.21	−.01	.21	.13	−.01
MASTERY	.22	−.02	.30	.15	.04
DEPRESS	.51	−.06	.20	.17	.06
POT	−.02	.12	−.13	−.09	−.09
IP DOWN	−.02	.11	−.09	−.00	−.05
THEFT	.06	.16	−.10	−.07	−.00
WEAOIB	−.02	.12	−.06	−.02	.03
BURGLARY	.04	.09	−.01	.03	.00
DRUGS	−.03	.10	.00	.00	.01
ROBBERY	.06	.11	−.15	−.06	.05
PRIORS	.02	.22	−.15	−.18	−.10
INCAR	.01	.05	−.15	−.12	−.06
DRUGALC	.00	.13	−.22	−.15	−.12
PROGRAMS	.09	.06	.16	.12	.05
PERSON	.06	.11	.05	.03	−.04
TSERVE	.07	.30	−.08	−.04	−.07

- RELIG is related both to INFRACS and to ADJUST. This suggests that each measure of adjustment is associated with an inmate's self-reported religiousness.
- ADJUST and INFRACS are unrelated, confirming our idea that these were distinct aspects of prison adaptation. These variables also exhibit different patterns of correlation with other variables.
- The inmate's age, time served, and participation in certain prison programs relate to both ADJUST and INFRACS. These findings are consistent with prior studies of prison adjustment.
- ADJUST relates to all three psychological variables (self-esteem, self-mastery and depression), underscoring the psychological nature of that measure of adjustment. INFRACS does not relate to these variables.
- INFRACS tends to relate to justice system variables that in previous studies have been related to risk of institutional misbehavior: drug use, security level, prior record, and current offense.
- Prior record relates negatively to RELIG. This is consistent with the comments of inmates that more experienced inmates begin to take religion more seriously.

Because the pattern of these results is consistent both with prior studies and with logic, we are encouraged to place confidence in the data, despite the problems of measurement and sampling. There appear to be no inexplicable anomalies in the data that would warn us to disregard the relationships contained within.

Table 2 presents the results of a stepwise, OLS-regression of adjustment (ADJUST) on the variables correlated with it at the bivariate level. This is an appropriate way to determine if ADJUST shares any unique variance with religion that is not already shared with other variables. In fact, this is not the case. Depression, ethnicity and age are all significantly associated with ADJUST; after these variables are entered into the equation, RELIG is not significantly associated with total adjustment. Older, non-Whites who are less depressed seem to be more well-adjusted to prison, regardless of their religious participation.

Analyses of variance further explore this idea. The inmates are divided into two groups based on their total religiousness score (RELIG). The first group, who might be thought of roughly as the "devout," are those 20% who score highest on that instrument. The second group is all others. (The 20% cut-off was selected based upon answers to our question about the proportion of inmates who were "sincere" in their religious views.)

A one-way analysis of variance on ADJUST shows that the top 20% are significantly more likely to be adjusted than the rest (p = .05). Table 3 is an analysis of variance, with depression, ethnicity and age entered as co-variates. This table shows that, once again, the demographic and psychological indicators explain variance in ADJUST better than religious grouping.

☐ **Table 2: Stepwise Regression of "ADJUST" on Demographic and Personal Correlates**

Variable	B	Beta	P
DEPRESS	.60	.49	.00
ETHNICITY	−1.64	−.13	.00
AGE	.59	.09	.02
RELIG	ns	ns	ns
ESTEEM	ns	ns	ns
MASTERY	ns	ns	ns
PROGRAMS	ns	ns	ns
PERSONS	ns	ns	ns
TSERVE	ns	ns	ns

☐ **Table 3: ANOVA of "ADJUST" with "GROUP" (Religious Group) and Co-variates**

Source	df	Sum of squares	F	p
GROUP	11	11.41	.40	.53
AGE	1	117.52	4.16	.02
ETHNICITY	1	351.35	12.45	.00
ESTEEM	1	50.17	1.75	.19
DEPRESS	1	4024.75	140.65	.00

Adjustment as Measured by Institutional Infractions

Table 4 presents selected results from a stepwise, OLS-regression of total number of institutional infractions (INFRACS) on the variables significantly related to it in bivariate analysis. Model 1 includes those variables in the final OLS equation. It can be seen that a number of variables form an equation for infractions, with total religion score (RELIG) entering the equation first (indicating it is the single, most powerful, univariate predictor).

As a further test of the power of religion as related to infractions, we reconstructed the equation in Model 2, forcing first into the equation the variables that entered *after* the religion score. We then entered RELIG as a second step. The results demonstrate that RELIG remains an important variable even after all the other important correlates are factored in. Not only does RELIG remain important, but the Beta indicates it is more important than any other variable except PRIORS in explaining the variance in INFRACS.

☐ **Table 4: Regression of "INFRACS" on Its Correlates–Two Models**

Variable	B	Beta	p
Model 1			
RELIG	−.03	−.23	.00
PRIORS	.41	.21	.00
PERSON	1.14	.20	.00
AGE	−.03	−.11	.01
THEFT	.02	.11	.01
Model 2			
POT	.34	.06	.09
THEFT	.02	.09	.02
PRIORS	.41	.21	.00
AGE	−.03	−.10	.03
RELIG	−.03	−.20	.00

The multivariate analyses may be summarized in a very straightforward manner: religiousness is directly and negatively associated with infractions; inmate religiousness and adjustment are also related, but less directly. The relationship between inmate religiousness and adjustment appears to be mediated by inmate depression.

Intrinsic and Extrinsic Orientations

One of the recurrent themes in our qualitative research was the distinction between *intrinsic* and *extrinsic* orientations toward religiousness. When our interviewees talked about sincere and insincere inmates, we interpreted their views as confirming our own earlier observations about the importance of I/E orientations.

The Prison Religion Survey provides sub-scales that may be extracted and used to calculate intrinsic and extrinsic orientations toward religiousness. The *intrinsic* items are: *I try hard to grow in my faith; My religious beliefs are really what lie behind everything I do. Religion is most important to me because it gives my life meaning.* The *extrinsic* items are: *It is a person's social duty to worship in the faith of his choice; The place of worship is very important as a place to meet people and make good friends; Being in a religious group gives me a place of safety when I need it.*

When we summed the Likert-type scale scores for these items (renamed as INTRINS and EXTRINS), we obtained two variables with the following characteristics:

- INTRINS: Mean = 11.7; Interquartile range = 10 to 13; Standard Deviation = 2.8
- EXTRINS: Mean = 11.3; Interquartile range = 10 to 12; Standard Deviation = 2.6

The two sub-scales are skewed to the left and correlated at r = .49. Their correlation with the religion measure (when the subscale items are subtracted out, called RELIG2) was for INTRINS, r = .62, and EXTRINS, r = .30. This indicates that the two subscales measure related but different constructs, though INTRINS is a closer measure of the general, overall religion score.

As earlier indicated, Table 1 displays the correlation matrix of INTRINS and EXTRINS with selected variables; a correlation of .09 or higher is significant at approximately the .10 level. The relationships of these variables with DEPRESS (which is interpreted as: the higher the score, the less the depression) are interesting in light of the earlier regression that shows that depression is most associated with adjustment. The pattern in this table suggests that inmates who feel less depression will be more concerned with intrinsic aspects of their religion, but depression will have no impact on concerns for extrinsic orientations toward religion. The data also suggest that as inmates become more experienced (as indicated by INCARS–"prior incarcerations") they tend to be less interested in intrinsic religious motivations. This is true even though older inmates are more intrinsic, regardless of prior correctional experience.

In order to determine if the religious orientations of an inmate further explain adjustment patterns, we recalculated the multivariate equations for ADJUST and INFRACS identified in earlier analyses. In neither case did the additional variables add explanatory power in the previous equations.

Institutional Variations

One of our most important findings had to do with institutional variations of religious program operations in the prison. Our prisons were very different in the way religious programs operated, and in their effects. The correlations between the two measures showed a remarkable variation across the facilities in our sample, and indicated that vastly different patterns of relationships exist in different facilities.

It was this powerful variation that led us to revisit some of the facilities in our sample in order to learn more about the prisons, the prisoners who live there and the religious programs in the facilities. We visited the eight facilities from which we had received enough completed inmate questionnaires to support quantitative analysis of the questionnaire results. During the course of each site visit we:

- Conducted group interviews of religious and non-religious inmates.
- Interviewed chaplains, correctional officers, and others associated with institutional programming (administrators, counselors, etc.).
- Conducted group administrations of the Wright "institutional climate" questionnaire to inmates and to staff.
- Compiled data about the facility, its population and its staff.

These visits enabled us to develop profiles of the major facilities in our study, including both quantitative and qualitative characteristics.

Based on these profiles, institutions were given a "score" on various attributes, including such environmental concerns as "safety" and "freedom of movement" and also including all the dimensions of the Wright profile and the security level of the facility.

Table 5 presents a summary of some of the characteristics of these institutions we visited. This table shows that four institutions had a significant relationship between ADJUST and RELIG, but *not* between INFRACS and ADJUST, while four institutions had the reverse pattern. (As can be seen from Table 5, some of these correlations are quite strong, on the order of .50 or higher.) Every prison displayed a relationship between one of our adaptation measures and religion, but *only that one.* This raised for us the possibility that there was some kind of "switching mechanism," in which religious participation results in increased adjustment to prison or a reduction in infractions, but not both.

In order to determine whether the "switching mechanism" observed at the institutional level of analysis would hold true at the individual level, we separately examined the relationships for inmates from prisons where the RELIG-ADJUST relationship was significant and inmates from prisons where the INFRACS-RELIG relationship was significant. Table 6 is a correlation matrix for RELIG, ADJUST and INFRACS for these two groups. It demonstrates very strong evidence of a "switching pattern." In institutions where religiousness is associ-

☐ **Table 5: Selected Characteristics of Institutions in the Sample**

	Adjustment vs. Religion	Infractions vs. Religion	Infractions vs. Adjustment	Mean Age	Mean Prior Record
Southwest 6	Y	N	N	23	1.9
Southeast 2	Y	N	N	23	1.5
Southeast 3	Y	N	*Y	28	1.8
Midwest 1	Y	N	N	32	2.5
Southwest 1	N	Y	N	33	2.1
Northwest 1	N	Y	N	39	3.0
Northeast 1	N	Y	*Y	34	2.7
Northeast 2	N	Y	N	36	2.5

- *Notes: Y = Coefficient of correlation reaches statistical significance. N = Coefficient of correlation fails to reach statistical significance. Whether significant or not, all coefficients fell in the expected direction. * Indicates coefficient = .50/.50+.*

☐ **Table 6: Correlations for the Grouped Institutions**

Variable	Religion vs. Adjustment Institution	Religion vs. Infractions Institution
RELIG2	120	123
ADJUST	37.4	37.6
INFRACS	1.5	2.5
INTRINS	12.0	11.2
EXTRINS	11.8	10.8
Correlation		
RELIG VS. ADJUST	.28	.00
N	320	187
p	.00	.98
RELIG VS. INFRACS	−.09	−.41
N	329	186
p	.12	.00
INFRACS VS. ADJUST	.04	.02
N	368	218
p	.41	.79

ated with disciplinary infractions, religious participation has no relationship to individuals' adjustment to prison. In those prisons where religiousness does relate to increased adjustment (through reduced depression), the impact of religiousness on infractions is small and statistically insignificant.

This is a powerful and surely unexpected pattern. Our earlier tables demonstrated that religion is associated with both adjustment and infractions. But it now appears that is because our sample included prisons representing a variety of settings; and in fact, religiousness relates to one or the other, but not both. That is, religion is associated with both measures of inmate adjustment, but the institution seems to "filter" this pattern to determine which actually exists.

This table also shows that while the RELIG-ADJUST institutions' inmates scored higher on both the I and E scales, they did not score any higher on the overall RELIG2 score, nor were they any better adjusted, overall. The only difference is the overall level of infractions–in the RELIG-INFRACS institutions, inmates had *more* infractions. This suggests that in these facilities, infractions may represent more of an issue for all inmates. The inmates involved in religion may find religious activities to be a helpful way to overcome the more serious challenge of infractions in these facilities. The suggestion is that there is something *unique* about the type of challenge the institution represents to the religious inmate, and the inmate will adapt his religious involvement to better meet that challenge.

We further investigated this idea by then looking at all the quantitative measures we had gathered on each of the institutions, and found that the following characteristics applied to RELIG-ADJUST institutions:

- Smaller facilities
- Younger inmates
- Fewer Whites
- Inmates with fewer incarcerations
- Older correctional officers
- Fewer assaults
- Fewer infractions, overall
- Less perceived institutional support (Wright)
- Less perceived emotional feedback (Wright)
- Chaplain seen as "important" by inmates
- Religious programs provide more: emotional support, material comfort, self-worth needs

These variables indicate a pattern of the type of environment-person interaction that sets the stage for religion to play a role in adjustment. What is remarkable is the "switching" nature suggested by these data. Religion as an adjustment tool is used either to help the inmate feel better emotionally about his confinement, or else it helps him to avoid the kinds of confrontations that lead to infractions.

Interactions in Religion and Inmate Adjustment

The foregoing analysis indicates that the relationship between religiosity and inmate adjustment is strongly influenced by person-place interactions. This is demonstrated by the fact that the adjustment effect occurs in one way in some prisons, and in another in the rest. Some prisons provide a setting in which the younger, less experienced prisoners tend to become depressed by imprisonment. In these prisons, religious commitment seems to reduce depression and provide the support needed to counteract the strains of a hostile environment. In other prisons, the presence of more experienced, older inmates perhaps contributes to an environment in which infractions and other types of "trouble" are more common. In these prisons, religious programs tend to provide the type of support men need to stay out of trouble. Differences in the way the prison environment deprives the inmate of what he seeks will therefore color the type of religious response occurring in that prison.

There is also a "person" aspect to religion and adjustment. We have shown, for example, that changes in religiosity are with correlated differences in age, ethnicity, faith, and religious orientation. That is, the inmate "imports" a set of religious values and needs into the prison setting, where his predisposition interacts with the prison environment and its religious programs to "produce" the adjustment effect. In this section, we explore further selected person-place interactions.

Table 7 provides an investigation of the interaction between ethnicity, age (broken at the age of 26 or higher) in the religion-adjustment relationship. This table displays several important patterns. First, again non-Whites report higher religiosity than Whites regardless of age, though the older inmates in both ethnic groups score higher than their younger counterparts. Young Whites are less well-adjusted (ADJUST) to prison than any other group. Again, the "switching mechanism" is indicated by the fact that each group exhibits a relationship between either RELIG and ADJUST, *but not both*. For only younger non-White inmates is there an impact of religion on adjustment, while for every other group there is an impact of religion on infractions.

The experience of young, non-White males is different than the others. For them, religiosity aids in adjustment to the harsh realities of prison life–for most of them, this is the first time in prison (INCARS =

Table 7: Age-Ethnicity Interaction for Selected Variables

		Young Non-Whites	Old Non-Whites	Young Whites	Old Whites
RELIG	N	113	238	86	200
INTRINS		145	150	134	141
EXTRINS		12.2	12.2	0.7	11.1
INFRACS		12.1	12.0	10.5	10.3
ADJUST		2.1	2.0	1.7	1.7
INCARS		37.4	38.3	38.4	37.9
RELIG vs. INFRACS		1.2	2.0	1.3	2.7
	r	−.04	−.23	−.32	−.34
	p	.65	.00	.00	.00
RELIG vs. ADJUST					
	r	−.26	.02	.10	.08
	p	.01	.79	.35	.25

1.2). They do not adjust as well to prison as the other groups, and religion appears to have little impact on their adjustment.

DISCUSSION

A significant relationship exists between inmate religiousness and multiple measures of inmate adjustment to the prison environment. Increasing levels of religiousness, as measured by a self-report questionnaire, are associated with higher levels of in-prison adjustment, as measured by the Wright prison adjustment questionnaire. Similarly, inmate religiousness (as measured by the same self-report questionnaire) is also significantly related to the number of times inmates report being placed in disciplinary confinement for violation of prison rules. Higher levels of inmate religiousness are associated with fewer self-reported disciplinary confinements. These relationships exist when inmate religiousness is treated as both a continuous and a categorical variable. Inmate religiousness does not appear to be significantly related to the number of self-reported prison rule infractions.

The significant relationships between inmate religiousness and these two measures of inmate adjustment to the in-prison environment appear to be unique and characteristically different from one another. This is perhaps a reflection of the fact that the two measures of adjustment are themselves quite dissimilar. The Wright prison adjustment scale is based on inmates' self-reported psychological comfort level in prisons. As such, it is reflective of the inmate's perceptual reality and his state of mind about his incarcerative experience. It asks an inmate how he feels in prison, not how he behaves.

In contrast, the number of times an inmate is placed in disciplinary confinement is a more behaviorally oriented measure of adjustment. Rather than tapping inmates' feelings, it merely asks about the frequency of a specified event, a disciplinary confinement. The event, the disciplinary confinement, is dependent not only on the action of the inmates, but also on the action of the guards, who must initiate the confinement. As such, this measure is also likely to be sensitive to changes in management styles and enforcement priorities and levels within each prison.

The relationship between inmate religiousness and the Wright adjustment measure does not appear to be a direct, causal association. Rather, when other variables were introduced as alternative independent variables in regression models predicting the Wright adjustment measure, or as co-variates in analyses of adjustment measure variance between religiousness groups, the observed relationships between inmate religiousness and the Wright adjustment measure which existed at the bivariate level were no longer significant.

The depression variable was a significant controlling variable in all of the multivariate analyses involving the Wright adjustment measure and appears to be a principal determinant of scores on the adjustment scale. The less depressed inmate tends to score higher on the adjustment questionnaire. Results from the multivariate analyses indicate that the measures of self-esteem and self-mastery (which are both highly correlated to the depression measure) also play important roles in determining scores on the adjustment questionnaire.

Inmates who report low levels of adjustment and high levels of self-mastery and self-esteem are likely to score high on the Wright adjustment scale. Religious inmates, in turn, report generally lower levels of depression and higher levels of self-esteem and self-mastery than non-religious inmates. Thus, because less depressed inmates with comparatively high levels of self-esteem and self-mastery are more well-adjusted to prison, religious prisoners also report higher levels of adjustment to the prison environment. This means that a central aspect of understanding the relationship between inmate religiousness and in-prison adjustment is understanding the nature of the relationship between religiousness, depression, self-mastery and self-esteem. At least three possible scenarios for this relationship are possible. First, increasing involvement in religious practices and adoption of religious values and beliefs may actually result in decreased feelings of depression and increased perceptions of self-esteem and self-mastery among prison inmates. In this sense, religiousness may cause a decrease in depression and increases in self-esteem and self-mastery among inmates.

Second, it may be that people who become involved in religious practices and who adopt religious values and beliefs are people with low levels of depression and high levels of self-esteem and self-mastery to begin with. In this sense, depression, self-esteem and self-mastery don't "cause" religiousness, but they are necessary preconditions. A third possible scenario is that religiousness, depression, self-esteem and self-mastery aren't directly related at all, but rather are each influenced independently by a fifth variable.

Unfortunately, the testing of each of these plausible alternative scenarios isn't possible with the data at hand. This is primarily due to the fact that the present data are cross-sectional, collected at one point in time. With data of this type, there is no way to establish whether religiousness preceded reduced depression and increased self-esteem and self-mastery or vice versa. What are needed are longitudinal data, collected over time, which would allow the researcher to examine the temporal order of different levels of the various variables.

The regional analysis, however, provides an important additional view of the nature of the relationship between religiousness and in-prison adjustment, as measured by the Wright scale. When treated as a continuous measure, the religiousness scale score was significantly correlated to the Wright adjustment scale score in only one region, the Central region. Here, the correlation coefficient between the two measures was fairly large (r = .53). In two of the other three regions (where the correlations were non-significant), however, the correlations were much weaker (r = .00 and .22) and in one, the coefficient had a negative sign, indicating an inverse relationship between religiousness and adjustment.

When treated as a categorical variable, religiousness was significantly related to the Wright adjustment scale scores in both the Central and Southwest regions, although the significance of the association was higher in the Central than the Southwest region. These results indicate that the significant relationship between religiousness and in-prison adjustment (as measured by the Wright scale) which was found in the entire study sample may exist in some institutions, but not in others. The relationship between religiousness and adjustment in the institutions in which the relationship exists, however, may be strong enough to produce significant effects when subjects from those institutions are grouped with subjects from prisons in which the relationship does not exist. One indication that this might have occurred in the present case is the fact that the correlation between the religiousness scale scores and the Wright adjustment scale scores in the Central region (r = .53) was considerably greater than the correlation for the study sample as a whole (r = .12).

This raises the question of what characteristics differentiate prisons where the relationship between religiousness and adjustment is significant from prisons where the relationship is not significant. One might be tempted to conclude from the regional analysis presented here that geographical location is an important determinant. In this study, however, only two prisons were located in the Southwest region and only one prison was located in the Central region. Thus, the regional analysis may have tapped more inter-prison differences than inter-regional differences. It could be that prison size, management style, staff to inmate ratio, support for religious programming, or some other institutional characteristics influence the association between religiousness and adjustment, not geographical location of the prison.

Unfortunately, the small number of subjects who came from some of the institutions included in this study would make conclusions based on statistical analysis at the institutional level insupportable. The level of security analysis may also have been just a mask for inter-prison differences. The three prisons from the Central and Southwest regions were all medium security facilities. Thus, it was not surprising that the association between religiousness and adjustment appeared strongest in medium security facilities.

As stated, the relationship between religiousness and the alternative measure of adjustment, number of disciplinary confinements, appears to be unique from the relationship between religiousness and adjustment as measured by the Wright scale. Principally, there appear to be two differences. First, the religiousness variable remained significant in three multivariate analyses incorporating other independent variables. It would therefore appear that the relationship between religiousness and this measure of adjustment is more direct.

Second, the type of independent variable which was significant in the multivariate analyses involving number of disciplinary confinements as a dependent variable was characteristically different than the measures of depression, self-esteem and self-mastery, those variables which were significant in the multivariate analyses using the Wright scale scores as the dependent variable. Sentence length and behavioral measures like number of prior property and person offenses were most often significant independent variables or co-variates in the analyses involving number of disciplinary confinements.

As with any research project, there are caveats to consider before drawing any conclusions from the study results. *First*, it is not known to what extent the sample is representative of prison inmates generally, or religious inmates specifically. The prisons from which study subjects were recruited were purposely selected. Likewise, study subjects were not randomly selected, but rather volunteered to participate in the project. The sample, with the exception of one facility, also excludes inmates who were housed in segregation. The extent to which the study sample is representative of prison inmates, and thus the extent to which study findings are generalizable to other prisons and inmates, is not known. One limitation is quite obvious, this study was limited to male prisoners, and would clearly not be generalizable to populations of female inmates.

Second, the objective of this study was to examine the possibility that a relationship exists between inmate religiousness and adjustment to the in-prison environment. Data collection in this study relied on self-report measures rather than official institutional records. While other studies of inmates have relied on data from inmates' institutional files, this method was problematic in this study for two reasons: (1) Apart from recording the inmate's religious denomination, many institutions do not maintain records of participation in religious programs or other indicators of inmate religiousness; (2) Official prison records are often incomplete and/or recorded inconsistently. Finally, institutional records of inmate adjustment (i.e., disciplinary infractions) may reflect the subjective biases of prison officials. Thus, while the use of self-report measures was the preferred approach for this study, the validity of these measures with this sample is not known.

CONCLUSION

A relationship does appear to exist between inmate religiousness and psychological adjustment to the in-prison environment such that inmates who report higher levels of religiousness also report higher levels of adjustment. This relationship may exist in some prisons, but not in others. The characteristics of prisons in which this relationship does exist are yet to be determined. Additionally, rather than being direct and causal, the relationship between religiousness and adjustment is a by-product of the relationships between depression, self-esteem, self-mastery and adjustment and religiousness.

There also appears to be a relationship between inmate religiousness and a more behaviorally oriented measure of inmate adjustment: the number of times an inmate reports being placed in disciplinary confinement. Religious inmates report being placed in confinement less often than non-religious inmates. While other variables, including sentence length and number of prior offenses, appear to mediate this relationship, religiousness often remains a principal determinant of the number of disciplinary confinements, even after these other variables are controlled for.

These relationships were found to exist in prisons of some security levels and in prisons in certain regions of the country, but not in others. Thus, it may be the relationships between religiousness and these two measures of in-prison adjustment occur in some situations, but not in others. Additional research, preferably incorporating longitudinal data from a larger number of institutions, is needed to further investigate the nature of the relationships between these variables and the environmental factors which influence these relationships.

REFERENCES

Albrecht, S. L., Chadwick, B. A., and Alcorn, D. S. 1977. Religiosity and Deviance: Application of an Attitude-Behavior Contingent Consistency Model. *Journal for the Scientific Study of Religion.* 16: 263-274.

Babbie, E. 1998. *The Practice of Social Research, 5th ed.* Belmont, CA: Wadsworth.

Bainbridge, W. S. 1989. The Religious Ecology of Deviance. *American Sociological Review.* 54(2): 288-295.

Benda, B. 1995. The Effect of Religion on Adolescent Delinquency Revisited. *Journal of Research in Crime and Delinquency.* 32(4): 446-466.

Benda, B. 1997. An Examination of a Reciprocal Relationship Between Religiosity and Different Forms of Delinquency Within a Theoretical Model. *Journal of Research in Crime and Delinquency.* 34(2): 163-186.

Berger, P. and Luckmann, T. 1963. Sociology of Religion and Sociology of Knowledge. *Sociology and Social Research.* 47: 417-27.

Black, T. R. 1993. *Evaluating Social Science Research: An Introduction.* Thousand Oaks, CA: Sage.

Brownfield, D. and Sorenson, A. M. 1991. Religion and Drug Use Among Adolescents: A Social Support Conceptualization and Interpretation. *Deviant Behavior.* 12(3): 259-276.

Burkett, S. R. and White, M. 1974. Hellfire and Delinquency: Another Look. *Journal for the Scientific Study of Religion.* 13: 455-62.

Carroll, L. 1974. *Hacks, Blacks, and Cons: Race Relations in a Maximum Security Prison.* MA: Heath.

Chadwick, B. A. and Top, B. L. 1993. Religiosity and Delinquency Among LSD Adolescents. *Journal for the Scientific Study of Religion.* 32(1): 51-67.

Clear, T., Stout, B., Dammer, H., Kelly, L., Hardyman, P., and Shapiro, C. 1992. *Prisoners, Prisons and Religion: Final Report.* Newark, NJ: School of Criminal Justice, Rutgers University.

Clemmer, D. 1958. *The Prison Community.* New York: Rinehart.

Cochran, J. K. 1988. The Effect of Religiosity on Secular and Ascetic Deviance. *Sociological Focus.* 21: 293-306.

Cochran, J. K. 1989. Another Look at Delinquency and Religiosity. *Sociological Spectrum.* 26(3): 147-162.

Cochran, J. K. and Akers, R. 1989. Beyond Hellfire: An Exploration of the Variable Effects of Religiosity on Adolescent Marijuana and Alcohol Use. *Journal of Research in Crime and Delinquency.* 26(3): 198-225.

Cochran, J. K., Wood, P. B., and Arneklev, B. J. 1994. Is the Religiosity-Delinquency Relationship Spurious? A Test of Arousal and Social Control Theories. *Journal of Research in Crime and Delinquency.* 31: 92-123.

Comstock, G. L. 1995. *Religious Autobiographies.* Belmont, CA: Wadsworth.

Cooper, H. M. 1989. *Integrating Research: A Guide for Literature Reviews*. New Park, CA: Sage.

Cornwall, M. 1989. The Determinants of Religious Behavior: A Theoretical Model and Empirical Test. *Social Forces*. 68(2): 572-592.

Cunningham, L. S., Kelsay, J., Barineau, R. M., and McVoy, H. J. 1995. *The Sacred Quest: An Invitation to the Study of Religion*. Englewood Cliffs, NJ: Prentice Hall.

Durkheim, E. 1915. *The Elementary Forms of the Religious Life: A Study of Religious Sociology*. New York: Macmillian.

Elifson, K. W., Peterson, D. M., and Hadaway, C. K. 1983. Religiosity and Delinquency: A Contextual Analysis. *Criminology*. 21: 505-27.

Ellis, L. 1985. Religiosity and Criminality: Evidence and Explanations of Complex Relationships. *Sociological Perspectives*. 28(4): 501-520.

Ellis, L. 1987. Religiosity and Criminality from the Perspective of Arousal Theory. *Journal of Research in Crime and Delinquency*. 24: 215-232.

Ellis, L. and Peterson, J. 1996. Crime and Religion: An International Comparison Among Thirteen Industrial Nations. *Personality and Individual Differences*. 20(6): 761-768.

Ellis, L. and Thompson, R. 1989. Relating Religion, Crime and Arousal and Boredom. *Sociology and Social Research*. 73(3): 132-139.

Ellwood, R. 1978. *Introducing Religion: From Inside and Outside*. Englewood Cliffs, NJ: Prentice-Hall.

Evans, T. D., Cullen, F. T., Burton, V. S., and Dunaway, R. G. et al. 1996. Religion, Social Bonds, and Delinquency. *Deviant Behavior*. 17(1): 43-70.

Evans, T. D., Cullen, F. T., Dunaway, R. G., and Burton, V. S. 1995. Religion and Crime Reexamined: The Impact of Religion, Secular Controls, and Social Ecology on Adult Criminality. *Criminology*. 33: 195-224.

Evans-Pritchard, E. E. 1965. *Theories of Primitive Religion*. Oxford, UK: Clarendon.

Fernquist, R. M. 1995. A Research Note on the Association Between Religion and Delinquency. *Deviant Behavior*. 16(2): 169-175.

Free, M. D. 1994. Religious Affiliation, Religiosity and Impulsive and Intentional Deviance. *Sociological Focus*. 25 (1): 77-91.

Gaer, J. 1929. *How the Great Religions Began*. Scranton, PA: Haddon Craftsmen.

Garofalo, J. and Clark, R. 1985. The Inmate Subculture in Jails. *Criminal Justice and Behavior*. 12(4): 415-434.

Glock, C. Y. 1973. *Religion in Sociological Perspective: Essays in the Empirical Study of Religion*. Belmont, CA: Wadsworth.

Goodstein, L. and MacKenzie, D. (Eds.) 1989. *The American Prison: Issues in Research and Policy*. New York: Plenum.

Goodstein, L. and Wright, K. 1989. Inmate Adjustment to Prison. In L. Goodstein and MacKenzie, D. (Eds.), *The American Prison: Issues in Research and Policy*. New York: Plenum.

Grasmick, H.G., Cochran, J. K., Bursik, R. J., and Kimpel, M. 1993. Religion, Punitive Justice, and Support for the Death Penalty. *Justice Quarterly*. 10 (2): 289-314.

Grasmick, H. G., Davenport, E., Chamlin, M., and Dursik, R. 1992. Protestant Fundamentalism and the Retributivist Doctrine of Punishment. *Criminology*. 30: 21-45.

Grasmick, H. G., Kinsey, K., and Cochran, J. K. 1991. Denomination, Religiosity, and Compliance with the Law: A Study of Adults. *Journal for the Scientific Study of Religion.* 30(1): 99-107.

Grasmick, H. G. and McGill, A. L. 1994. Religion, Attribution Style, and Punitiveness Toward Juvenile Offenders. *Criminology.* 32 (1): 23-46.

Greek, Cecil E. 1992. *The Religious Roots of American Sociology.* New York: Garland.

Hair, J. F., Anderson, R. E., Tatham, R. L., and Black, W. C. 1998. *Multivariate Data Analysis,* 5th ed. Upper Saddle River, NJ: Prentice Hall.

Hall, W. T. (Ed.) 1978. *Introduction to the Study of Religion.* New York: Harper and Row.

Heffernan, E. 1972. *Making It in Prison: The Square, The Cool, and The Life.* New York: Wiley.

Higgins, P. C. and Albrecht. N. 1977. Hellfire and Delinquency Revisited. *Social Forces.* 52: 952-958.

Hirschi, T. and Stark, R. 1969. Hellfire and Delinquency. *Social Problems.* 17: 202-213.

Hopfe, L. M. and Woodard, M. R. 1998. *Religions of the World. 7th ed.* Upper Saddle River, NJ: Prentice Hall.

Irvin, J. and Cressey, D. 1962. Thieves, Convicts, and the Inmate Culture. *Social Problems.* 10: 142-155.

Jacobs, B. 1976. Stratification and Conflict Among Prison Inmates. *Journal of Criminal Law and Criminology.* 66: 476-482.

James, W. 1936. *The Varieties of Religious Experience: A Study in Human Nature.* Toronto: Random House.

Jenson, G. F. and Erickson, N. 1979. The Religious Factor and Delinquency: Another Look at the Hellfire Hypothesis. In R. Wuthnow, *The Religious Dimension: New Directions in Quantitative Research.* New York: Academic.

Johnson, B. R. 1984. *Hellfire and Corrections: A Quantitative Study of Florida Prison Inmates.* Tallahassee, FL: Unpublished Doctoral Dissertation. Florida State University.

Johnson, B. R. 1987. Religiosity and Institutional Deviance: The Impact of Religious Variables Upon Inmate Adjustment. *Criminal Justice Review.* 12: 21-30.

Johnson, B. R., Larson, D. B., and Pitts, T. C. 1997. Religious Programs, Institutional Adjustment, and Recidivism Among Former Inmates in Prison Fellowship Programs. *Justice Quarterly.* 14: 501-521.

Johnson, R. 1976. *Culture and Crisis in Confinement.* Lexington, MA: Lexington Books.

Johnson, R. A., Wallwork, E., Green, C., Vanderpool, H. Y., and Santmire, H. P. 1990. *Critical Issues in Modern Religion.* Englewood Cliffs, NJ: Prentice Hall.

Junger, M. and Polder, W. 1993. Religiosity, Religious Climate, and Delinquency Among Ethnic Groups in The Netherlands. *British Journal of Criminology.* 33(3): 416-435.

Knudten, R.D. and Knudten, M. S. 1971. Juvenile Delinquency, Crime, and Religion. *Review of Religious Research.* 12:130-152.

Marett, R. R. 1932. *Faith, Hope, and Charity in Primitive Religion.* New York: Macmillian.

Maxfield, M. G. and Babbie, E. 1995. *Research Methods for Criminal Justice and Criminology.* Belmont, CA: Wadsworth.

O'Dea, T. F. 1966. *Sociology of Religion.* Englewood Cliffs, NJ: Prentice-Hall.

Paden, W. E. 1992. *Interpreting the Sacred: Ways of Viewing Religion.* Boston: Beacon.

Parisi, N. (Ed.) 1982. *Coping with Imprisonment.* Beverly Hills, CA: Sage.

Pettersson, T. 1991. Religion and Criminality: Structural Relationships Between Church Involvement and Crime Rates in Contemporary Sweden. *Journal for the Scientific Study of Religion.* 30(3): 279-291.

Porporino, F. and Zamble, E. 1984. Coping with Imprisonment. *Canadian Journal of Criminology.* 26(4): 403-421.

Ramirez, J. 1983. Race and the Apprehension of Inmate Misconduct. *Journal of Criminal Justice.* 11: 413-417.

Ross, L. E. 1994. Religion and Deviance: Exploring the Impact of Social Control Elements. *Sociological Spectrum.* 14 (1): 5-17.

Sloane, D. and Potvin, R. 1986. Religion and Delinquency: Cutting Through the Maze. *Social Forces.* 65: 87-105.

Slosar, J. 1978. *Prisonization, Friendship, and Leadership.* MA: Lexington Books.

Smart, N. 1983. *Worldviews: Cross-Cultural Exploration of Human Beliefs.* New York: Prentice-Hall.

Stark, R. 1984. Religion and Conformity: Reaffirming a Sociology of Religion. *Sociological Analysis.* 45(4): 273-282.

Stark, R., Kent, L., and Doyle, D. P. 1982. Religion and Delinquency: The Ecology of a "Lost" Relationship. *Journal of Research in Crime and Delinquency.* 14: 4-23.

Sumter, M. T. and Clear, T. R. 1998. An Empirical Analysis of Literature Examining the Relationship Between Religiosity and Deviance since 1985. Tallahassee, FL: Unpublished Document, School of Criminology, Florida State University.

Sykes, G. 1958. *The Society of Captives: A Study of Maximum Security Prisons.* Princeton, NJ: Princeton University Press.

Sykes, G. M. and Messinger, S. L. 1960. The Inmate Social System. In R. Cloward, S. L. Messinger and G. M. Sykes. (Eds.), *Theoretical Studies in the Social Organization of the Prison.* New York: Social Science Research Council.

Thomas, C., Petersen, D. M., and Zingraff, R. M. 1978. Structural and Social Psychological Correlates of Prisonization. *Criminology.* 16(3): 383-393.

Tittle, C. R. and Welch, M. 1983. Religiosity and Deviance: Toward a Contingency Theory of Constraining Effects. *Social Forces.* 61: 653-682.

Welch, M. R. and Tittle, C. R. 1991. Religion and Deviance Among Adult Catholics: A Test of the "Moral Communities" Hypothesis. *Journal for the Scientific Study of Religion.* 30 (2): 159-172.

Zamble, E. and Porporino, F. 1988. *Coping, Behavior, and Adaptation in Prison Inmates.* New York: Springer-Verlag.

AUTHORS' NOTES

Todd R. Clear is Distinguished Professor at John Jay College of Criminal Justice, City University of New York. His PhD in criminal justice is from The University at Albany, State University of New York. Among his publications are *Harm in American Penology* and *Controlling the Offender in the Community.* His current research interests include incarceration policy, alternatives to imprisonment, and community justice.

Melvina T. Sumter is an assistant professor at Old Dominion University, Norfolk, Virgina. Her PhD is from the School of Criminology and Criminal Justice at Florida State University. Her current research interests include efforts to control crime through capital reinvestment in disadvantaged communities, religion and prison, and community justice.

The study described in this report was funded by the PEW Charitable Trusts.

Address correspondence to Dr. Todd R. Clear, Department of Law and Police Science, John Jay College of Criminal Justice, 899 Tenth Avenue, New York, NY 10019 (E-mail: tclear@ jjay.cuny.edu).

Religion, the Community, and the Rehabilitation of Criminal Offenders. Pp. 161-183.
© 2002 by The Haworth Press, Inc. All rights reserved.

Religiosity and Drug Use Among Inmates in Boot Camp: Testing a Theoretical Model with Reciprocal Relationships

BRENT B. BENDA

University of Arkansas at Little Rock

NANCY J. TOOMBS

Department of Correction, Wrightsville, Arkansas

SUMMARY The present investigation is one of the first theoretical studies of young persons entering boot camp. The sample in the present study consists of 326 males, aged 15 to 24 years, in the only boot camp in Arkansas. The purpose of the study is to examine the effects of religiosity within a hypothesized theoretical model with reciprocal relationships of drug use among boot camp inmates. This model is tested with two-stage least squares regression, and all hypothesized relationships, with two exceptions, are supported. The findings show that attachment to caregivers is inversely related to associations with peers who engage in illicit behavior, whereas being abused by an adult is positively related to these associations. These associations have inverse reciprocal relationships with religiosity and secular beliefs, and are positively related to use of excuses for illicit acts, which are positively related to drug use. Drug use increases with advances in age and among white persons (versus persons of color), and use of drugs has positive reciprocal relationships with selling illicit substances and carrying a gun. Conceptual and practice implications of the study are discussed. *[Article copies available for a fee from The Haworth Document Delivery Service: 1-800-HAWORTH. E-mail address: <getinfo@haworthpressinc.com> Website: <http://www.HaworthPress. com> © 2002 by The Haworth Press, Inc. All rights reserved.]*

KEYWORDS Boot camp, religion, drugs, delinquency, juvenile

Data from two recent national surveys, the 1995 Household Survey on Drug Use (Gfroerer, 1996) and the Monitoring the Future Study (Johnston, O'Malley, & Bachman, 1996), show a significant increase in illicit drug use among young persons in this country. The sharp rise in prevalence rates of marijuana, cocaine, heroin, hallucinogen, and meth-amphetamine use are of particular concern to many professionals because of the aversive outcomes associated with these drugs such as addiction, crime, spread of sexually-transmitted diseases, and death (Akers, 1992; Decker & Rosenfeld, 1992; Leavitt, 1995; Lurigio & Davis, 1992; Stimmel, 1993).

Despite the magnitude of youthful drug use and associated problems, the precise nature and sequence of processes leading to use and abuse of drugs remain uncertain (Akers, 1992; Leavitt, 1995). Yet, effective intervention relies on theory as a guide for what motivations are most likely to lead to behavioral change (Andrews & Bonta, 1994). In fact, evidence indicates that programs based on useful theory are five times more effective than are those lacking an underlying theoretical framework (Izzo & Ross, 1990). Yet, while drug users are entering boot camps in increasing numbers because of their high proportion among youths who qualify for boot camp programs, a thorough review of the literature indicates that there are no theoretical studies of persons entering boot camps (Cronin, 1994; Zhang, 1998). The present investigation is the first theoretical study of persons in boot camp, and it is relevant to program design in confirming what factors are influencing drug-using, criminal lifestyles.

HYPOTHESIZED THEORETICAL MODEL

The hypothesized model (see Figure 1) is constructed based on conceptualization in related literature on youthful offenders (Notes 1, 2; see reviews by Akers, 1992, 1997; Bartol & Bartol, 1998; Elliott, Huizinga, & Ageton, 1985; Elliott, Huizinga, & Minard, 1989; Walters, 1994), and on experiential knowledge of boot camps. The present study examines elements of control (Durkheim [1897]1951; Hirschi, 1969) and social learning (Akers, 1992, 1997) theories thought to be the most useful to conceptual understanding and to program design. Also, reviews of the

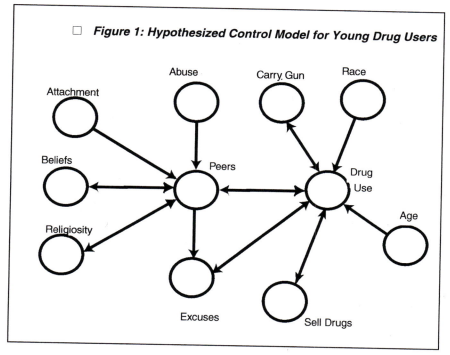

Figure 1: Hypothesized Control Model for Young Drug Users

literature on boot camps suggest that these theories are likely to be the most useful to boot camp programs (Cronin, 1994; Zhang, 1998).

The model is constructed using theoretical elaboration (Thornberry, 1989) instead of attempting to fully integrate (see Akers, 1997) two theories that rest on contradictory assumptions about motivations for drug use and crime (see Agnew, 1995). A true integration of these theories would require resolution of differences in assumptions (see Hirschi, 1979), whereas theoretical elaboration requires that propositions of the hypothesized model be consistent (Thornberry, 1989). The hypothesized model tested represents an elaboration of control theory (Durkheim 1897/1951; Hirschi, 1969) using essential elements from social learning theory (Akers, 1997; Benda, 1997). The fundamental assumption underlying the model is that drug use occurs among persons with weak inner controls over natural urges for euphoria induced by use of substances studied (Hirschi, 1969; Nye, 1958). Unlike classical control theory (Kornhauser, 1978), however, the assumption is that weak restraint allows, but does not motivate, illicit use of drugs (Akers, 1992;

Benda, 1997; Elliott et al., 1985). Succinctly stated, data support the argument that certain elements of control theory are necessary but not sufficient to explain youthful drug use (Walters, 1994). Evidence indicates that a primary motivation for illicit use of drugs is social learning that occurs in associations with peers who teach excuses or rationalizations for drug use (Akers, 1992; Walters, 1994). Persons drift into these peer associations to fill an emotional void left by insecure attachments to parents or other caregivers (Patterson & Dishion, 1985). Insecure familial attachments lead to underdeveloped social skills which are rejected by more socially-skilled youths (Simons, Whitbeck, Conger, & Conger, 1991).

The elaboration of control theory with elements of social learning theory requires a softening of the control assumptions of an invariant natural motivation for drugs and of only conventional sources of socialization (see Kornhauser, 1978). However, genetic and intergenerational studies indicate predispositions and susceptibilities to drug use, and many young persons are socialized by others who use illicit drugs (Akers, 1992; Walters, 1994). Control theory is useful in providing a valuable explanation for why some individuals differentially associate with persons who regularly use illicit drugs (Benda, 1997; Elliott, Huizinga, & Ageton, 1985). Aside from the elaboration of control theory with elements of social learning, the explanatory model shown in Figure 1 is based on two other major assumptions that recently have emerged in the literature on construction of theoretical models of drug use (Benda, 1997; Thornberry, 1997): (1) the relevance of religiosity and (2) reciprocal relationships.

Despite the legacy of religion in social control theory (Durkheim, 1897/1951; Weber, 1905/1958), many scholars remain skeptical about the impact of religious beliefs and commitment on drug use and other illegal behavior (Benson, 1960; Merton, 1957; President's Commission, 1967; Schur, 1969; Sutherland & Cressey, 1978). Indeed, the preeminent control theorist (Hirschi, 1969), who formulated his theory out of Durkheimian (1897/1951) thought, dismissed religion as an important element of that theory, based on his findings that church attendance and belief in supernatural sanctions are unrelated to self-reported delinquency (Hirschi & Stark, 1969). These particular findings became, for many researchers (see reviews, Burkett, 1993; Stark, Kent, & Doyle, 1982), the accepted conclusion to a long-debated issue in the literature (e.g., Barnes & Teeters, 1951; Bonger, 1916; Ellis, 1910; Lombroso, 1911; Steiner, 1924). For other researchers, however, these results have become a catalyst for a resurgence of investigations into the relationship between personal religiosity and drug use and other illegal acts (e.g., Benda, 1995, 1997; Burkett, 1993; Burkett & Warren, 1987; Chadwick & Top, 1993; Cochran & Akers, 1989; Cochran, Wood, & Arneklev, 1994; Evans, Cullen, Dunaway, & Burton, 1995).

More recent research has begun to show support for the relevance of religiosity to illicit behavior such as use of "street drugs" (see Benda, 1997; Burkett, 1993; Evans et al., 1995). At the same time, there are arguments that religiosity is relevant only for behaviors where there are ambiguous societal values and norms and clear proscriptions in religion (see reviews, Benda & Corwyn, 1997a; Burkett, 1993; Cochran, 1988; Evans et al., 1995). The clearest examples typically given are use of alcohol, tobacco, and even marijuana by adolescents (Cochran & Akers, 1989; Cochran et al., 1994). A caveat is in order at this juncture, however, that a major problem with this argument is that no one has conceptually or operationally defined which behaviors are covered by the argument.

A second major argument concerning the importance of religiosity is that it is not a significant element of any theoretical explanation when examined together with the major influences on drug use and other unlawful offenses (see Cochran et al., 1994). At the same time, there have been very few attempts to formulate an explanatory model of interrelationships that involves any effects of religiosity on unlawful behavior (Cochran et al., 1994; Evans et al., 1995). Conceptualization of where religiosity fits into any system of interactional relationships is practically non-existent. Moreover, there is inconsistent evidence regarding the arguments that religiosity is an influence only on behaviors that are more clearly prohibited in religious doctrine, or that religion ceases to be relevant when more important factors are considered (Benda, 1995, 1997; Burkett, 1993; Cochran et al., 1994; Evans et al., 1995).

The present study rests on the assumptions that these inconsistent findings result, in large measure, from failure to conceptualize what relationships exist between religiosity, other important influences, and drug use, and from failure to examine reciprocal relationships. Indeed, Thornberry (1987) has made a cogent argument for his interaction theory that explanatory systems are dynamic in reality and contain many bi-directional or reciprocal relationships. Subsequently, reciprocal relationships have been empirically validated in models of drug use and other unlawful behaviors (Benda, 1997; Benda & Corwyn, 1997; Burkett & Warren, 1987; Jang & Smith, 1997; Thornberry, Lizotte, Krohn, Farnworth, & Jang, 1994).

For example, some writers argue that all persons, to varying degrees, receive some inculcation in religion and beliefs in the moral validity of societal laws and norms (Matsueda, 1989; Sykes & Matza, 1957). Based on social control theory (Durkheim, 1897/1951; Hirschi, 1969), it is hypothesized that religiosity and societal beliefs insulate young persons from peer associations that encourage unlawful behavior (Benda, 1997; Benda & Corwyn, 1997b; Matsueda, 1989). At the same time, it has been shown that peers who engage in unlawful acts provide alternative beliefs that diminish commitment to religion and to societal beliefs (Benda, 1997; Burkett, 1993; Matsueda, 1989). Hence, inverse reciprocal relationships are hypothesized in Figure 1 between beliefs and peer association and between religiosity and peer association.

According to the preeminent control theory (Hirschi, 1969), parental attachment is the initial element of bonding to form, and is an empathic identification with parents that fosters acceptance of parental expectations, including peers with whom one associates (Patterson & Dishion, 1985). Based on control theory (Hirschi, 1969; Nye, 1958), secure attachments are hypothesized to affect drug use through encouraging peer associations that tend to shun illegal behavior (see Figure 1). Conversely, physical abuse from parents results in weak and insecure attachments and limited interpersonal skills (Bartol & Bartol, 1998; Boney-McCoy & Finkelhor, 1995; Brezina, 1998). Limited ability to interact with others resulting from this trauma typically leads to peer associations (Figure 1) which encourage indulgence of natural desires for pleasures of drugs and criminal activity (Walters, 1994). Individuals with a history of physical abuse from adults are three times more likely to abuse drugs than their peers (Finkelhor & Dziuba-Leatherman, 1995).

Because the majority of young persons, to differing degrees, are inculcated with religious and societal beliefs (Akers, 1997; Matsueda, 1989; Stark & Bainbridge, 1997), peers who engage in illicit acts offer excuses that provide episodic release from the guilt induced by behaving in ways contrary to one's beliefs (Sykes & Matza, 1957). Also, differential peer association with those who regularly participate in illicit acts encourages, and is encouraged by, unlawful behavior. Hence, Figure 1 shows a reciprocal relationship between peer association and unlawful behavior.

The remaining aspects of the model shown in Figure 1 are based on experiential knowledge of at least this boot camp (Note 1). For example, due to differential use of drugs and administrative processing in the correctional system, white youths are hypothesized to have a greater frequency of drug use than persons of color. Many persons of color processed into the Arkansas Department of Correction are gang members, and use of drugs is seen as a sign of weakness and unreliability by gang members. Most of these gangs are involved, to varying extents, in drug traffic, and members do not want persons who are unreliable because of drug abuse (Baumer, 1994). Also, statewide data clearly show that persons of color are given longer sentences for drug-related offenses than are white youths, making them ineligible for boot camp (Note 2). These observations about Arkansas are supported by data from other areas of the country (Baumer, 1994; Pope & Clear, 1994; Wallace & Bachman, 1991).

To be eligible for the boot camp studied, persons have to be first-admissions to the correctional system for adults who have no recorded violent offenses as an adult. Therefore, first-admissions who regularly use drugs tend to be older persons because younger offenders who frequently consume illicit drugs typically commit other offenses, including violence, that result in longer sentences than allowed by the boot camp. Hence, age is expected to have a positive relationship to drug use. Carrying a gun and selling drugs are hypothesized to have reciprocal relationships to all three forms of problem behavior studied. The nexus of contemporary criminal lifestyles typically involves interrelationships between selling of drugs and carrying a gun, and consumptions of illicit substances as well as property and person crimes (Baron & Hartnagel, 1998; Baumer, 1994; Walters, 1994).

METHOD

Sample

The sample in the present study consists of 326 males, aged 15 to 24 years, from 25 classes in the only boot camp in Arkansas. Persons are eligible for this boot camp if they: (1) are a first-time referral to the adult correctional system in Arkansas, (2) are sentenced to 10 or less years, (3) have no recorded violent offenses as an adult, (4) have an IQ above 70, and (5) have no physical or psychological problems that would preclude military training. Participation in boot camp is an option to prison for those who are eligible. The drop-out rate is approximately 20 percent, and at the time of the study only males were placed in the one boot camp for adults in the state. The boot camp program has five major components described elsewhere (Toombs, Benda, & Corwyn, 1997).

Characteristics of the study subjects are shown in Table 1. To summarize, the respondents range in age from 15 years to 24 years, with a mean of 20.3, a median of 20, and a mode of 19 (39 percent). It should be noted at this juncture that only nine percent are under 18 years of age. Because the vast majority (94 percent) of the persons of color are African Americans, the discussion of analyses reflects this distribution.

Dependent Variable

The outcome or dependent variable analyzed in this study is use of illicit drugs. The drug measure consists of six items that asked respondents if they ever had used the following drugs: (1) marijuana; (2) cocaine; (3) heroin, Paregoric, Meperidine, Methadone, Morphine, opium; (4) LSD, mescaline, Peyote, or other hallucinogens (acid); (5) barbiturates; and (6) amphetamines. The same 5-point scale was used for all six forms of drug use (1 = no, 2 = 1 to 2 times, 3 = 3 to 5 times, 4 = 6 to 9 times, and 5 = 10 times or more), and examples of street names were provided for all drugs, such as speed, yellow jackets, pink hearts, and cross tops for amphetamines. Cronbach's (1951) alpha for those drugs is .88, and the item-to-total correlations range from .60 to .89.

Theoretical Measures

Attachment. The same three items (5-point scales ranging from very much to very little) are used to measure both attachment to mother and to father: (1) how much do you like to be with, (2) how close do you feel to, and (3) how much do you want to be like–(or female and male caregiver). Beliefs are measured with four items (5-point scales ranging from strongly disagree to strongly agree) asking if: (1) it is okay to sneak into a movie or ball game without paying, (2) it is important to obey rules and laws, (3) it is wrong to damage others' property, and (4) it is important to pay for all things taken from a store. These are commonly used measures adapted from Hirschi (1969) and Marcos and Bahr (1988). Religiosity was five items adopted from Woodroof (1985) measuring (5-point scales): (1) church attendance (ranging from once a month or less to three times a week); (2) prayer (ranging from never to daily); (3) church activity (ranging from never involved to very involved); (4) talk about religion (ranging from never to daily); and (5) trying to convert someone (ranging from never to frequently). Abuse was measured with two items (4-point Likert scales from never to more than 10 times) asking how often respondents had been physically abused by any

☐ Table 1. Selected Background Characteristics of Subjects

Age (in years)	Mean: 20.3	Range: 15-24
Race	Number	Percent
Caucasian	146	44.8
African American	170	55.1
Asian American	2	0.6
Hispanic American	4	0.9
Other	5	1.5
Family structure before age = 12 years		
Both biological parents	117	35.9
Biological and step	67	20.6
Mother only	93	28.5
Father only	6	1.8
Other	43	13.2
Family structure after age = 12 years		
Both biological parents	89	27.3
Biological and step	65	19.9
Mother only	102	31.3
Father only	7	2.1
Other	63	19.3
Mother's education*		
Less than high school diploma	89	27.3
High school diploma	132	40.5
Some college	68	20.9
College graduate	26	8.0
Graduate school	2	0.6
Missing data	3	0.9
Carry gun		
Never	158	48.5
Once or twice	61	18.7
Several times	47	14.4
Very often	58	17.8
Missing data	2	0.6
Sold drugs		
Never	76	23.3
Once or twice	42	12.9
Several times	64	21.7
Very often	112	34.4
Missing data	32	9.8

Father's education was nearly identical to mother's education.

adult (1) before 12 years of age and (2) after 12 years of age. Abuse was defined as any physical contact that resulted in severe cuts, bruises, welts, or other marks that took a few days to disappear; in concussions or breaking of bones; or in scalding or burns.

From social learning theory, peer association (peers) is measured by five items (5-point Likert scale from none to four or more) asking how many close friends: (1) had been picked up by police; (2) use illegal drugs regularly; (3) drink three or more beers or glasses of liquor or wine in a day regularly; (4) steal regularly; and (5) have used a weapon on someone. Excuses were measured with five items (4-point Likert scales from strongly disagree to strongly agree) stating: (1) heavy drinking of alcohol does not harm anyone; (2) use of illegal drugs does not harm anyone; (3) stealing is all right since everyone does it; (4) using illegal drugs is all right since most people use them; and (5) stealing from someone who can afford it is okay since it does not hurt them much. These social learning measures were taken from Akers (1992, 1997).

Among other theoretical factors, selling illegal drugs was measured with one item asking how often they had sold these drugs (1 = never, 2 = 1 or 2 times, 3 = several times, 4 = very often). Carrying a gun was measured by asking how often they carried a gun (same scale as previous item). Race was dichotomized as: 0 = white youth, 1 = persons of color.

Otherwise, the dependent and theoretical variables are represented by summated scores. An intercorrelation matrix and tolerance tests do not indicate a problem with multicollinearity. Maximum likelihood factor analyses, with oblimin rotation, reveal that items load on separate factors as theorized. Factors are coded for theoretical concordance (e.g., high score on religiosity is high religiosity, whereas high score on excuses means use of excuses for deviant behavior). The psychometric properties of the theoretical measures are shown in Table 2.

Procedure and Data

The 150-item questionnaire was administered to each class of 15 to 30 boot camp participants by a staff psychologist), who had eight research associates available to monitor each table of five respondents to clarify wording or to answer questions, and to interview those who could not read. The questionnaires were administered approximately halfway through the 105-day program, when discipline has been instilled and rapport has developed with the psychologists who conduct group discussions with all inmates (Note 3). Only five persons refused

Table 2. Psychometric Properties Associated with Theoretical Factors

	Mean	SD	Alpha	r's*	Factor Analysis	Kurtosis	Skewness
Attachment	12.3	5.30	.90	.88-.93	.79-.90	−0.9	0.7
Beliefs	1.8	.77	.72	.66-.79	.41-.76	2.0	1.2
Religiosity	3.2	.86	.75	.60-.75	.44-.73	−0.5	−0.1
Physical abuse	1.4	.82	(–)	.89-.91	(–)	2.9	2.0
Peer association							
(PEERS)	2.6	1.00	.80	.67-.82	.59-.79	−0.9	0.2
Excuses	1.6	.48	.82	.44-.80	.40-.99	1.8	1.4

Note: Both biological parents residing in the home most of the time after 12 years of age; mother's education is "no high school diploma" versus "had high school diploma." SD is standard deviation, alpha is Cronbach's (1951) alpha, ranges are shown for item-to-total correlations and for maximum likelihood factor analyses with oblique (oblimin) rotation.

*Reports value of coefficients of correlation between Items and Totals.

to participate in the study. About 85 percent of the 150 items on the questionnaire had no missing information, and most of the others were missing from one to 10 cases. Parents' education had seven percent missing data and selling drugs had nine percent missing cases.

Statistical Procedures

Prior research has relied almost exclusively on (OLS) ordinary least squares regression procedures to test unidirectional relationships between predictors and various forms of deviant behavior. However, the algorithm involved in OLS procedures wrongly attributes some of the theoretically unexplained variance in deviant behavior to the effect of predictors because of this correlation when there is a reciprocal or feedback effect involved (see Intriligator, 1978). If it is assumed that beliefs and peer association are reciprocally related, then it is highly possible that some unmeasured influences on beliefs are related to peer association and vice versa. The simple correlation does not permit differentiation between the effect of beliefs on peer association (or the reverse effect) and a spurious relationship between these factors induced by an unmeasured variable or variables.

Hence, the initial step in the development of a nonrecursive structural model is to introduce other variables into the system to measure or at least control for the influences of unmeasured variables (Kmenta,

1971). A critical condition for employing two-stage least squares regression in correlational studies is a clear theoretical model that specifies the presumed relationships among factors (Intriligator, 1978).

FINDINGS

Two-stage least squares regression procedures (Intriligator, 1978) are used to examine the system of interrelationships shown in Figure 1. In Table 3 are presented the analyses of drug use among youth in the study. As an orientation to reading the table, all factors with arrows pointing to peer associations (see Figure 1) are significantly (alpha = 0.05) related to these associations as hypothesized. For example, beliefs, religiosity, and attachment are inversely related to peer association (in parenthesis) with those who engage in unlawful behavior, whereas being abused is positively related to these associations (top tier of Table 3). Together, these factors account for 11 percent (adjusted R^2) of the variance in peer association. In the next tier, peer association with those involved in delinquency, as hypothesized, is positively related to use of excuses for unlawful behavior, accounting for seven percent of the variance in excuses. As also hypothesized, the next two tiers show that these peer associations have negative reciprocal relationships with religiosity and beliefs. The remainder of the table reveals that drug use has reciprocal relationships with all hypothesized factors except peer association. Whereas drug use is positively related to association with delinquent peers, this association is not relevant to drug use. The model shown in Figure 1 explains 45 percent of the variance in use of drugs among these boot camp inmates.

DISCUSSION

This study of 326 boot camp participants, aged 15 to 24 years, was designed to test a hypothesized theoretical model of illicit drug use among persons entering a boot camp (Note 4). Of particular concern were the importance of religiosity and reciprocal relationships to the explanatory model proposed. There appears to be an emerging consensus in the literature that religiosity is relevant only to behaviors for which there are clear religious proscriptions and ambiguous societal values and norms, such as use of alcohol by adolescents or marijuana use (Cochran & Akers, 1989). Also, it has been assumed that any relation-

☐ **Table 3. Two-Stage Least Squares Analysis of Drug Use Among Young Offenders**

Predictors (PEERS)		B*	Beta*	t	p
Beliefs		−.19	−.12	−2.77	.0057
Abused > 12		.50	.10	2.51	.0090
Religiosity		−.12	−.11	−2.65	.0062
Attachment		−.10	−.10	−2.53	.0085
Multiple	*R*	.25			
Adjusted	*R²*	.11			
	F	8.01			
	p	.0000			
(EXCUSES)					
Peer Association*		.30	.57	6.46	.0000
Multiple	*R*	.27			
Adjusted	*R²*	.07			
	F	41.74			
	p	.0000			
(RELIGIOSITY)					
Peer Association*		−.46	.57	5.82	.0000
Multiple	*R*	.24			
Adjusted	*R²*	.06			
	F	33.84			
	p	.0000			
(BELIEFS)					
Peer Association*		−.34	−.56	−6.01	.0000
Multiple	*R*	.25			
Adjusted	*R²*	.06			
	F	36.22			
	p	.0000			
(SOLD DRUGS)					
Drug use*		.34	.56	6.25	.0000
Multiple	*R*	.36			
Adjusted	*R²*	.13			
	F	39.08			
	p	.0000			
(PEER ASSOCIATION)					
Drug use*		.15	.24	3.91	.0001
Multiple	*R*	.27			
Adjusted	*R²*	.07			
	F	41.74			
	p	.0000			
(CARRY GUN)					
Drug use*		.03	.19	3.05	.0024
Multiple	*R*	.12			
Adjusted	*R²*	.02			
	F	9.27			
	p	.0024			

	□ **Table 3 (continued)**			
Predictors	B*	Beta*	t	p
(EXCUSES)				
Drug use*	.01	.03	0.39	.6952
Multiple R	*.02*			
Adjusted R²	*.01*			
F	*0.15*			
p	*.6952*			
(DRUG USE–dependent variable)				
Peer	.02	.05	0.89	.1526
Excuses	.27	.13	2.23	.0122
Carry gun	1.01	.15	3.04	.0007
Sold drugs	1.78	.28	7.89	.0000
Race**	−9.33	−.58	−17.91	.0000
Age	.25	.21	6.05	.0000
Multiple R	*.67*			
Adjusted R²	*.45*			
F	*89.71*			
p	*.0000*			

*These are reciprocal feedback effects. B = unstandardized regression coefficient; Beta = standardized regression coefficient. **Race code = Caucasian = (0), Person of color = (1).*

ship between religiosity and unlawful behavior becomes irrelevant if other major influences are introduced into the analysis. However, the present study was based on the assumption that both of these generalizations, to a large extent, arise from the lack of conceptualization of an explanatory model that involves religiosity and reciprocal relationships.

In contrast to most prior research, this study examines a hypothesized theoretical model that includes religiosity and reciprocal relationships. Every hypothesized relationship, with two exceptions, is supported in the two-stage least squares analysis.

The exceptions are that peer associations do not have direct effects on use of substances, and drug use does not affect the use of excuses. Instead, peer associations affect drug consumption indirectly through their influence on use of excuses for illicit behavior. This atypical finding on the direct effects of peer association on use of drugs may result from the measure used. That is, peer association is measured with items concerning values and norms of peers rather than a more direct measure of how many of their friends use illicit drugs. Hindsight suggests that this more direct measure may have been a better indicator of the influence of peer association. On the other hand, it seems plausible that excuses allow drug use without frequent use of these drugs enhancing the necessity of excuses. However, future research is needed to verify this suggested sequence.

Before launching further into a discussion of findings and their implications, other limitations of the study need to be addressed at this juncture. Foremost, this is an initial theoretical study of drug use among those entering boot camps. While there are studies that examine explanatory models of drug use among youthful offenders (e.g., Benda, 1997; Burkett, 1993; Free, 1994; Marcos & Bahr, 1988), there are no published theoretical studies of young persons entering boot camp. Hence, the hypothesized model examined in this study is based on extrapolation from research on the general population of youthful drug users.

This lack of precedence is of special importance because the study involves a convenience sample from one boot camp, and boot camps vary in admission criteria. Hence, the sample characteristics may not generalize to other boot camps. Another salient limitation of this study is the cross-sectional design, which does not allow an examination of the developmental sequence. Furthermore, multiple measures and sources of information would have strengthened the study. It should be noted that the boot camp studied screens out those persons who are seriously addicted to drugs and need special drug treatment programs. At the same time, the fit of a complex model lends credibility to its validity.

Data on age and race corroborate experience and other data from the same facility that indicate that regular drug users who enter boot camp tend to be older white males (Note 4; Toombs et al., 1997).

Typically, these persons sell illicit substances to afford to use drugs, which promotes peer associations with other drug users, but these associations do not directly influence drug use. Another interpretation of these findings on peer association and drug use, aside from measurement issues just discussed, is that any direct influence of peer association per se may lessen with advances in age, and yet peers indirectly influence drug use through excuses. Drug use also is influenced by and influences carrying a gun and selling drugs. These reciprocal relationships are the result of the dangerous lifestyle involved in use of illicit substances and the amount of cash that can be made in selling these substances to purchase drugs for one's own use (Baron & Hartnagel, 1998; Walters, 1994).

As hypothesized, secure attachments to parents or caregivers are inversely related to associations with peers who are engaged in unlawful behavior, whereas abuse by adults is positively related to these associations. These findings lend support to the theories that relationships between children and their caregivers have long-lasting effects on outcomes like drug use (Bartol & Bartol, 1998). Also, beliefs in the moral validity of societal laws and norms, instilled by caregivers and others from infancy, have a reciprocal relationship with peer association. The human development literature and criminological studies indicate that peers often assume greater influence than parents or other adults in identity formation and beliefs of young persons (Feldman & Elliott, 1990; Thornberry, 1997). Societal beliefs instilled early in life often are undermined by contrary beliefs presented by peers who engaged in illicit acts. As observed by Agnew (1995), researchers need to distinguish between unconditional alternative beliefs and conditional excuses in conceptualizing a theoretical model of unlawful behavior.

Of particular interest in the present study is the relevance of religiosity to drug use among young persons entering boot camp. As hypothesized, the findings indicate that religiosity, like secular beliefs, has a negative reciprocal relationship to association with peers who engage in unlawful behavior. Succinctly stated, high religiosity is related to less of these peer associations, and more of these associations is related to lower religiosity. Association with peers who engage in unlawful behavior, in turn, is related to increased drug use through use of excuses for illicit acts. Hence, this study indicates that religiosity is a major influence leading to use of drugs, albeit an indirect influence. A direct relationship between religiosity and drug use is not hypothesized based on the assumption that during this stage of the life span religiosity, for youths who tend to experiment enough with drugs to enter a correctional system for adults, is a precursor to other more direct influences. However, this does not mean, as is often stated in the literature, that religiosity has a spurious relationship to unlawful behavior or that it is superfluous when other factors are considered (see review, Evans et al., 1995). Instead, religiosity would seem to be one of the key factors that influences peer associations which do lead to unlawful behavior such as drug use. In other words, religiosity, beliefs, attachment to caregivers, and abuse are factors that help explain why some youths differentially associate with peers who are involved in illicit acts.

IMPLICATIONS OF THE PRESENT STUDY

Keeping in mind the limitations of the study, the findings offer support to the underlying assumption of the investigation that religiosity is a significant factor in the processes leading to illicit drug use among first-admissions to the correctional system for adults. This study does not augur well for the prevalent arguments that religiosity is relevant only to illicit acts like underage drinking where there are ambiguous societal values, or only as long as the major predictors are not considered. Use of the drugs studied is not typically included in the argument about ambiguity of societal values, and the factors analyzed are considered among the strongest predictors of drug use (Akers, 1992; Walters, 1994). A more cogent argument would seem to be that more conceptualization and research attention needs to be given to how religiosity influences the system of interrelated factors leading to unlawful behavior such as use of drugs. The lack of theoretical attention to religiosity in the criminological literature would appear to result from several inconsistencies in findings (see reviews, Burkett, 1993; Evans et al., 1995), as well as some ideological biases. Illustratively, Schur (1969: 85-86) argues that organized religion may "be held partly responsible for the magnitude of the American crime problem through its frequent support for translating standards of private morality into criminal laws." More generally, the ideological bias seems to be represented in the common use of church attendance as an indicator of religiosity. Gorsuch (1988) has shown that these single-item measures do not fully measure the complex domain of religiosity. Church attendance is only one aspect of religiosity and is not a good indicator of commitment to religious practices which are more likely relevant to unlawful behavior. There seems to be an ideological bias that attendance represents commitment to religion despite evidence that people attend church for many reasons other than commitment such as familial pressure or fear of eternal damnation (Kirkpatrick & Shaver, 1990; Tittle & Welch, 1983).

Aside from the limitations in conceptualization of explanatory models of drug use presented by the lack of attention to religiosity, religion is useful in intervention. Indeed, meta-analyses (e.g., Harland, 1996; Izzo & Ross, 1990) have begun to identify essential components that differentiate effective and ineffective programs. Among the most important components is the conceptual framework out of which the program is developed, and the most effective programs are based on interpersonal identity, cognitions or beliefs, and on peer associations (Gendreau, 1996; Izzo & Ross, 1990; Sherman et al., 1997).

MacKenzie and Shaw (1990) hypothesize, that, in fact, the stress and disorientation of the initial stages of boot camp may actually provide a window of opportunity to make substantial attitudinal and behavioral changes because of the heightened feelings of vulnerability and insecurity induced by an unfamiliar environment controlled by intimidating drill instructors and unrelenting military regimens. The two essential aspects of identity development for Marcia (1980) include crisis, an intense period of stress requiring significant alteration in thinking in a relatively short period of time, and finding meaning in life. The high stress induced by entry into a boot camp may constitute the type of crisis during which new thinking about life is precipitated. Insightful professionals and staff have the opportunity to raise questions that cause young adults to reevaluate their beliefs and excuses. The boot experience, often referred to as "shock incarceration," may present a unique crisis and opportunity for adolescents and young adults to develop attachments that encourage positive identities, a change in beliefs, and less peer associations that lead to illegal behavior (MacKenzie, Shaw, & Gowdy, 1993). For some persons, religion can offer a sense of identity and attachment to other believers and to God, and a set of beliefs that give meaning to life. Religion can provide a sense of security and of control over natural impulses through divine providence (Kirkpatrick, 1997; Stark & Bainbridge, 1997). Religion also consists of a system of beliefs about why people should exercise control over natural urges such as drug use (Worthington, 1993).

NOTES

1. The authors have conducted several research projects at this boot camp for several years. The conceptualization also relies on extensive discussions with professionals working in this boot camp for many years.

2. The authors have analyzed statewide data in Arkansas on differential processing of racial groups. These analyses are to be reported in future publications.These hypothesized relationships regarding race and age are based on over 1000 psychosocial histories that have been taken by the same psychologist since the only boot camp for adults was opened in Arkansas ten years ago (Toombs, Benda, & Corwyn, 1997).

3. The study was conducted on Sunday afternoons when there is a more relaxed day off from the military routine and questions were read by the psychologist who sees inmates for counseling and runs groups on drug education.

4. The socidemographic characteristics observed at this boot camp are very similar to those reported in the literature for other boot camps (see review, Cronin, 1994).

REFERENCES

Agnew, R. (1995). Testing the leading crime theories: An alternative strategy focusing on motivational processes. *Journal of Research in Crime and Delinquency, 32,* 363-99.

Akers, R. L. (1992). *Drugs, alcohol and society: Social structure, process and policy.* Belmont, CA: Wadsworth.

Akers, R. L. (1997). *Criminological theories: Introduction and evaluation* (2nd ed.). Los Angeles, CA: Rosbury.

Andrews, D. A., & Bonta, J. (1994). *The psychology of criminal conduct.* Cincinnati, OH: Anderson.

Barnes, H., & Teeters, N. K. (1951). *New horizons in criminology.* Englewood Cliffs, NJ: Prentice-Hall.

Baron, S. W., & Hartnagel, T. F. (1998). Street youth and criminal violence. *Journal of Research in Crime and Delinquency, 35,* 166-192.

Bartol, C. R., & Bartol, A. M. (1998). *Delinquency and justice: A psychosocial approach* (2nd ed.). Upper Saddle River, NJ: Prentice-Hall.

Baumer, E. (1994). Poverty, crack, and crime: A cross-city analysis. *Journal of Research in Crime and Delinquency, 31,* 311-327.

Benda, B. B. (1995). The effect of religion on adolescent delinquency revisited. *Journal of Research in Crime and Delinquency, 32,* 446-466.

Benda, B. B. (1997). An examination of a reciprocal relationship between religiosity and different forms of delinquency within a theoretical model. *Journal of Research in Crime and Delinquency, 34,* 163-186.

Benda, B. B., & Corwyn, R. F. (1997a). Religion and delinquency: The relationship after considering family and peer influences, *Journal for the Scientific Study of Religion, 36,* 81-92.

Benda, B. B., & Corwyn, R. F. (1997b). A test of a model with reciprocal effects between religiosity and various forms of delinquency using 2-stage least squares regression. *Journal of Social Service Research, 22,* 27-52.

Benson, P. H. (1960). *Religion in contemporary culture.* New York: Harper and Row.

Boney-McCoy, S., & Finkelhor, D. (1995). Psychosocial sequelae of violence in the juvenile justice system. *Journal of Consulting and Clinical Psychology, 63,* 726-736.

Bonger, W. A. (1916). *Criminality and economic conditions.* Bloomington: Indiana University Press.

Brezina, T. (1998). Adolescent maltreatment and delinquency: The question of intervening processes. *Journal of Research in Crime and Delinquency, 35,* 71-99.

Burkett, S. R. (1993). Perceived parents' religiosity, friends' drinking, and hellfire: A panel study of adolescent drinking. *Review of Religious Research, 35,* 136-154.

Burkett, S. R., & Warren, B. O. (1987). Religiosity, peer association, and adolescent marijuana use: A panel study of underlying casual structures. *Criminology, 25,* 109-131.

Chadwick, B. A., & Top, B. L. (1993). Religiosity and delinquency among LDS adolescents. *Journal for the Scientific Study of Religion, 33,* 51-67.

Cochran, J. K. (1988). The effect of religiosity on secular and ascetic deviance. *Sociological Focus, 21,* 293-306.

Cochran, J. K., & Akers, R. L. (1989). Beyond hellfire: An examination of the variable effects of religiosity on adolescent marijuana and alcohol use. *Journal of Research in Crime and Delinquency, 26,* 198-225.

Cochran, J. K., Wood, P. K., & Arneklev, B. J. (1994). Is the religiosity-delinquency relationship spurious? A test of arousal and social control theories. *Journal of Research in Crime and Delinquency, 31,* 92-123.

Cronbach, L. J. (1951). Coefficient alpha and internal structure of tests. *Psychometrica, 16,* 297-334.

Cronin, R. C. (1994). *Boot camps for adult and juvenile offenders: Overview and update.* Washington, DC: Department of Justice.

Decker, S., & Rosenfeld, R. (1992). Intravenous drug use and the AIDS epidemic: Findings from a 20-city sample of arrestees. *Crime & Delinquency, 38,* 492-509.

Dembo, R., Williams, L., Wothke, W., Schmeidler, J., Getreu, A., Berry, E., & Wish, E. W. (1992). The generality of deviance: Replication of a structural model among high-risk youth. *Journal of Research in Crime and Delinquency, 29,* 200-216.

Durkheim, E. (1897/1951). *Suicide: A study in sociology.* Glencoe, IL: Free Press. (Originally published as *Le suicide* [1897]).

Elliott, D. S., Huizinga, D., & Ageton, S. S. (1985). *Explaining delinquency and drug use.* Beverly Hills, CA: Sage.

Elliott, D. S., Huizinga, D., & Menard, D. (1989). *Multiple problem youth: Delinquency, substance use and mental health problems.* New York: Springer-Verlag.

Ellis, H. (1910). *The criminal.* New York: Walter Scott.

Evans, D. T., Cullen, F. T., Dunaway, R. G., & Burton, V. S. (1995). Religion and crime reexamined: The impact of religion, secular controls, and social ecology on adult criminality. *Criminology, 33,* 195-217.

Feldman, S. S., & Elliott, G. R. (Eds.) (1990). *At the threshold: The developing adolescent.* Cambridge, MA: Harvard University Press.

Finkelhor, D., & Dziuba-Leatherman, J. (1994). Victimization of children. *American Psychologist, 49,* 183-193.

Gendreau, P. (1996). Offender rehabilitation: What we know and what needs to be done. *Criminal Justice and Behavior, 23,* 144-161.

Gfroerer, J. (1996). Preliminary estimates from the 1995 National Household Survey on Drug Abuse (SAMHSA Publication No. 18). Rockville, MD: Substance Abuse and Mental Health Services Administration, Office of Applied Statistics.

Harland, A. T. (Ed.) (1996). *Choosing correctional options that work.* Thousand Oaks, CA: Sage.

Hirschi, T. (1969). *Causes of delinquency.* Berkeley: University of California Press.

Hirschi, T. (1979). Separate and unequal is better. *Journal of Research in Crime and Delinquency, 16,* 34-37.

Hirschi, T., & Stark, R. (1969). Hellfire and delinquency. *Social Problems, 17,* 202-213.

Intriligator, M. D. (1978). *Econometric models, techniques and applications.* Englewood Cliffs, NJ: Prentice-Hall.

Izzo, R. L., & Ross, R. R. (1990). Meta-analysis of rehabilitation program for juvenile delinquents. *Crime & Delinquency, 17,* 134-142.

Jang, S. J., & Smith, C. A. (1997). A test of reciprocal causal relationships among parental supervision, affective ties, and delinquency. *Journal of Research in Crime and Delinquency, 34,* 307-336.

Johnston, L. D., O'Malley, P. M., & Bachman, J. G. (1996). National survey results on drug use from the Monitoring the Future Study, 1975-1994. Vol. 1. Rockville, MD: National Institute on Drug Abuse.

Kirkpatrick, L. A. (1997). A longitudinal study of changes in religious belief and behavior as a function of individual differences in adult attachment style. *Journal for the Scientific Study of Religion, 36*, 207-212.

Kirkpatrick, L., & Shaver, P. R. (1990). Attachment theory and religion: Childhood attachments, religious beliefs, and conversion. *Journal for the Scientific Study of Religion, 29*, 315-334.

Kmenta, J. (1971). *Elements of econometrics*. New York: Macmillan.

Kornhauser, R. R. (1978). *Social sources of delinquency: An appraisal of analytic models*. Chicago: University of Chicago Press.

Leavitt, F. (1995). *Drugs & behavior* (3rd ed.). Thousand Oaks, CA: Sage

Lombroso, C. (1911). *Crime, its causes and remedies*. Boston: Little Brown.

Lurigio, A. J., & Davis, R. C. (Eds.) (1992). Drugs and crime [Special Issue]. *Crime & Delinquency, 38*.

MacKenzie, D. L., & Shaw, J. W. (1990). Inmate adjustment and change during shock incarceration: The impact of correctional boot camp programs. *Justice Quarterly, 7*, 125-150.

MacKenzie, D. L., Shaw, J. W., & Gowdy, V. B. (1993). An evaluation of shock incarceration in Louisiana. National Institute of Justice Research in Brief (NCJ 140567), U. S. Department of Justice.

Marcia, J. E. (1980). Identity in adolescence. In J. Adelson (Ed.), *Handbook of adolescent psychology* (pp. 159-177). New York: Wiley.

Marcos, A. C., & Bahr, S. J. (1988). Control theory and adolescent drug use. *Youth & Society, 19*, 395-425.

Matsueda, R. L. (1989). The dynamics of moral beliefs and minor deviance. *Social Forces, 68*, 428-457.

Merton, R. K. (1957). *Social theory and social structure* (rev. ed.). Glencoe, IL: Free Press.

Nye, F. I. (1958). *Family relationships and delinquent behavior*. New York: Wiley.

Patterson, G. R., & Dishion, T. J. (1985). Contribution of families and peers to delinquency. *Criminology, 23*, 63-79.

Pope, C., & Clear, T. (Eds.) (1994). Race and punishment [Special Issue]. *Journal of Research in Crime and Delinquency, 31*.

President's Commission of Law Enforcement and Administration of Justice (1967). Task Force Report: Corrections. Washington, DC: U. S. Government Printing Office.

Schur, Edwin M. (1969). *Our criminal society*. Englewood Cliffs, NJ: Prentice Hall.

Sherman, L. W., Gottfredson, D. C., MacKenzie, D., Eck, J., Reuter, P., & Bushway, S. (1997). *Preventing crime: What works, what doesn't, what's promising*. Washington, DC: U. S. Department of Justice, Office of Justice Programs.

Simons, R. L., Whitbeck, L. B., Conger, R. D., & Conger, K. (1991). Parenting factors, social skills, and value commitment as precursors to school failure, involvement with deviant peers, and delinquent behavior. *Journal of Youth and Adolescence, 20*, 645-663.

Stark, R., & Bainbridge, S. (1997). *Religion, deviance & social control*. New York: Routledge.

Stark, R., Kent, L., & Doyle, D. P. (1982). Religion and delinquency: The ecology of a "lost" relationship. *Journal of Research in Crime and Delinquency, 19*, 4-24.

Steiner, J. F. (1924). *Religion and roguery*. New York: Truth Seekers.

Stimmel, B. (1993). *The facts about drug use*. New York: The Haworth Medical Press.

Sutherland, E. H., & Cressey, D. R. (1978). *Principles of criminology* (10th ed.). Chicago: J. B. Lippincott.

Sykes, G., & Matza, D. (1957). Techniques of neutralization: A theory of delinquency. *American Sociological Review, 22*, 664-670.

Thornberry, T. P. (1987). Toward an interactional theory of delinquency. *Criminology, 25*, 863-869.

Thornberry, T. P. (1989). Reflections on the advantages and disadvantages of theoretical integration. In S. F. Messner, M. D. Krohn, & A. E. Liska (Eds.), *Theoretical integration in the study of deviance and crime* (pp. 31-45). Albany: State University of New York Press.

Thornberry, T. P. (Ed.) (1997). *Advances in criminological theory: Developmental theories of crime and delinquency*. New Brunswick, NJ: Transaction Books.

Thornberry, T. P., Lizotte, A. J., Krohn, M. D., Farnworth, M., & Jang, S. J. (1994). Delinquent peers, beliefs, and delinquent behavior: A longitudinal test of interaction theory. *Criminology, 32*, 47-84.

Tittle, C. R., & Welch, M. R. (1983). Religiosity and deviance: Toward a contingency theory of constraining effects. *Social Forces, 61*, 653-682.

Toombs, N. J., Benda, B. B., & Corwyn, R. F. (1997). Recidivism among Arkansas boot camp graduates after 12 months. *Journal of Offender Rehabilitation, 26*, 3/4, 141-160.

Wallace, L. E., & Bachman, E. (1991). Explaining racial/ethnic differences in adolescent drug use: The impact of background and lifestyle. *Social Problems, 38*, 333-357.

Walters, G. D. (1994). *Drugs and crime in lifestyle perspective*. Thousand Oaks, CA: Sage.

Weber, M. (1958). *The protestant ethic and the spirit of capitalism*. New York: Scribner (Originally published in [1905]).

Woodroof, J. T. (1985). Premarital sexual behavior and religious adolescents. *Journal for the Scientific Study of Religion, 24*, 343-366.

Worthington, E. L. Jr. (Ed.) (1993). *Psychotherapy and religious values*. Grand Rapids, MI: Baker.

Zhang, S. X. (1998). In search of hopeful glimpses: A critique of research strategies in current boot camp evaluation. *Crime & Delinquency, 44*, 314-334.

AUTHORS' NOTES

Dr. Brent Benda is a professor, School of Social Work, University of Arkansas at Little Rock, Little Rock, Arkansas, and has published articles on religiosity and crime and drug use in *Journal of Research in Crime and Delinquency, Journal for the Scientific Study of Religion, Journal of Adolescence, Social Work Research*, and *Journal of Social Service Research*.

At the time of this study, Dr. Nancy Toombs served as a psychologist at the boot camp studied. She now teaches psychology at the University of Arkansas at Little Rock and is also in private practice.

Address correspondence to Dr. Brent Benda, School of Social Work, University of Arkansas at Little Rock, Little Rock, AR 72204.

Religion, the Community, and the Rehabilitation of Criminal Offenders. Pp. 185-198.

Denominational Differences in Self-Reported Delinquency

LEE ELLIS

Minot State University

SUMMARY How much does religion help to preserve societal order, especially in terms of preventing crime and delinquency? If religion promotes law-abiding behavior, it is reasonable to ask whether some denominations are more effective in doing so than others. To explore this question, the present study compared the self-reported delinquency of more than 11,000 United States and Canadian college students belonging to 18 different religious groups (henceforth called *denominations*). With analyses performed separately for males and females, only about half of the offense categories yielded significant denominational differences. Particularly surprising was a failure to find any significant denominational differences for either gender regarding violent offenses. The most definitive differences were found with respect to illegal drug use, with atheists/agnostics reporting the highest rates. Otherwise, some property offense categories exhibited significant differences, with female atheists/agnostics being particularly prone to report the highest offending rates. In no case did those who claimed to have no religious preference report high offending rates to significant degrees. The only religious denomination whose members reported the lowest offending rates in more than one offense category was Greek Orthodox. *[Article copies available for a fee from The Haworth Document Delivery Service: 1-800-HAWORTH. E-mail address: <getinfo@haworthpressinc.com> Website: <http://www.HaworthPress.com> © 2002 by The Haworth Press, Inc. All rights reserved.]*

KEYWORDS Religion, denomination, delinquency, crime

One of the most sensitive aspects of research into the relationship between religiosity and delinquency/criminality involves the possibility that offending rates differ according to religious denomination. Nonetheless, searching for denominational differences in offending rates could help to identify some of the social forces impinging on delinquent and criminal behavior, and might even lead to more effective prevention and treatment programs.

Since around the turn of the twentieth century, numerous studies have compared rates of delinquency and crime for various religious denominations. The results of these studies are summarized in Tables 1 and 2. Table 1 pertains to research based on official data, whereas Table 2 pertains to findings derived from self-reports. In both tables, the numbers assigned under each denomination indicates the denomination's rank in terms of any significant differences in offending, with "1" representing greatest involvement, "2" representing second greatest, etc.

OFFICIAL DELINQUENCY AND CRIME

As Table 1 indicates, nearly all studies of official delinquency and crime have been limited to western countries based on the three main religious groups–Jews, Catholics, and Protestants–with the latter often subdivided into two or more denominational categories. A typical design for the studies represented in Table 1 would involve comparing the religious preferences of a group of offenders (e.g., inmates) with that of the general population from which they came.

The results of these studies have consistently shown that Christians (Catholics and Protestants combined) are significantly more likely than Jews to be identified as offenders. These differences cannot be attributed to prejudice or discrimination, since all of the countries in which the studies were conducted were predominantly Christian. Even studies in Germany in years leading to the Second World War indicated that Jews exhibited significantly lower rates of offending than Christians.

Table 1 identifies seven studies which compared official crime/delinquency rates of Catholics and Protestants, all of which reported Catholics exhibiting significantly higher rates (Bonger 1936; Hersch 1936; Kvaraceus 1944a; Lunden 1942; Gillin 1946; von Hentig 1948b; Glueck & Glueck 1950). One additional study compared Catholic rates with rates for Lutherans, finding higher official crime rates for Catholics (Aschaffenburg 1933).

Table 1: Religious Affiliation and Criminal Behavior as Gauged from Studies Based on Official Data

Place	Offense Type	Rank	Group	Source
Nigeria	Delinquency	1	Christian	
		2	Muslim	Asuni, 1963
Austria	General, unspecified	1	Christian	
		2	Jewish	Herz, 1908
Germany	General, unspecified	1	Christian	
		2	Jewish	Von Mayr, 1917; Exter, 1939-67
	General, unspecified	1	Catholic	
		2	Lutheran	
		3	Jewish	Aschaffenburg, 1933-38
Hungary	General, unspecified	1	Christian	
		2	Jewish	Thon, 1907
Netherlands	General, unspecified	1	Catholic	
		2	Protestant	
		3	None	
		4	Jewish	Bonger, 1936
Poland	Delinquency	1	Christian	
		2	Jewish	Hersch, 1937, 1945
Eastern Europe		1	Catholic	
		2	Protestant	
		3	Jewish	Hersch, 1936
United States	Delinquency	1	Catholic	
		2	Protestant	
		3	Jewish	Glueck & Glueck, 1950
	General, unspecified	1	"Other"	
		2	Jewish	Levinger, 1940
	General, unspecified	1	Protestant	
		2	Jewish	Linfield, 1940
California	Delinquency	1	"Other"	
		2	Jewish	Goldberg, 1950
Massachusetts	General, unspecified	1	Catholic	
		2	Protestant	Von Hentig, 1948b
New Jersey	Delinquency	1	Catholic	
		2	Protestant	
		3	Jewish	Kvaraceus, 1944a
	General, unspecified	1	Christian	
		2	Jewish	Kvaraceus, 1945
New York	Delinquency	1	"Other"	
		2	Jewish	Maller, 1932; Peck et al., 1955; Robinson, 1958
Pennsylvania	General, unspecified	1	Catholic	
		2	Protestant	
		3	Jewish	
		4	None	Lunden, 1941
Wisconsin	General, unspecified	1	Catholic	
		2	Protestant	
		3	Jewish	
		4	None	Gillin, 1946

□ **Table 2: Religious Affiliation and Criminal Behavior as Gauged from Studies Based on Self-Report Data**

Place	Offense Type	Rank	Group	Source
England	Overall	1	Christian	
		2	Jewish	Belson et al., 1975
Canada	Illegal drug use	1	None*	
		1	Jewish*	
		2	Christian	Smart et al., 1970
	Illegal drug use	1	Protestant	
		2	Catholic	Fejer, 1971
United States	Illegal drug use	1	"Other"	
		2	Jewish	Milman & Su, 1973
	Illegal drug use	1	Catholic*	
		1	Protestant*	
		1	"Other"*	Sarvela & McClendon, 1988
	Overall, by whites	1	None	
		2	Muslim	
		3	Catholic	
		4	Baptist	
		5	Conservative Protestant	
		6	Liberal Protestant	
		7	Jewish	
	Overall, by Blacks	1	Catholic	
		2	None	
		3	Baptist	
		4	Conservative Protestant	
		5	Liberal Protestant	
		6	Muslim	Rhodes & Reiss, 1970
Arizona	Overall	1	Catholic	
		2	Protestant	
		3	Mormon	Jensen & Erickson, 1979
Wisconsin	Overall	1	Conservative Protestant	
		2	Liberal Protestant	Free, 1994

* Indicates no difference in rank *or* a tie in absolute data.

If one tries to go beyond the Jewish-Christian and Catholic-Protestant comparisons, generalizations become more tenuous. So far, three studies have compared persons with no religious preference with those who stated they were Christian. These studies report lower official crime rates among those with no religious preference (Bonger 1936; Lunden 1942; Gillin 1946), although the two studies that included data on Jews found their crimes to be lower than those with no religious affiliation. To date, the only study to examine official crime rates among Muslims was conducted in Nigeria (Asuni 1963:188). It found Muslim crime rates to be significantly lower than those for Christians.

SELF-REPORTED DELINQUENCY AND CRIME

In the 1970s, studies began to be published linking religiosity with self-reported offending. These studies generally measure far less serious types of offending than do official data. Studies have indicated that the most persistent and serious offenders underreport offending to a greater degree than do those least involved (Farrington 1982:194; Mieczkowski et al. 1993; Cervenka et al. 1996:206). Furthermore, nearly all self-report studies of offending behavior are conducted among college or high school students, populations where serious and persistent offenders are substantially underrepresented. Despite these drawbacks to self-reported offending, they still provide much more complete information about delinquent/criminal behavior than do official data, especially regarding drug offenses.

Table 2 makes a distinction between two types of self-reports. One type is specific to drug offending, such as the use of marijuana or other illegal substances. The other type of self-report studies is more global; it includes illegal drug use, but also covers assaults, thefts, vandalism, as well as age-contingent status offenses (such as underage drinking and truancy).

The picture provided by Table 2 is less clear than in the case of Table 1. Regarding Jewish-Christian comparisons, four studies were located. One of the two studies pertaining strictly to illegal drug use found Christians more involved than Jews (Milman & Su 1973), while the other study found the opposite (Smart et al. 1970). The two remaining studies, which included the entire spectrum of criminal/delinquent offenses, found Christians self-reporting higher offending rates than Jews (Belson et al. 1975; Rhodes & Reiss 1970). Turning to Catholic-Protestant comparisons, one study found higher rates of overall offending among Catholics (Jensen & Erickson 1979:165), while another study found lower rates of drug offenses among Catholics (Fejer 1971). A third study found no significant difference in drug offending (Sarvela & McClendon 1988), and a fourth found quite different denominational patterns for overall offending depending on the race of the subjects (Rhodes & Reiss 1970). At the present time, one would be hard pressed to generalize about the nature of any denominational differences in self-reported offending, despite the consistent differences that have appeared in the official data.

THE PRESENT STUDY

The purpose of the present study was to look for denominational differences in self-reported offending using an unusually large data set from United States and Canadian college students. Ultimately, these and similar studies could not only improve social science understanding of the causes of delinquency, but also lead to improved preventive measures.

Methods

This study was based on a convenience sample of 3,978 male and 7,822 female students attending 22 colleges/universities throughout the United States and Canada between 1988 through 1997. In alphabetical order, the colleges and universities were as follows: Arizona State University, Boise State University (Idaho), Bowling Green State University (Ohio), California State University at San Francisco, Christopher Newport College (Virginia), Florida Atlantic University, Iowa State University, McNeese State University (Louisiana), Minot State University (North Dakota), Riverside City College (California), St. John's University (Minnesota), University of British Columbia, University of Colorado at Colorado Springs, University of Delaware, University of Lethbridge (Alberta, Canada), University of Louisville (Tennessee), University of Missouri at Columbia, University of Richmond (Virginia), University of Rio Grande (Ohio), University of South Dakota, University of Southern Maine, and Western Illinois University.

The average age for the males was 23.0 (SD = 6.1) and the average for the females was 22.3 (SD = 5.6). Regarding marital status, 80.4% of the males and 79.1% of the females were single, while 10.9% of the males and 13.7% of the females were married. The remaining subjects were either divorced (1.6% of the males and 3.9% of the females) or widowed (0.1% of the males and 0.2% of the females) or failed to respond to this particular question (6.8% of the males and 2.7% of the females).

Denominations/Religious Groupings

Subjects responded to the question about "religious preference" by writing in the names of 71 different religious denominations or other preferences. These responses were consolidated into 18 categories using the following rules: If more than 50 subjects (males and females combined) identified themselves as members of a specific religion, these individuals were grouped separately. If fewer than 50 subjects identified themselves as members of some religious group, they were put into one of the following four groups: other conservative Christian, other liberal Christian, other non-Christian, or unknown.

Following a classification system developed by Smith (1990), the denominations primarily comprising Other Conservative Christian were Evangelical, Seventh Day Adventist, Mennonite, Dutch Reform, Alliance, and Unity. Other Liberal Christian denominations consisted largely of Congregationalist, Nondenominational, Quaker. Other Non-Christians were mainly comprised of Unitarian, Muslim, Buddhist, Hindu, and Wicca. Four responses could not be coded due to the use of unrecognizable abbreviations.

One non-denominational religiosity measure was also examined with regard to juvenile offending. It involved responses to a question regarding self-assessed "religiousness" on a 100-point scale, with "100" meaning extremely religious, and "1" meaning the opposite. The mean response of males was 48.95 (SD = 28.54) and for females, 54.41 (SD = 28.14).

Self-Reported Delinquency

Subjects were presented with an extensive list of offenses, and asked to report the number of times they recalled committing one or more of the offenses within each of eight categories during three periods in their lives: between ages 10 and 15, between ages 16 and 18, and after age 19 (copies of the questionnaire items are available upon request). In the present analysis, coverage was limited to the first two of these age categories, which closely parallels the age range covered by nearly all juvenile delinquency statutes. Offenses were consolidated into the following eight categories:

1. Serious violence–assaulting others to the point of their requiring medical treatment;
2. Less serious violence–assaulting others short of their requiring medical treatment;
3. Vehicle theft–stealing a motor vehicle;
4. Thefts–stealing other than motor vehicles;

5. Vandalism–damaging or destroying other people's property;
6. Illegal entry–burglarizing a residence or business;
7. Illegal drugs–using illegal drugs (not including under-age drinking);
8. Illegal commerce–selling illegal drugs or stolen property, or writing bad checks.

ANALYSIS AND RESULTS

Offending rates for all denominations were compared separately for males and females using ANOVA. Means in the present context can be sometimes misleading because self-reported offense frequencies were usually skewed to the upper values. Nevertheless, because of the large samples involved in this study, denominational variations in the means can still be a useful basis of comparison.

Gender Differences and Denominational Preferences

It is well established that males are more involved in serious and persistent offending than females (reviewed by Ellis & Walsh 2000:102). Entirely consistent with this evidence, Table 3 shows gender differences in self-reported offending, with males being more than three times as likely as females to be involved in serious violent offenses (i.e.,

---

□ Table 3: Gender Differences in Self-Reported Offending

Type of Offense	N Males*	Mean	N Females*	Mean
Serious violence	3762	0.31	7666	0.09
Less serious violence	3767	0.72	7659	0.53
Vehicle theft	3766	0.11	7663	0.05
Theft	3752	0.56	7647	0.41
Vandalism	3762	0.47	7653	0.23
Illegal entry	3760	0.33	7660	0.15
Illegal drugs	3096	0.49	6201	0.40
Illegal commerce	2920	0.19	5944	0.11

* In each case, only valid responses are enumerated.

injuring another person to the point of the victim requiring medical attention). For most of the property offenses, males were about twice as likely to be involved. Only in the case of drug offenses were the gender differences in offending modest (i.e., 49% for males vs. 40% for females).

Table 4 reflects gender differences in denominational affiliation. The main difference in this regard is that whereas 2.4% of males identified themselves as atheists/agnostics, only 1.0% of females did so. Similarly, 6.9% of males said they had no religious preference, compared to 4.7% of females. These differences are consistent with other studies suggesting that males are less religious than females (e.g., Nelson & Potvin 1981; de Vaus & McAllister 1987).

Gender-Specific Denominational Differences in Offending

Motor Vehicle Theft. In the case of motor vehicle theft, no significant denominational differences were found for males (F = 1.040, p = .410).

□ **Table 4: Denominational Affiliations of Subjects Arrayed by Gender**

Affiliation	N Males	%	N Females	%
No response	529	13.3	623	8.0
Atheist/agnostic	96	2.4	82	1.0
Baptist	240	6.0	631	8.1
Catholic	1239	31.1	2679	34.2
Church of Christ	50	1.4	113	1.4
Eastern Orthodox	15	0.4	41	0.5
Episcopalian/Anglican	60	0.5	162	2.1
Jewish	62	1.6	151	1.9
Lutheran	565	14.2	1253	16.0
Methodist	213	5.4	530	6.8
Mormon	62	1.6	70	0.9
None/no preference	275	6.9	371	4.7
Other Conservative Christian	47	1.2	77	1.0
Other Liberal Christian	53	1.3	137	1.8
Other Non-Christian	75	1.9	118	1.5
Pentecostal	63	1.6	132	1.7
Presbyterian	92	2.3	200	2.6
Protestant, unspecified	243	6.1	453	5.8
Total	3979	100.0	7823	100.0

However, for females, significant differences were found (F = 1.867, p = .019), with Other Non-Christians exhibiting the highest rates and several denominational categories exhibiting virtually zero rates.

Theft (Other than Motor Vehicle Theft). A wide assortment of thefts other than those of motor vehicles comprised this widely reported type of offending. ANOVA revealed significant denominational differences for both genders. For males, Atheists/Agnostics and Mormons were both unusually high in thefts, while Jews, Other Liberal Christians, and Church of Christ members were unusually low (F = 2.252, p = .003). Regarding females, Atheists/Agnostics had the highest rate, while Eastern Orthodox and Other Liberal Christians had the lowest rates (F = 1.686, p = .042).

Vandalism. Neither males nor females exhibited significant denominational differences in their involvement in vandalism. For males, the F score was .925 (p = .539), and for females the F score was .975 (p = 482).

Illegal Entry. Data pertaining to burglarizing homes or buildings revealed no significant denominational differences as far as males were concerned (F = .556, p = 9.18). For females, however, significant denominational differences were found (F = 1.738, p = .034), with the highest rates reported by Mormons and Unspecified Protestants, and the lowest rates by Eastern Orthodox and Pentecostals.

Illegal Drug Use. Very significant denominational differences were found for both males (F = 3.422, p = 000) and females (F = 5.122, p = 000) in the case of illegal drug use. For males, the highest rate of illegal drug use was reported by Other Liberal Christians and the lowest rate was by Eastern Orthodox. In the case of females, illegal drug use was most prevalent among Atheists/Agnostics and lowest among members of the Church of Christ.

Illegal Commerce. Illegal commerce pertains largely to the sale of illegal drugs and stolen property. Among males, the highest self-reported rates were exhibited by Other Liberal Christians, and the lowest by Eastern Orthodox, with the results being statistically significant (F = 1.695, p = .045). For females, Atheists/Agnostics reported engaging in the highest rates of illegal commerce, while Eastern Orthodox had the lowest rates. The difference between these two groups was very significant (F = 2.440, p = .001).

Self-Rated Religiosity

In light of the surprising nature of the findings, a separate analysis based on the responses to a 100-point scale of overall self-perceived religiosity was performed. Responses to this question were then individually correlated with involvement in each of the eight offense categories for males and females (as reported in Table 5).

Two of the coefficients were significant for males, while four were significant for females. The correlations suggest that among males, illegal drug use and illegal commerce were less likely for those who were most religious. Among females, strong religiosity was associated with low involvement in illegal drug use, illegal commerce, theft, and vandalism. For neither gender was evidence found to suggest that high religiosity inhibited violent offending. In fact, three of the four correlation coefficients were positive rather than negative. The general directions in patterns on overall religiosity and offending shown in Table 5 are in substantial agreement with the denominational differences in terms of the types of offenses that seem to be inhibited by religiosity: Religiosity may at least marginally inhibit drug use and sale among males and these offenses plus property offenses among females.

CONCLUSIONS

Using a large sample of North American college students, this study explored variations in self-reported juvenile delinquency according to denominational affiliation. All analyses of denominational differences were performed separately for males and females.

☐ **Table 5: Correlations Between Self-Rated Religiosity and Eight Categories of Delinquency Among 11,802 Subjects**

Composite Offense Category	Males	Females
Serious violence	0.027	0.018
Less serious violence	0.025	0.011
Vehicle theft	−0.014	0.001
Theft	−0.030	*−0.050
Vandalism	0.009	*−0.024
Illegal entry	0.010	−0.012
Illegal drug use	**−0.096	**−0.126
Illegal commerce	*−0.042	*−.050

*p = .05. ** p = .01

The analysis suggests that there are no general denominational differences in self-reported offending. The closest to an exception involved respondents identifying themselves as being atheists/agnostics and Eastern Orthodox. Atheists/agnostics reported especially high offending rates in the case of females for thefts and for illegal drug use. Regarding the Eastern Orthodox, the lowest offending rates were found for four gender/offending categories: female illegal entry, male illegal drugs, and both male and female illegal commerce. No other denominational grouping exhibited either the highest or the lowest offending rates (where differences were statistically significant) in more than one category. Particularly surprising was the finding that in no case were those professing to have no religious preferences unusually high in offending for any specific category.

These findings call into question the view that commitment to a particular set of religious teachings inhibits most forms of crime and delinquency, especially regarding violent offending. The main exception that was established in the present study was in the case of illegal drug use and sale, and possibly some forms of property offenses. For these offenses, an inhibiting effect of religious commitment was found, especially in the case of females, albeit of small absolute magnitude. Additional research on this topic is obviously in order.

REFERENCES

Aschaffenburg, G. (1933). *Das Verbrechen und seine Bekampfung.* Heidelberg: Carl Wingers Universitatstiuchhandlung.

Asuni, T. (1963). Preliminary study of juvenile delinquency in western Nigeria. *Proceedings of the 12th International Course in Criminology, 1,* 186-194.

Belson, H. A. (1975). *Juvenile theft: The causal factors.* New York: Harper and Row.

Bonger, W. A. (1936). *An introduction to criminology.* London: Methuen.

Cervenka, K. A., Dembo, R., & Brown, H. C. (1996). A family empowerment intervention for families of juvenile offenders. *Aggression and Violent Behavior, 1,* 205-216.

de Vaus, D., & McAllister, I. (1987). Gender differences in religion: A test of the structural location theory. *American Sociological Review, 52,* 472-481.

Ellis, L., & Walsh, A. (2000). *Criminology: A global perspective.* Boston: Allyn & Bacon.

Ellis, L., & McDonald, J. N. (2001). Crime, delinquency, and social status: A reconsideration. *Journal of Offender Rehabilitation, 32,* 23-52.

Exner, F. (1939). *Kriminalbiologie in ihren grundzugen.* Hamburg, Germany: Hanseatische Verlagsanstalt.

Farrington, D. P. (1982). Longitudinal analyses of criminal violence. In M. E. Wolfgang & N. A. Weiner (Eds.), *Criminal violence*. Beverly Hills, CA: Sage.

Fejer, D. (1971). *Drug use among high school students in North Bay, Ontario*. Toronto, ON: Addiction Research Foundation.

Forthun, L. F., Bell, N. J., Peek, C. W., & Sun, S. W. (1999). Religiosity, sensation seeking, and alcohol/drug use in denominational and gender contexts. *Journal of Drug Issues, 29*, 75-90.

Free, M. D., Jr. (1994). Religiosity, religious conservatism, bonds to school, and juvenile delinquency among three categories of drug users. *Deviant Behavior: An Interdisciplinary Journal, 15*, 151-170.

Gillin, J. L. (1946). *The Wisconsin prisoner*. Madison, WI: University of Wisconsin Press.

Glueck, S., & Glueck, E. (1950). *Unraveling juvenile delinquency*. Cambridge, MA: Harvard University Press.

Goldberg, N. (1950). Jews in the police records of Los Angeles, 1933-1947. *Yivo Annual of Jewish Social Science, 5*, 266-291.

Hersch, L. (1936). Delinquency among Jews. *Journal of Criminal Law and Criminology, 27*, 515-516.

Hersch, L. (1937). Complementary data on Jewish delinquency in Poland. *Journal of Criminal Law and Criminology, 27*, 857-873.

Herz, F. O. (1908). *Verbrechen und verbrechertum in Oesterreich*. Tubingen: Mohr.

Jensen, G. F., & Erickson, M. L. (1979). The religious factor and delinquency: Another look at the hellfire hypothesis. In R. Wuthnow (Ed.), *The religious dimension* (pp. 157-177). New York: Academic Press.

Kvaraceus, W. C. (1944). Delinquent behavior and church attendance. *Sociology and Social Research, 28*, 284-289.

Kvaraceus, W. C. (1945). *Juvenile delinquency and the school*. New York: World Books.

Levinger, L. J. (1940). A note on Jewish prisoners in Ohio. *Jewish Social Studies, 2*, 209-212.

Linfield, H. S. (1940). Jewish inmates of the state prisons of the United States. *American Jewish Yearbook, 33*, 203-211.

Lunden, W. A. (1942). *Statistics on crime and criminals*. New York: Stevenson Foster.

Maller, J. B. (1932). Juvenile delinquency among the Jews in New York. *Social Forces, 10*, 542-549.

Mieczkowski, T. M., Launders, H. J., Newel, R., & Coletti, S. D. (1993). Testing hair for illicit drug use. *National Institute of Justice–Research in Brief, NCJ 138539* (January).

Milman, D. H., & Su, W. (1973). Patterns of illicit drug and alcohol use among secondary school students. *Journal of Pediatrics, 83*, 314-320.

Nelson, H. M., & Potvin, R. H. (1981). Gender and regional differences in the religiosity of Protestant adolescents. *Review of Religiosity Research, 22*, 285-288.

Peck, H. B., Harrower, M., Hariri, C., Beck, M. B., Maryjohn, J. B., & Roman, M. (1955). A new pattern for mental health services in a children's court: Round table 1954. *American Journal of Orthopsychiatry, 25*, 1-50.

Rhodes, A., & Reiss, A., Jr. (1970). The religious factor and delinquent behavior. *Journal of Research in Crime and Delinquency, 7,* 83-98.

Robinson, S. M. (1958). A study of delinquency among Jewish children in New York City. In M. Sklare (Ed.), *The Jews: Social patterns of an American group* (pp. 535-542). Glencoe, IL: Free Press.

Sarvela, P. D., & McClendon, E. J. (1988). Indicators of rural youth drug use. *Journal of Youth and Adolescence, 17,* 335-347.

Smart, R. G., Fejer, D., & White, W. J. (1970). *The extent of drug use in metropolitan Toronto Schools: A study of changes from 1968-1970.* Toronto: Addiction Research Foundation.

Smith, T. (1990). Classifying Protestant denominations. *Review of Religious Research, 31,* 225-245.

Thon, J. (1907). Kriminalitat der Christen und Juden in Ungarn im Jahre 1904. *Zeitschrift, 2,* 16-26.

von Hentig, H. (1948). *The criminal and his victim.* New Haven, CT: Yale University Press.

von Mayr, G. (1917). *Statisik und gesellschaftslehre.* Tubingen: Mohr.

AUTHOR'S NOTE

Lee Ellis (PhD, Florida State University) is professor of sociology at Minot State University. His research interests have centered around criminal behavior and social status. Most recently, he has co-authored an introductory text with Anthony Walsh, entitled *Criminology: A Global Perspective* (Allyn & Bacon, 2000). His previous books include *Crime in Biological, Social, and Moral Contexts* (Praeger, 1990) and *Social Status and Socioeconomic Inequality, Volumes I & II* (Praeger, 1993, 1994).

The author thanks Myrna Nelson, Robert Thompson, and Alan Widmayer for commenting on drafts of this article, and Christopher Ficek for assisting in the analysis.

Address correspondence to Dr. Lee Ellis, Division of Social Science, Minot State University, Minot, ND 58707 (E-mail: ellis@minotstateu.edu).

Religion, the Community, and the Rehabilitation of Criminal Offenders. Pp. 199-214.

Evaluating Religious Initiatives
in a Correctional Setting:
Do Inmates Speak?

ANDREW SKOTNICKI, O.CARM.

St. Patrick's Seminary, Menlo Park, California

SUMMARY Social scientific accounts of inmate behavior, generally, and inmate religious behavior, particularly, have, by and large, failed to account for the critical questions raised by philosophical hermeneutics and linguistics. This paper uses insights from key figures in each discipline as foci in investigating the methods criminologists employ in reporting what inmates say about the carcereal experience. These methods are mainly found to magnify the voice of the report writers to such a degree that often inmates themselves do not speak. *[Article copies available for a fee from The Haworth Document Delivery Service: 1-800-HAWORTH. E-mail address: <getinfo@haworthpressinc.com> Website: <http://www.HaworthPress.com> © 2002 by The Haworth Press, Inc. All rights reserved.]*

KEYWORDS Evaluation methodology, religion, inmates, hermeneutics, linguistics

Who is talking when social scientists and theoreticians present and analyze what inmates say in correctional institutions? Specifically, who is talking in reports on what inmates say in relation to their religious beliefs? The answers to these questions are critical since the analytical data derived from inmate speech often serves in the creation, maintenance, or termination of penal policy.

To speak for another is a task fraught with certain pitfalls. To report accurately what one has heard is one thing. In this regard, the methods used by criminologists in the collection of data are highly refined and safe-guarded by the standards imposed by the academic profession and the journals that convey the results of scholarly research. However, significant doubts arise as to how meaning is derived from what has been recorded.

The pitfalls that present themselves here are linguistic and hermeneutical. They involve not so much errors in reporting, as in interpretation; not so much in content, as in how the content is organized in a meaningful way; not so much in faithfully recording as in understanding. The result in such cases is that the meaning of what is spoken is often lost in the translation. Translation involves the need to take into account, and to harmonize, two symbolic worlds: that of the inmates, and that of those who report on the inmates. "We are all natives now," as Clifford Geertz (1971) reminds us. Social scientists are just as exotic as those they study. This insight, it seems to me, has been a difficult one to embrace as I scan the numerous journals given to the analysis of the correctional experience and what inmates have to say about it.

It is the contention of this essay that inmates themselves often do not speak to any significant degree due to a lack of attentiveness to translation, context, and meaning which has clouded many sociological reports. One is left wondering whose significative world shapes the words one is reading.

A related problem concerns the question of professional distance in the analysis of religion. Using the analogy of the game as employed by John Searle (1969) and Hans Georg Gadamer (1976), one must enter in some committed way into a community of faith in order to gain accurate insights into what transpires there. Much of the literature on religion and deviance reveals a caricature, or anecdotal understanding, of religious involvement and, as such, provides no real help in exploring this complex and potentially fruitful area of study.

The first section of this paper presents basic insights developed by some of the key figures in both linguistics and hermeneutics. The second section seeks to show the general weakness of the criminological literature in accounting for and accurately conveying what inmates are truly saying. The third section brings together the ideas of the first two sections to specifically critique the treatment of religion as it applies to the correctional setting.

CULTURE, LANGUAGE
AND THE CREATION OF BOUNDARIES

Gadamer (1976) suggests that our prejudices or ideologies define who we are (9). Much like Geertz (1983), and Karl Mannheim (1936) before him, Gadamer (1976) does not necessarily use "prejudice" in a pejorative way. He is reminding us that all language has an "unconscious teleology" operating within it . . . Our language constitutes who we are and how we see the world. It is socially transmitted and thus we do not "preside" over it. Rather, we find ourselves within the world of meaning that it presents to us. Gadamer argues that we do not "possess" ourselves, nor are we capable of "free self-realization." We only come to discover the nexus of symbols that condition our view of the world through a process of interpretation (55). A hermeneutical understanding is required if we are to name the prejudices, constraints, and boundaries of the particular language that we speak.

To speak is to learn a highly complex set of rules. As Searle (1969) states, it is not unlike learning a game such as baseball (14). Learning to play the game properly requires the internalization of rules, largely an intuitive process: i.e., one knows to run to first base rather than to third not by checking the rule book but intuitively. One internalizes the rules and the endless subtleties of the game by playing the game. In the same way, one learns the complex rules that govern a language by speaking. One does not understand the speaker by simply learning the rules that govern communication. One must recognize that rules cannot be separated from their use in active situations, or what Searle (1969) terms "speech acts" (17).

Gadamer proposes that in the process of a game a way of thinking and acting develops that subordinates the subjective attitudes of the participants to itself (54). Only in the back and forth movement between the players does something ascend that "obeys its own set of laws" (53). This view recalls Wittgenstein's (1958, 144) understanding of language games and his belief in the particular power that language has in fixing our perception of what we see:

> The child learns to believe a host of things . . . Bit by bit there forms a system of what is believed, and in that system some things stand unshakably fast and some are more or less liable to shift. What stands fast does so, not because it is intrinsically obvious or convincing; it is rather held fast by what lies around it.

Searle (1969) states that there are two sets of rules that govern the actions related to speech: regulative and constitutive rules. The former relate to activities that exist independent of the rules (33). One might think of the rules governing table manners as an example. Eating beans with one's fingers or drinking soup from the bowl are proscribed by the code of etiquette, but also exist independently of those constraints. Such behavior may offend one's host and may result in one eating alone; but the regulative rules are not integral to how one chooses to eat.

Constitutive rules, on the other hand, are essential to the activity itself. They not only name and regulate the activity; they create and sustain the activity (34). Once again, one might think of baseball. Here the rules constitute the activity and within the field of action that they create, new possibilities, strategies, and understandings emerge. The more one plays, the greater is one's facility. The more one is submerged within the self-forgetting context of the interplay, the more new and intricate possibilities are discovered. The participants develop a consciousness that cannot be known from the outside. It remains obscure and largely impenetrable to one who would attempt to judge the activity through the lens of regulative rules. Language, Searle (1969) argues, is fundamentally a set of constitutive rules (37).

Searle (1969) also develops the distinction between what he terms "brute facts" and "institutional facts." The model for brute facts is the natural sciences (50). They consist of empirical observations of sense experiences, the type so often found in analytical reports concerning inmates in correctional institutions. Like regulative rules, brute facts exist independently of the conditions that govern the activities themselves. One could patiently and accurately describe the activities that one sees on a field as someone throws a ball, and another hits it and begins to run toward a stationary point. But such a description would be inadequate since the meaning of the activity cannot be understood by simple empirical observation. Searle (1969) maintains that institutional facts are created and sustained by a network of constitutive rules. Once again, these rules are learned in the process of ongoing participation in the activity. Languages are systems of constitutive rules that take place in various institutional contexts. The observation of behavior and the attentiveness to words spoken in a given environment must take into account "the inadequacy of the brute fact conception of knowledge to account for institutional facts" (52). Yet one often finds, as Searle (1969) claims, the tendency to offer "analysis of languages armed with only a conceptual structure of brute facts and ignoring the institutional facts that underlie the brute regularities" (52-53).

These observations provide a significant challenge to those who seek to analyze the speech of those confined in correctional institutions. An inmate inhabits several cultural worlds: his or her native linguistic and cultural community, as well as the variegated set of social relations and linguistic forms common to the prison environment. One must also take into account the researcher and the research assistants who so often assist in the creation of reports. Each of these speech communities bears witness to the production and reproduction of complex cultural and linguistic codes or, as Geertz (1983, 182) puts it, "webs of signification." These codes cannot be unlocked by "social mechanics" or a "physics of judgment," but only lie open within the context of "cultural hermeneutics."

Inherent in the speaking of a language and analogous to the concept of prejudice is the creation of boundaries. The system of constitutive rules and institutional facts, the particular self-understanding that one discovers in the process of linguistic interchange, reinforces the connection between native speakers, binding them into a single speech community and "excluding outsiders from intragroup communication" (Saville-Troike, 1982, 21).

Normal and Abnormal Discourse

The preceding analysis is meant to suggest that the meaning and intentions of a particular speaker require interpretation despite the seemingly transparent character of what is spoken. As Searle (1969, 15) attests, "everything I have ever read in the philosophy of language" relies "on the intuitions of the speaker." A rather daunting interpretive process would be entailed in deciphering the meaning of an interview with, e.g., a Spanish-speaking, Catholic immigrant attending a fundamentalist Bible study in a correctional institution in Texas. The analysis would seem to require a preliminary explication of the process by which agreement can be reached between the symbolic world of the researcher, and that of the inmate whose words he or she seeks to report. Geertz (1983) terms "normal discourse" the type that proceeds under a set of rules, assumptions, criteria, and beliefs which, in principle, tell us how to go about settling issues and resolving the disparity of viewpoints caused by factors such as culture, religion and social location (222).

Abnormal discourse, on the other hand, proceeds from a standpoint that these agreed-upon, or at least enunciated, criteria are not "the axis upon which communication turns" (222). In such discourse "the evaluation of disparate views in terms of some accepted framework within which they can be objectively assessed and commensurated one with the other is not the organizing aim" (223). Muriel Saville-Troike (1982) contends that cross-cultural research must begin from the perspective that interpretations of meaning are "problematic rather than given" (48).

J. L. Austin's (1962) concepts of locutionary, illocutionary and perlocutionary acts further demonstrate the need to exercise caution in seeking to interpret what another is saying. He carefully outlines the differences between a descriptive or locutionary statement, "Juan attended the Bible study," a forceful or illocutionary statement, "The chaplain suggested that Juan attend the Bible study," and an effectual or perlocutionary statement, "At the urging of the chaplain, Juan attended the Bible study" (102). Austin goes on to say: "When we perform a locutionary act, we use speech: but in what way precisely are we using it on this occasion? . . . It makes a great difference whether we were advising or merely suggesting, or actually ordering, whether we were strictly promising or only announcing a vague intention" (99). Austin also speaks of "happy" and "unhappy" utterances. These terms refer, in essence, to the linguistic guidelines we have been discussing and are ascribed to the extent that these guidelines are followed or violated. He writes that the "ways we can do wrong, speak outrageously, in uttering conjunctions of 'factual statements,' are more numerous than merely by contradiction" (47). He further states (144):

> It is essential to realize that "true" and "false," like "free" and "unfree," do not stand for anything simple at all; but only for a general dimension of being a right or proper thing to say as opposed to a wrong thing, in these circumstances, to this audience, for these purposes and with these intentions.

Rules of speech–regulative and constitutive, brute and institutional facts, happy and unhappy locutions–all affect the spirit of the spoken word. Without careful attention, they can distort the meaning intended by the speaker. They can lead, in the case at hand, to such confusion over the interpretation of what inmates are saying that the inmates themselves, in effect, do not speak.

INMATE SPEECH IN CRIMINOLOGICAL LITERATURE

Numerous studies report on what residents of correctional institutions are saying, and there have been a growing number of studies probing both the causes and effects of religious faith and practice in the penal environment. While the interest of criminologists in religion shares elements in common with the sociology of religion, there is a certain urgency to many of the former reports that reflects the specific concerns of the criminological community. Crime, like religion, may be here to stay, but in Durkheimian terms religion is a "social fact," while crime is a symptom of social chaos. Much of what is written regarding crime from the scholarly viewpoint has a prescriptive tone normally not found in the sociology of religion. This stance reflects not only the frustration of a crime-ridden society and exasperated penal and government officials, but also reflects what Geertz (1983) calls "the general revolution of rising expectations" that the "culture of scientism has induced in us all" (171). He argues that scientific accounts, and the fact-based methodologies that underlie them, have given rise to a general sense that stubborn and intractable social issues can be ameliorated, if not solved (171).

For all of their methodological rigor and clarity, quantitative methodologies must still contend with hermeneutical and linguistic questions if they are to report accurately what inmates are saying. Once again, Gadamer's (1976, 11) concept of prejudice comes into play:

> [T]he anticipatory character of the questions statistics answer make it particularly suitable for propaganda purposes. Indeed, effective propaganda must always try to influence initially the judgment of the person addressed and to restrict his possibilities of judgment. Thus what is established by statistics seems to be a language of facts, but which questions these facts answer and which facts would begin to speak if other questions were asked are hermeneutical questions.

Within the discipline of criminology some scholars have raised questions concerning the adequacy of the methodological tools employed to adequately capture the essence of the prison experience. Ray Pawson (1997) calls for more "ontological depth" than is found in the "time-honored experimental design" of pre-test, post-test, and one control group. He writes that the "evaluation research itself has failed to deliver a clear enough knowledge base on what we know and can know about how programmes work" (151). Matthews and Pitts (1997) call for more "qualitative and intensive data" than is found in the "quantitative" process that "concentrates on correlations and the patterning of variables."

Jacobs and Wright (1999, 149-150) look directly at the meaning question in relation to criminal motivation, calling it "criminology's dirty little secret." They go on to critique the "positivistic tradition of finding the one factor, or set of factors that accounts for it." Marenin and

Worrall (1998) argue that this conceptual and methodological narrowness is reproduced by graduate criminal justice programs and journals that are not "comfortable with multiple sources, disciplines and materials" and refuse to "integrate various theoretical strands into a common enterprise."

From a hermeneutical standpoint, the scientific discourse used to convey the attitudes of inmates regarding religion must be understood as a language representing the world in which the researcher lives. All languages feature self-forgetfulness. Within this self-forgetfulness are contained what Harold Garfinkel (1967, 35) calls the "massive facts" that condition the eyes and ears of scholars, the assumptions that shape the world that lies before them as they awake, that they carry with them, and to which they return after a day in the field. Wittgenstein (1969, 103) states:

> And now if I were to say "It is my unshakeable conviction that, etc.," this means . . . that I have not consciously arrived at the conviction by following a particular line of thought, but that it is anchored in all my questions and answers, so anchored that I cannot touch it.

Against this background, studies of inmate attitudes generally, and with regard to religion particularly, are frustrating to read. For example, "well-trained criminal justice graduate students" can interview over 1,000 felons, nearly two-thirds of whom were Hispanic or African American, presenting them "with 11 pairs of hypothetical criminal sanctions," and it is assumed that reliable data has been produced on the meaning of what was said (Crouch, 1993, 72-73). "Twelve trained female interviewers using a computer-assisted interviewing system" can investigate 80 female felons "with histories of mental illness," with diverse racial, ethnic and educational backgrounds, to ascertain their "at risk" behaviors (Brewer et al., 1998). In another study, students asked subjects to "expand on their initial responses to questions when these responses did not reveal their underlying reasoning." The students' qualifications for discovering the underlying reasoning of 109 White, Black and Hispanic Texas prison inmates, besides their graduate courses, were conducting "several pilot interviews before beginning the study." Furthermore, they were told "not to ask leading questions or introduce new materials."

These examples raise more questions than answers. One is left wondering what are the "massive facts," the institutional rules, the locutionary parameters that condition the world that the various groups of inmates see upon awaking each morning. The guiding assumption seems to be that controlling for race, language, culture and education are sufficient in themselves to provide the interpreter with the information required to decipher the meaning of what has been spoken.

From a hermeneutical standpoint, the questions the interviewers ask *are* new materials. How the data is recorded is new material. The interpretation of what was said in terms of the information being sought is new material. The language in which the report is written is new material.

Similar cautionary flags should be raised with other methods of data collection in many reports of what inmates are saying. Few questions are raised as to how one can report with some degree of accuracy the meaning found in true-false questionnaires, save that the data was gender specific and checked against control groups (Houston et al., 1988). Self-report surveys filled out anonymously may insure a degree of authenticity, but, as Wood et al. (1997) observe, how can one then interpret "the feelings and sensations people experience when committing specific types of crimes" when one knows nothing of their personal history, education, race, or culture? As Benaquisto and Freed (1996) suggest, inmates from different minority groups can be asked to give their "personal perspective" on vignettes reflecting the carcereal experience, but how does one interpret what was said when inmates are "honestly speaking their minds"?

The Likert-type scale (Note 1) similarly does more than reflect attitudes; it creates responses on a scale that can be measured. But what exactly is being measured? How does one approximate the internal process that is taking place in a given respondent? In Austin's terms, how one discerns the meaning of an illocutionary act must take several factors into consideration. Among these are "the specific way in which each is intended," whether they are "in order or not in order," whether in this instance they are "right" or "wrong," what terms of approval and disapproval are used for each, and what meaning is ascribed to them (1962, 145-46). Similarly, Wittgenstein (1958) states that the meaning of a phrase is "characterized by the use we make of it." Words, like hammers and chisels, can only be understood in reference to how they are used in a particular circumstance.

One might recall Gadamer's (1976, 28) idea that "in the sciences of understanding" often the interpreter does not see him or herself "in relationship to the hermeneutical situation." Rather, interpreters often act as if their "own understanding does not enter into the event." One might also recall Searle's contention that the sciences record "brute facts" but a greater involvement is required if one is to penetrate the constitutive rules of discrete speech communities within penal institutions.

The Rational Prisoner

There seems to be a sense in some reports that listening to inmates is not unlike listening to ourselves. Arnulf Kolstad (1996, 325) states that "the best way to understand inmates is to start listening to them." Next, we must "interpret what they are saying in light of their situation and interests." What are they saying and what are their interests? Kolstad insists that "they want their freedom and opportunities for a normal, law-abiding life." He seems to assume that one can know the depth and nuances of terms such as freedom, normalcy and law, when he states that prisoners "have to be understood as rational human beings"; and contends that there are "rational reasons for their deviation" and that since offending is similar to other types of antisocial behavior, the theories and methods relating to "uncommon" behavior "can be applied to the study of crime." In somewhat similar fashion, Benaquisto and Freed (1996, 499) were confident that they had ascertained the meaning and intentions of Massachusetts prison inmates who were discussing the validity of legal sanctions because the respondents talked "freely, openly, and honestly about their perceptions."

Rationality in these reports seems to have a magical, universal quality that gives the scientist a privileged insight into the world of another that somehow escapes the conditioning and the boundaries created by the language that is being spoken.

One of the programs designed to combat criminogenic tendencies is the Cognitive Skills Program. It seeks to replace "faulty" thinking by "straight" thinking and operates on the assumption that "faulty" thinking in the form of diminished reasoning capacity produces antisocial traits (Matthews and Pitts, 1998). Here, the hermeneutical process is sidestepped due to the erroneous belief that the administrator or analyst of a prison program stands within the same cognitive framework as the inmates being studied. The independent variable seems to be the mind of the interpreter which becomes the norm judging between deficient and proper thinking. A similar mind-set seems to be revealed when researchers interview offenders convicted of homicide and conclude: ". . . in most cases interviewers had little trouble gaining the trust of the inmates to be interviewed" (Spunt et al., 1994, 160).

In these and similar reports, criminologists seek to match the social location of the inmates to how they think and speak, "running causal arrows from somewhere in the recesses of the second in the general direction of the first." There is no indication among these authors that the mind of the interpreter, like the language, rituals and stories of the inmates, is itself socially created. Geertz (1973, 153) claims that understanding does not proceed from "rationalists wearing square hats sitting in square rooms thinking square thoughts; they should try sombreros." For all that some criminologists (Van Voorhis et al., 1997) claim that "it seems tragic to continually ignore" those confined in correctional institutions, much of the research unwittingly does just that in assuming a value-free environment safeguarded by reason that pays little attention to the constitutive facts of the worlds of both researcher and inmate.

PARTICIPATION AND THE UNDERSTANDING OF RELIGION

Inmates cannot speak until what they are saying is understood. Evaluating the effectiveness of religious programs in the correctional context requires an understanding similar to Gadamer's (1976) metaphor of the game, and Searle's (1969) concepts of constitutive rules and institutional facts. Such a study also requires a realization that academics play their own game with its own language and "webs of meaning" that are virtually impenetrable to the outside observer. Inmates could no more enter an academic seminar and derive a meaningful understanding of what is taking place than most of us could join a prayer circle or bible study on a prison tier and take away an accurate understanding of what was said. Each group would possess a set of "brute facts" and may well possess knowledge of the regulative rules that obtain for one seeking to participate in the other's world. But a host of deeper meanings would be lost. And while what was reported might be "orally" accurate, the context, the symbols, the language and the rituals would be more reflective of the interpreter's life-world than that of those being interpreted.

What is constitutive to religious experience is faith, or at least the desire to possess faith. Faith creates a certain kind of understanding, a way of seeing that is unknowable from the outside, or the sidelines. Much like the interplay between two players on an athletic field, it is instinctual, and recalling William James (1961, 299-300), ineffable and noetic. Faith cannot be described to those who are not playing in that experiential field; it comes to possess those actively involved within the community that seeks to learn its subtleties and become conversant with its demands. This level of self-forgetting participation, as Gadamer (1976, 54) claims, is difficult for the rationalist to accept since the type of knowledge based on scientific procedures "tolerates no restrictions of its claim to universality."

A further constitutive element of religion is the language of faith. The relation of faith to its foundational text and the proclamation of the specific language proclaimed within that text is essential. The world comes to us as language and it is through the language that we speak that we see and interpret the world. As Wittgenstein (1958) avers, no one can speak a private language. It is only through training and membership in a particular community that people learn linguistic practices (Fogelin, 1987, 177-185). In this case, only as a committed member of a community of people whose language is based on their faith, can one appreciate and understand that way of speaking and have the capacity to reveal accurately what has been spoken.

These provisional guidelines are noticeably absent from many of the reports on inmate religious practice. Many theorists, despite a basic humility with regard to their own ability to detect a "true" religious consciousness (e.g., Clear and Myhre, 1995; Johnson, 1987), tend to equate the authenticity of religious commitment to its functional validity (Note 2). Religion is often studied, and evaluated, in relation to its ability to pacify the imprisoned or aid in their "adjustment" to the penal environment. In other studies, religious devotion is measured and authenticated in relation to its effects on rearrest and reconviction rates (Johnson et al., 1997; O'Connor et al., 1998).

Despite the intentions of the authors, what often emerges in their presentations is a distortion of the profound behavioral and psychological complexity of the religious life. One wonders how a study of inmates in the jail in Birmingham, Alabama would have evaluated the "salience" of religion in the life of a repeat offender like Martin Luther King.

It is also difficult to understand what is meant in studies of religion and crime that argue that religious communities hold no particular influence on the social behavior of their members (Cochran et al., 1994; Elifson et al., 1983). Language is the framework in which social views are created and sustained. What must be analyzed is not whether those whose significative world is dominated by religious language and imagery are influenced in their comportment by that language, but what specific language the particular person is speaking.

Inmates speak a distinctive language and, as Gadamer (1976, 87) claims, "one must master a language, if one is to express oneself to another in that language." He goes on to say that to master a language one must "live within it." If the language inmates speak is a religious language, then the constitutive rules and institutional facts that pertain to that language cannot be fathomed by simple observation. Nor can they be verified simply in functional terms, any more than the worth of a player to a team can be measured simply by looking at his or her statistics. A brute fact analysis cannot provide an accurate measure of the depth of an "institutional" commitment.

CONCLUSION

In his essay on the nature of sympathy, Max Scheler (1992) tells the story of a couple holding their dead child in their arms. He goes on to describe the various reactions that observers might experience as they view that poignant scene. He concludes that these reactions are borne of the particular history and psychology of the observers. The attainment of sympathy, "a community of feeling," is related to entering compassionately, and to some significant degree, the life-world of the couple. It would require a measure of understanding that is the product of patience, care and attentiveness (54-57).

Whatever is happening when inmates gather to pray cannot be known or accurately revealed without careful attention to the insights provided by linguistics and hermeneutics. To probe the relationship between religion and the offender, one must first take note of one's own language, its prejudices, and the way its particular web of symbols refracts the images that one sees.

Only with an understanding of the "all encompassing" nature of language can one begin the process of delineation and accommodation that would be required to understand the meaning of the "speech acts" of another. The sphere of the "we" in which language takes place requires an immersion in the world of those one studies. If Scheler is correct, that immersion must bring with it a degree of tenderness as well as analytical rigor. This approach dismisses the claims to rational universality as a screen that distorts the words and intentions of the subjects under study; it does so in such a way that one learns more about the researcher in the process of the report than about those putatively under observation.

Inmate culture, and specifically inmate religious culture, is a symbolic world with its own constitutive rules. These rules can only be understood when one has trimmed one's analytical expectations, and considered the possibility that the language of faith is a precondition for understanding the experience of faith. It is a precondition for determining the meaning of its rituals, its behavioral expectations, and what possibilities and sanctions emerge with the failure to live according to those expectations.

In Greek mythology, Hermes was the interpreter of the word of the gods to humankind. Heidegger argues that poets and prophets have a similar task. Those of us who seek to understand the meaning of religion in the correctional context may be carrying the message of lesser gods but we do well to bear that message humbly and as accurately as we can.

NOTES

1. A Likert-type scale measures attitudes on a number scale, often ranging from one to five, with *5 = strongly agree* to *3 = neutral* to *1 = strongly disagree*. See, e.g., Erez, 1988; Van Voorhis, Browning, Simon, & Gordon, 1997; Zimmerman & Valhov, 1991.

2. Among the authors who give evidence of the multi-faceted nature of religious experience is Byron Johnson (1987). He states, "In fact, one does not have to look too far to see examples of where crime/deviance have been religiously motivated and/or based on church doctrine."

REFERENCES

Austin, J.L. (1962). *How to Do Things with Words*. Cambridge: Harvard University Press.

Benaquisto, L., & Freed, P.J. (1996). The myth of inmate lawlessness: The perceived contradiction between self and other in inmates' support for criminal justice sanctioning norms. *Law and Society Review*, 30, 481-511.

Brewer, V.E., Marquart, J.W., Mullings, J.L., & Crouch, B.M. (1998). AIDS-related behavior among female prisoners with histories of mental impairment. *Prison Journal*, 78 (2), 101-17.

Clear, T.R., & Myhre, M. (1995). A study of religion in prison. *IARCA Journal on Community Corrections* (June), 20-25.

Cochran, J.K., Wood, P.B., & Arneklev, B.J. (1994). The religiosity-delinquency relationship spurious? *Journal of Research in Crime and Delinquency*, 31 (2), 92-123.

Crouch, B.M. (1993). Is incarceration really worse? Analysis of offenders' preference for prison over probation. *Justice Quarterly*, 10 (2), 67-88.

Elifson, K.W., Peterson, D.M., & Hadaway, C.K. (1983). Religiosity and delinquency. *Criminology*, 21 (7), 504-527.

Erez, E. (1988). The myth of the new female offender: Some evidence from attitudes toward law and justice. *Journal of Criminal Justice*, 16, 499-509.

Fogelin, R.J. (1987). *Wittgenstein*, 2nd ed. London: Routledge.

Gadamer, H.G. (1976). *Philosophical hermeneutics* (Linge, David E., Trans.). Berkeley, CA: University of California Press.

Garfinkel, H. (1967). *Studies in Ethnology.* Englewood Cliffs, NJ: Prentice Hall.

Geertz, C. (1973). *The Interpretation of Cultures.* New York: Basic Books.

Geertz, C. (1983). *Local Knowledge.* New York: Basic Books.

Houston, J.G., Gibbons, D.C., & Jones, J.F. (1988). Physical environment and jail social climate. *Crime and Delinquency,* 34 (9), 449-466.

Jacobs, B.A., & Wright, R. (1999). Stick-up, street culture, and offender motivation. *Criminology,* 37, 149-173.

James, W. (1961). *The Varieties of Religious Experience.* New York: Collier Books. [Reissued; originally published 1902]

Johnson, B. (1987). Religiosity and institutional deviance: The impact of religious variables upon inmate adjustment. *Criminal Justice Review,* 12, 21-31.

Johnson, B.R., Larson, D.B., & Pitts, T.C. (1997). Religious programs, institutional adjustment, and recidivism among former inmates in prison fellowship programs. *Justice Quarterly,* 14 (4), 145-165.

Kolstad, A. (1996). Imprisonment as rehabilitation: Offenders' assessment of why it does not work. *Journal of Criminal Justice,* 24, 323-335.

Mannheim, K. (1936). *Ideology and Utopia* (Wirth, Louis, & Shils, Edward, Trans.). New York: Harcourt, Brace, & Co.

Marcus, D.K., Amen, T.M., & Bibace, R. (1992). A developmental analysis of prisoners' conceptions of AIDS. *Criminal Justice and Behavior,* 18 (4), 174-188.

Marenin, O., & Worrall, J. (1998). Criminal justice: Portrait of a discipline in progress. *Journal of Criminal Justice,* 26, 465-480.

Matthews, R., & Pitts, J. (1997). Rehabilitation, recidivism and realism: Evaluating violence reduction programs in prison. *Prison Journal,* 78, 390-405.

O'Connor, T., Ryan, P., & Parikh, C. (1998). A model program for churches and ex-offender rehabilitation. *Journal of Offender Rehabilitation,* 28 (3/4), 107-126.

Pawson, R. (1997). Evaluation methodology: Back to basics. In G. Mair (Ed.), *Evaluating the Effectiveness of Community Penalties.* Aldershot, UK: Avebury.

Saville-Troike, M. (1982). *The Ethnography of Communication.* Oxford: Blackwell.

Scheler, M. (1992). *On Feeling, Knowing, and Valuing.* Chicago: University of Chicago Press. [Reissued; originally published 1912]

Searle, J. (1969). *Speech Acts.* London: Cambridge University Press.

Spunt, B., Goldstein, P., Brownstein, H., Fendrich, M., & Langley, S. (1994). Alcohol and homicide: Interviews with prison inmates. *Journal of Drug Issues,* 24 (3), 143-163.

Van Voorhis, P., Browning, S. L., Simon, M., & Gordon, J. (1997). The meaning of punishment: Inmates' orientation to the prison experience. *Prison Journal,* 77, 135-167.

Wittgenstein, L. (1958). *The Blue and Brown Books.* New York: Harper. [Reissued; originally published 1902]

Wittgenstein, L. (1969). *On Certainty.* New York: Harper. [Original publication from re-constituted class notes]

Wood, P.B., Gove, W.R., Wilson, J.A., & Cochran, J.K. (1997). Non-social reinforcement and habitual criminal conduct: An extension of learning theory. *Criminology,* 35, 335-365.

Zimmerman, S.E., & Valhov, D. (1991). AIDS knowledge and risk perceptions among Pennsylvania prisoners. *Journal of Criminal Justice,* 19, 239-256.

AUTHOR'S NOTE

Andrew Skotnicki, O.Carm., is professor of social ethics at St. Patrick's Seminary of the Archdiocese of San Francisco.

Address correspondence to the author at 320 Middlefield Road, Menlo Park, CA 94025.

Religion, the Community, and the Rehabilitation of Criminal Offenders. Pp. 215-230.

Shame and Religion as Factors
in the Rehabilitation of Serious Offenders

KENNETH D. JENSEN

Western Oregon University

STEPHEN G. GIBBONS

Western Oregon University

SUMMARY In a qualitative study of twenty adult ex-offenders, all having served lengthy sentences for serious crimes, the authors found that religiosity and strong expressions of shame played a prominent role in their ability to live productive lives after the prison experience. Those who have reintegrated into the community were compared with individuals who either committed new crimes or violated the conditions of their parole. *[Article copies available for a fee from The Haworth Document Delivery Service: 1-800-HAWORTH. E-mail address: <getinfo@haworthpressinc.com> Website: <http://www.HaworthPress.com> © 2002 by The Haworth Press, Inc. All rights reserved.]*

KEYWORDS Shame, prison, religion, reintegration, inmate, forgiveness

This paper describes an in-depth study of ex-offenders who have "gone straight." Although no one knows better than ex-offenders why they have desisted from crime, there are few studies that treat them as the experts in this matter. This is perhaps due to the practical and ethical problems inherent in such research. Of the few who have studied the ex-offenders themselves (see, for example, Meisenhelder, 1977; Shover, 1985; Pinsonneault, 1985; Liebrich, 1996; Maruna, 2001), some valuable and important information on going straight has been obtained.

However, save for Maruna's, each of these studies investigated relatively minor offenders and therefore the results may not be applicable to more serious offenders.

The present study looks at men and women who either committed very serious crimes or were career criminals. In this study we draw upon the work of Spradley (1970), Carpenter et al. (1988), and Fleisher (1995) in designing an informal, personal research strategy. We are also influenced by Irwin (1970) and his pioneering work on the stages and problems of reentry. We ask ex-felons to describe their experiences and perceptions of the world. We are therefore treating these men and women as the experts and are empowering their voices. It is in this way that we hope to enlighten our understanding of the world "outside" and what it takes to "make it" there.

METHOD

Twenty adult subjects who have served at least five years in an Oregon prison/correctional institution are interviewed. Eight of the 20 were institutionalized for murder, five for sex offenses, one for kidnapping, four were armed robbers, and two were drug dealers. Eight of the 20 also admitted to serious drug addiction prior to their incarcerations and five acknowledged alcohol abuse as a contributing factor to their criminal behavior. The average time of incarceration of our sample was 12 years with the range being five to 25 years. Eighteen of the participants live in Oregon. The others live in California and in Washington state. They range in age from 33 to 52, with an average age of 42. Eighteen of the subjects are Caucasian, one is African-American, and one is Native American. Two are female. The amount of time our subjects have been out ranges from one to 12 years with an average of six years.

The interviewees were identified by the first author who has 20 years experience administering and teaching in a prison education program. He advised and taught the subjects of this research and has remained in contact with them since their release. The second author has been involved in correctional research for 25 years. Each participant was contacted by phone by the first author and the nature of the research was explained to him or her. Arrangements were then made for the time and location of the interview. Each subject was paid $50 for their participation, plus mileage if they had to drive, and was required to sign a confidentiality agreement. The participants were interviewed once, and both authors participated in all 20 interviews. The interviews lasted approximately two hours each but often continued over coffee or dinner with the tape recorder off.

The interview schedule followed a structured, open-ended format with predetermined topics guiding the interviewers. This ethnographic method assures that the interviews are open-ended and exploratory while asking a basic set of questions to gather comparable and quantifiable data from respondents (Kottak, 1999). Each interview began with a discussion of the goals of the research. We then asked the participants to tell us what he or she is doing now (where he is employed, what his job is, etc.). This provided an opportunity to discuss employment issues upon release–how hard, or easy, was it to find and keep a job–as well as other post-release experiences. In each interview, we ask about their experiences with their parole officers, amount of support (familial and otherwise) inside and outside the institution, program participation inside and outside the institution, and anything they think is relevant relative to their ability to stay out of prison.

The tape-recorded interviews were conducted between December, 1995 and October, 1998. The open-ended questions enabled the interviewers to listen to the subjects give answers in their own terms, unconstrained by the interview or the interviewer. It also allowed a broader discussion in explaining the details of the subjects' life experiences, thoughts, and feelings. Structuring the interviews this way reinforces our recognition of the subject as the expert and encourages his or her active participation.

This approach allows the participants to explain and discuss their perspectives, definitions, and interpretations in relationship to their behaviors and actions (Blumer, 1969; Irwin, 1970; Spradley, 1970; Burgess, 1984). Consequently, it was possible to observe the subjects' lives from their unique viewpoints and perspectives. This ultimately led to important questions which other methods may exclude (Becker, 1966). Through this research, we hope to eventually approximate a rare "insider" ethnographic view of the parolee's life and life-style.

The interview data were analyzed using a qualitative inductive approach (Bogdan and Biklen, 1982; Glaser and Strauss, 1967). For any given topic, all statements in the transcripts about the topic were located and then sorted according to emergent themes. Those themes became the basis for the analysis that presents the subjects' perspectives in the richness and complexity of their own stories. We therefore are not reducing their experiences and beliefs to variables or factors predetermined by hypotheses conceived separately from data collection. This paper is part of an ongoing research project exploring the process of "going straight." In earlier papers we identified familial support, successful employment experiences, and participation in institutional programs–drug and alcohol, education, and anger management–as being positively associated with successful integration into society (Gibbons and Jensen, 1996; Jensen and Gibbons, 1997). In a later paper (Gibbons and Jensen, 1998) we saw that experiences of shame and remorse prepared inmates for the difficult task of accepting responsibility for their crimes and, in turn, paved the way for their rehabilitation. In this paper, we investigate the role shame and religion play in preparing offenders for the life changes necessary to go straight.

NARRATIVES ON SHAME AND THE SHAMING PROCESS

In his theory of reintegrative shaming, Braithwaite (1989:12) makes an important distinction between shaming that "leads to stigmatization–to outcasting, to confirmation of a deviant master status–versus shaming that is reintegrative, that shames while maintaining bonds of respect or love, that sharply terminates disapproval with forgiveness, instead of amplifying deviance by progressively casting the deviant out." Braithwaite's concept of stigmatizing shaming is congruent with the public humiliation that is imposed on some offenders after their release from prison as a condition of their parole. These actions, while viewed as necessary to protect the public, can work against an offender's rehabilitation. For Clyde, an urban-born Native American convicted of a violent rape while in the military, both his attempts to work and continue his education were thwarted by the stigma of his crime and the strict requirements of his parole:

> One time I was actually hired by (a local) press at $9 an hour . . . went back after the interview and he said you start tomorrow and everything and I called my parole officer up and told him. I would have been violated if I hadn't, so I have to comply with his wishes and he called him (the boss) and said you're gonna have to put up posters all around the offices. 'Cuz he told me throughout our discussion, he asked if there was a woman anywhere on the premises. Well, yeah, somewhere in the office, I'm sure there's a secretary. Then we have to put a poster up about you. He said 'you gotta call him (the boss) up and tell him' and he (the boss) said don't show up tomorrow, sorry. I lost a $9 an hour job which would have been a vocational investment, a career opportunity.

Similar notification posters were going to be placed around the college campus Clyde was attending, prompting these comments:

> And there was no way I could attend class. The humiliation would be unbearable. But I really wanted to go to college, I felt so good. This was a step toward a future.

Although these notification posters are intended to inform and protect the public, their effect on an ex-offender's attempts to integrate back into society can be devastating. The effects of the sex offender notification posters are further illuminated by the experiences of Harold, a former crack addict convicted of raping his wife after she left him. Harold returned to his home town and his previous employment, expecting to fully integrate back into his community despite the fact that a condition of his parole forbid him from contacting his former wife and their two children. Shortly after his return, flyers describing him as a predatory sex offender were posted at area schools. Harold's initial reaction was that of anger and confusion, wondering why this was done when his crime had nothing to do with juveniles. He felt powerless and humiliated, yet he resigned himself to the public stigma associated with the flyers. It was as though "an iron cage had closed around my heart."

The stigmatizing shaming experienced by Clyde and Harold makes it harder to go straight, yet their lives have followed different courses. Clyde was never integrated into a Native American community, has few friends, is estranged from his natal family, and is unemployed. Without the support of a close-knit community to encourage him, Clyde is withdrawn and, at the time of the interview, felt his chance of a productive future is limited:

> Until I get off parole, I don't believe I have a future. I'm struggling, treading water, just trying to keep my head above, keep from being sent back to prison for the most obscure and absurd things they create. It never ends . . . Every footstep you take is challenged, you know. Why did you say hi to this person? Was you trying to groom them? Are you expecting to molest them or take advantage of them in some way? . . . Everything you do and say and breathe and think is subject to criticism . . . I want to hide in my own bedroom all the time. I want to shut the door, I want my bedroom door locked . . . Basically, I've isolated myself. I stay home . . . I think I'm digressing mentally, probably because of the lack of education and opportunity for assimilation.

Clearly, Clyde sees himself as powerless, with no support, and he feels unable to move beyond his crime. In his words,

> I cannot deal with the rage and the anger I have toward myself for committing this stupid act in the first place, the horrible thing that got me here.

Harold, on the other hand, is not discouraged. He has the support of a loving family and has accepted the embrace of his parents' religious community, thereby refusing to allow the stigma attached to this unwanted publicity to prevent him from achieving a successful integration into the community and from accomplishing his long-term goal of reuniting with his children.

Harold, in his narrative, also offered a strong testimonial of regret and shame:

> I made a conscious decision to stay out of jail (A) for my life, and (B) for my family. I wasn't going to put my family through, because it's not just you that goes to jail, it's your family. I hurt my family something fierce. I now look back and see the pain my mother went through, and she got cancer in the middle of all that . . . I could have lost my mom while I was sitting there, and I couldn't have done a thing about it. And my dad came in in the middle of all that when she had cancer, and he wasn't lashing out at me, but he was just trying to tell me you're killing your mom.

Later in the interview, Harold returned to the shame he felt while in prison for the agony he caused his family, especially his mother:

> Here I am in prison and realizing that look at what you did, you fool. You've got this woman that spent an enormous amount of her life caring and here you are breaking her heart . . . It's time to wake up and that's what keeps me being sane now is knowing that if nothing else, if I die tomorrow, I can be happy with the fact I made my folks happy and family happy. Them knowing I'm normal and not going to make them go through crap.

Harold's statements are reflective of the concept of reintegrative shaming identified by Braithwaite. Reintegrative shaming involves personal disgrace when one's behavior is exposed to those known, loved, and respected. It is also a deterrent to criminal behavior for some offenders. This socially imposed punishment is consistent with the concept of "attachment costs" discussed by Williams and Hawkins (1986) and Grasmick and Bursik's concept of "embarrassment" (1990). Liebrich (1996) provides ample evidence of this type of shame in her study of petty offenders.

In our study, the reintegrative shaming that Harold experienced is also evident in the narrative by Roger, a chronic alcoholic convicted of the violent rape of an employee. Roger responded strongly to the loss of esteem in the eyes of his children, especially a teenaged daughter:

> So the idea to ever allow myself to be put into a position to where I would give that kind of harm to my children again was enough to keep me from ever doing anything (criminal) . . . I laid awake a lot of nights in the pen thinking about my kids. That was a real strong motivation for me.

That motivation was strong. Roger is reunited with his children, is active in the Salvation Army Church, and has lived an alcohol-and-crime-free life for the thirteen years since his release.

A third kind of shame, private remorse, is not obviously apparent in Braithwaite's theory. However, Liebrich (1996) and Grasmick and Bursik (1990) do include this concept in their discussions of offenders' desistance from crime. Private remorse is a self-imposed punishment; it is offending one's own personal morality. In fact Liebrich (1996:294) found that "private remorse was the most important kind of shame" and "it is personal remorse which stops a person continuing to offend others" (299). This claim is consistent with what we found in three of the following four "remorse narratives."

Stan

Stan, a large, imposing man, graphically describes his crime as the actions of a "real bad guy":

> I robbed a cocaine dealer and I was wielding a pistol and I pistol whipped the guy and I sexually assaulted the woman that was there, and there was a couple other guys that lived there and I pistol whipped them and robbed them.

Stan felt disgust for what he'd done "because it was contrary to all of my own values." Later in the interview, he expresses the powerful punitive aspects of private remorse when, in a lengthy and impassioned response to a question about his first year inside, he dredged up the following agonizing memories:

> . . . the first year inside, because of my strong moral value system growing up in the country, I beat myself up for a good year, a good year, maybe even a little longer. But, about that time I realized that maybe up till then it served a purpose, for me. But beyond that it was serving no purpose because it was self-defeating. It was just self-defeating behavior, self-defeating thinking. So, to move on, to move past that, I couldn't retract what I had done; I couldn't take the harm back. But if I could have, I would have, gladly. But you can't. I can't. I can't take that back. So, I beat myself up for what I'd done. But I realized it was counterproductive and I had to move on. So, I did. What else could I do? Basically kinda where I was at, I was doing good in my mind, I was taking advantage of the lost years and that was all I could do. I could firmly commit myself not to harm anyone ever again; that was all I could do. That's all I could do to make it better.

Stan did take advantage of the "lost years" by making the prison experience a positive one. He enrolled in college classes and eventually completed a baccalaureate degree while at the same time holding down a full-time job in prison industries.

Marvin

For Marvin, convicted of murder when he was 18, the critical self-evaluation occurred somewhere around the seventh or eighth year of his incarceration when he started accepting responsibility for his actions:

> I think you start accepting responsibility for your actions when you stop denying things that happened . . . the merry-go-round of I'm innocent, I shouldn't be here, it wasn't me . . . that's just a real cute form of denial 'cuz you don't want to own up to what you've done.

Marvin "came clean" and admitted his guilt in a letter he wrote to his mother and father, and to an older brother:

I didn't own up to it till then. Writing it down was like, okay, here it is, you're committed . . . You shame yourself to the point that, you know, god, you don't want to look at yourself anymore . . . The act that put me in jail destroyed two families . . . the knowledge of what I did, none of it has faded, the experience of what I was has not faded. If anything, the compassion for things that are going on now is more.

Marvin has not let the memories fade. Since his release in 1992 he has been active in both AA and NA and has the support of fellow workers who are also AA/NA members. He describes his work environment as "an ongoing support group . . . I get a meeting every day with the people I work with. They call me every day."

Tim

Tim, a convicted drug dealer and heroin addict, continued his criminal activity while in prison with little interruption until he was confronted with a dilemma common to the trade, collecting unpaid debts. "It's kinda a expected thing that if somebody doesn't pay you you're supposed to do sumpin' to them." And when Tim realized a long-time customer was going to "bum pay him," he reacted in the expected way: "I'm gonna pike him in the furniture factory. I'm gonna pike him, you know what I mean?" But the contemplation of the violent blows he was about to deliver brought him to an unexpected realization:

I'm thinking this hateful shit, you know, and I had like a, in NA they call havin' a spiritual awakening . . . it is recognizing something about yourself you didn't know before . . . what they say happens when people do "steps." I don't know man, but I learned sumpin' there, that I didn't know a second before and that was I'm full of distrust, and poison, and anger. And I'm goin' insane here, man. I'm thinkin' about doin' things that I never think of doin' and I'm thinking of doin' it to people that don't even have it comin.' I'm goin' crazy. I decided I'm not gonna do this anymore, it's not worth it. So, I quit doin' that. And it wasn't like I was doin' it a lot. But I quit doin' that, which left more time to do sumpin' else, right?

And that something else was the beginning of Tim's transformation into a drug- and crime-free lifestyle. He found time to complete a religious study course in "Miracles," attend college-level classes and commit to the tenets of Narcotics Anonymous that anchor his life today.

Gloria

Volunteered expressions of remorse, however, do not always correlate positively with an individual living a crime-free life after release from prison (see Table 1). This is the case with Gloria, a female armed robber and heroin addict whose remorse is clear in her statement below:

> It was really hard for me . . . when I was doing those robberies I really didn't realize the impact I was having on other people until they got up to testify against me . . . I was so terrified myself, I didn't realize the fear I had instilled in other people, and I really wasn't out to hurt anybody, you know. But, when those people walked around me, and cried on the stand and came back months later and clapped when I got sentenced . . . Then, I think about the person I was and how I could have shot somebody. I could have, you know. I grew up in prison a lot. That's really not me; I'm not this cold-blooded whatever.

☐ **Table 1: Religiosity, Shame, and Recidivism**

Subject ID	Religiosity Expressed?	Shame Expressed?	New Crime or Parole Violation?
1	No	No	None
2	No	Yes	New crime
3	No	Yes	None
4	No	No	None
5	No	No	None
6	No	No	New crime
7	No	Yes	Parole violation
8	No	Yes	None
9	No	No	Parole violation
10	No	No	None
11	Yes	Yes	None
12	Yes	Yes	None
13	Yes	Yes	None
14	Yes	Yes	None
15	Yes	No	None
16	Yes	No	Parole violation
17	Yes	Yes	None
18	Yes	Yes	None
19	Yes	No	None
20	Yes	Yes	None

After her release, Gloria could not overcome the pull heroin had on her life, and eight months after being released from prison, she "started abusing":

> And the minute I started my whole life went in the toilet, like that quick, whereas before I could use for awhile and kinda function for a period of time. It went like that. It was devastating.

But no matter how desperate she became, there would be no returning to crimes that involved threat and intimidation–crimes that harmed others. Her personal morality dictated that:

> . . . robbery wasn't an option this time. But I was out there using, right. I didn't commit the major felonies, glaring felonies. I did commit a few felonies but they weren't the glaring ones.

After this short criminal episode she contacted her parole officer and "I turned myself in. I couldn't stop using drugs. I know that the only other time I've been able to stop using drugs is to be incarcerated." In the end, Gloria was left to confront her drug addiction alone. During her parole, she avoided her family, she was not active in NA, and lacked the social support of a drug-free community:

> And then I thought, well . . . how am I gonna fit in with a doctor/lawyer type relationship, a square person per se. I've done five years in prison, you know, I felt like a marked woman, you know, I really did. And I thought, you know, I mean it was like, I didn't fit really, especially when I was using, I didn't fit in the straight community.

ANALYSIS AND DISCUSSION

Since our interview cycle began in 1995, three subjects violated their parole and were reincarcerated for various periods of time. One of these three has been released and the other two remain incarcerated. Additionally, two subjects were convicted of new crimes: one for a property offense, requiring six months in a county jail; and another, a career criminal, is currently serving a federal sentence for armed robbery. Seventeen of our subjects live in their respective communities and appear to be crime free (see Table 1).

These are encouraging results. But can we conclude from the stories of our subjects that the presence of shame makes someone less likely to re-offend? Our results indicate this is not an either/or phenomenon. Ten respondents, in our sample of 20, expressed experiencing some form of shame. Eight of these are living a crime-free lifestyle while two have re-offended: one committed a parole violation and one served six months in a county jail for a relatively minor property crime. On the other hand, three of the 10 subjects who did not experience shame re-offended or violated their parole conditions. Shame is obviously not the only factor influencing one to remain crime free.

There are no easy answers. Going straight is often a gradual, incremental process that involves several variables in combination, including attachments to others, employment, life changes or crises while in prison, exposure to education and treatment programs, and religiosity, as well as personal feelings of shame. Clearly, shame can make a difference for some offenders. Our evidence indicates that shame is a sufficient, but not a necessary, condition for going straight.

As indicated above, several of our subjects have remained crime free without any evidence of shame or remorse. This does not mean they did not have any shame, just that our methodology did not uncover it. We made no attempt to directly elicit responses regarding feelings about the respondents' crimes. This is due to the potential "demand characteristics" inherent in our interview process. One of the researchers has had a long and positive association with the study population. If we had pressed the issue, the danger is the subjects may have responded in a manner designed to gain the researcher's approval. Rather, we allowed the topic to come to us, following the informal ethnographic model that guided our research.

We believe that volunteered responses are more legitimate and sincere. However, we recognize the potential problem of stereotyping former offenders, who either choose not to or who cannot revisit the agonizing experience of their crimes and incarcerations, as lacking remorse for their actions. We should not assume that because they do not express shame during the interview that they do not feel it.

We think it is also important to point out that in eight of 10 cases where shame was not expressed, the subjects either minimized, externalized or denied their guilt, distancing themselves from their victims and their crimes. For example, Douglas, convicted of killing a man in a bar altercation, externalizes his actions by suggesting that the victim's actions caused his own death:

> I tried to shoot him in the hip just to try and stop the whole situation, but he bent over and turned away and I fired. I don't feel that I have to be ashamed. It was something that happened in my life. I'm sorry that it happened, but I'm not ashamed of what happened.

On the other hand, Clyde clearly minimizes the impact of a brutal sex attack with the rationale that all crimes are alike, and that a victim's reaction to physical harm is no different than the psychological distress of losing one's property:

> I honestly feel it's unfair to categorize a sex offender as any more dangerous than somebody else, say a burglar. Many burglars sometimes hurt people trying to escape, or the emotional distress (they cause) stealing your wife's great-grandmother's wedding band. There's some severe emotional trauma there. So, I don't think that just because you physically hurt somebody it makes you any more worse.

The ethnographic method will not tell us everything. However, the method enabled us to uncover shame for some and various types of denial for others, all in the subject's own words. The expressions of shame and remorse by the former inmates often equate with an acceptance of culpability for the crimes they committed and a recognition that the prison sentences they received were deserved. Statements like "I basically deserved what I got," can be contrasted with the complaint of a less than remorseful murderer that "They done it to me. I was really bitter and rotten because there's no way I shoulda gotten a life beef."

But how do some individuals move beyond the criminal mind-set of denial, externalization, and minimization and come to accept responsibility for their crimes? Religion, with its emphasis on morality and individual responsibility plays a role for some. That is, of the 10 subjects in our study who expressed either negative or neutral attitudes toward religion, only three expressed shame; whereas seven of the 10 expressing religiosity volunteered statements of shame (see Table 1). We cannot claim that this finding has uncovered a causal relationship between religious beliefs and emotions of shame in which religion causes shame.

In fact, the opposite causal order could be argued and is more evident in our narratives. That is, a person commits a crime, after a time feels shame, and to further develop and understand those feelings, turns to religion. In Roger's case, described above, the shame and depression he experiences when his children reject him leads him to seek understanding and acceptance in a religious-based community initiated and controlled by inmates. The group combined the hard work of encounter with a pledge of confidentiality:

> I belonged to a group called Yokefellows . . . it comes from that New Testament parable about yoking yourself to Christ to pull through hard times. We normally kept about six to 10 men in the group. We kept it small intentionally. You get any more than that the group would be too big to do the good that we did.

The "good" that Roger refers to came about in an environment charged with confrontation and guided by the members' trust of each other:

> It was an encounter group, and we definitely encountered each other. Sometimes you'd think it would almost go to blows. If it was any other place in the penitentiary it would have gone to blows . . . In the institution, it is very tough to trust anybody, but we trusted each other. We never would let anything out of the group and no matter how bitter it would get or what the individual was I never knew a time that that was broke.

But as Roger's following words reveal, the work of healing and redemption would not go forward until he accepted the support of this close-knit community and "truly opened up."

> Even though I swore to open up . . . that doesn't mean that during those first two years I truly opened up. Because I was still beginning to open up to myself. First of all you have to see your own evil before you can really share it. Obviously, I thought I was all right before all that, meaning the crime, etc. Looking back, I see what a pathetic bastard I was.

In this paper we have presented narratives that reveal the pain of incarceration as former inmates describe their struggles to come to grips with their shame. Many of these stories became "redemptive narratives" as several of the interviewees later reflected on the process of revisiting experiences they had not confronted with anyone since their release. Clearly, shame can be a powerful and debilitating emotion. It was identified by several of the respondents as the major factor in their desire to go straight. And of the 10 respondents who experienced emotions of shame, only two re-offended. But even this number may distort the significant role shame plays in one's decision to lead a crime-free life.

The parole violation occurred when the individual turned herself in, and the new crime was a relatively minor property offense resulting in six months jail time. When shame and religiosity are both expressed by the same individual, the results are even more impressive. *As Table 1 clearly indicates, not one of the subjects who identified both variables committed a new crime or had his or her parole revoked.* Admittedly, this is a small sample, so any generalizations must be made with great caution. Also, and as noted above, the methodology may not uncover all those with shame, or those who are religious. It is also possible that there were criminal and parole violations not uncovered during the interview process, both by those expressing religiosity or shame and those who did not make such expressions. However, even with all these caveats, we feel that the combination of religiosity *and* shame does provide a buffer from further criminal activity.

REFERENCES

Becker, H. S. (1966). Introduction. In C. Shaw, *The Jack Roller* (2nd ed.). Chicago: University of Chicago Press.

Blumer, H. (1969). *Symbolic interactionism: Perspective and method.* Englewood Cliffs, NJ: Prentice-Hall.

Bogdan, R. C., & Biklen, S. K. (1982). *Qualitative research for education: An introduction to theory and methods.* Boston: Allyn and Bacon.

Braithwaite, J. (1989). *Crime, Shame and reintegration.* Cambridge, UK: Cambridge University Press.

Burgess, R. G. (1984). *In the field: An introduction to field research.* London: George Allen & Unwin.

Carpenter, C., Glassner, B., Johnson, B. D., & Loughlin, J. (1988). *Kids, Drugs and Crime.* Lexington, MA: D.C. Heath.

Fleisher, M. S. (1995). *Beggars and thieves: Lives of urban street criminals.* Madison: University of Wisconsin Press.

Gibbons, S., & Jensen, K. (1996). Institution-to-community experiences of ex-offenders. Paper presented at the annual meetings of the Academy of Criminal Justice Sciences, Las Vegas, March, 12-15.

Gibbons, S., & Jensen, K. (1998). The role of private remorse in going straight. Paper presented at the annual meetings of the Academy of Criminal Justice Sciences, Albuquerque, NM, March 11-14, 1998.

Glaser, B., & Strauss, A. (1967). *The discovery of grounded theory.* Chicago: Aldine.

Grasmick, H. G., & Bursik, R. J. (1990). Conscience, significant others, and rational choice: Extending the deterrence model. *Law and Society Review, 24* (3), 837-861.

Irwin, J. (1970). *The Felon.* Berkeley: University of California Press.

Jensen, K., & Gibbons, S. (1997). Ex-offender perspectives on the value of education and treatment programs. Paper presented at the annual meetings of the Academy of Criminal Justice Sciences, Louisville, March 11-14.

Kottak, C. P. (1999). *Assault on paradise: Social change in a Brazilian village.* Boston: McGraw-Hill.

Liebrich, J. (1996). The role of shame in going straight: A study of former offenders. In B. Galaway & J. Hudson (Eds.), *Restorative justice: International perspectives.* Monsey, NY: Criminal Justice Press.

Maruna, S. (2001) *Making good: How ex-convicts reform and rebuild their lives.* Washington, DC: American Psychological Association.

Meisenhelder, T. (1977). An exploratory study of exiting from criminal careers. *Criminology, 15*(3): 319-334.

Pinsonneault, P. (1985). Abandonment of the criminal career: Some evidence. *Criminologie Montreal, 18*(2): 85-116.

Shover, N. (1985). *Aging criminals.* Beverly Hills, CA: Sage.

Skotnicki, A. (1996). Religion and rehabilitation. *Criminal Justice Ethics, 15*(2): 34-43.

Spradley, J. M. (1970). *You owe yourself a drunk: An ethnography of urban nomads.* Boston: Little, Brown.

Tittle, C.R., & Welch, M. R. (1983). Religiosity and deviance: Toward a contingency theory of constraining effects. *Social Forces, 61*(3): 653-682.

Williams, K., & Hawkins, R. (1986). Perceptual research on general deterrence: A critical review. *Law and Society Review, 20*(4): 545-572.

AUTHORS' NOTES

Kenneth D. Jensen, PhD, is professor of anthropology at Western Oregon University. He spent 20 years in prison education and is currently working on research investigating the prison-to-community transition of adult offenders. He has served as a defense witness during the penalty phase in capital murder cases.

Stephen G. Gibbons, PhD, is professor and chair of the Criminal Justice Department at Western Oregon University. He is currently investigating the prison-to-community transition of adult offenders and has research interests in the politics of prison site selection, community policing, and juvenile crime prevention.

Data used in this study were gathered with the support of grants from the Western Oregon University Faculty Development Fund.

Address correspondence to Kenneth D. Jensen, PhD, Department of Anthropology, Western Oregon University, Monmouth, OR 97361.

Religion, the Community, and the Rehabilitation of Criminal Offenders. Pp. 231-247.

Social Theory, Sacred Text, and Sing-Sing Prison: A Sociology of Community-Based Reconciliation

VICTORIA LEE ERICKSON

Drew University

SUMMARY This paper examines the sociological component of the urban community-based professional education programs at New York Theological Seminary (NYTS), focusing on the auxiliary Master of Professional Studies program offered at Sing-Sing Prison. NYTS serves urban poor and socially marginal populations and is the only seminary in the country to require social theory and social research methods course work. Explored is the simultaneous use of social theory and sacred texts as teaching tools and intervention strategies in the educational and personal transformation processes of men incarcerated for violent crimes. A survey of NYTS Sing-Sing alumni further documents the impact of the MPS program and facilitates our conclusion that community faith-based corrections can be transforming encounters as demonstrated, by one important measure, in a low recidivism rate. *[Article copies available for a fee from The Haworth Document Delivery Service: 1-800-HAWORTH. E-mail address: <getinfo@haworthpressinc.com> Website: <http://www.HaworthPress.com> © 2002 by The Haworth Press, Inc. All rights reserved.]*

KEYWORDS Community religion, methodology, prison inmate, social theory

Michael Foucault: . . . the soul is the prison of the body.

St. Augustine: For so it is Oh Lord, My God, I measure it but what I measure, I do not know.

Sing-Sing Prison and New York Theological Seminary have drawn their clientele from the same populations for over a century. Both institutions claim to seek personal and social transformation.

Addressing the wayward, Sing-Sing Prison was built in 1825 with 1,000 cells and quickly became as notoriously violent as Devils Island, Alcatraz, and San Quentin prisons. Now called a "correctional facility," Sing-Sing operates under a social mandate supervised by the "justice system."

New York Theological Seminary (NYTS) was founded in 1900 to serve the poor immigrant communities of New York City. "Seminaries" are social institutions shaped by the faith "practices" of believers and the mandates of "religious traditions." In 1981, at the request of alumni, NYTS created a Masters in Professional Studies (MPS) for Christian, Muslim, Jewish, Hindu, Buddhist, Rastafarian, and many other, inmates with long sentences who would return to their respective prisons to work as chaplain's assistants. NYTS entered the social justice system as a community faith-based provider of educational services.

Enrollment in this highly competitive application and reference process nets on the average 75 system-wide applications. The admissions committee, made up of NYTS administration and alumni, select an average class size of 10-15. The MPS program requires simultaneously one year of field work and one year of pastoral counseling course work. The student is supervised in a prison setting. The standard professional requirements for field work and counseling are met. In addition to course work, the students write an integration paper.

Critical to the program's success is the fact that the Sing-Sing classroom is a NYTS classroom. The faculty value their classrooms equally and are held equally accountable for student success. All NYTS programs offer traditional and liberation-oriented ethics, church history, theology, and pastoral counseling course work that engage and revolve around the sacred texts that shape one's identity. Students are taught a variety of hermeneutical tools to exegete and interpret scripture and daily life. Racism, sexism and classism as sociological realities that construct their lives are routinely addressed.

Run as a mission of the school, the Sing-Sing MPS degree currently costs $70,000 per year or $4,667 per student. It is only in looking historically at the MPS program that we can say that it is a community-based corrections project. It is first and foremost a ministry. The MPS intervention strategy is largely dependent on the labors of its director, the Rev. Dr. George (Bill) Williams Webber.

A CLOSER LOOK AT COMMUNITY INTERVENTIONISTS

Explaining what motivates community people to intervene in the messy life stories and complicated social responses we call the "justice system" has pushed researchers into a language that sociologists seldom use or analyze because it is hard to measure. It is common for community corrections researchers and practitioners to use words like "mission, goodwill, virtue, peace, faith and spirit." These words describe the source of motivation that shapes the practice of community corrections. What connects socially conservative, liberal and radical people in community corrections is that the source of their motivations is *faith*–the faith they have in people to respond to human caring. In spite of the fact the humans are not "indefinitely malleable," it is on holy or "secular faith that human nature permits the possibility of wide social cooperation to bring about a just or egalitarian society" (Arneson, 1985:627). In short, for many interventionists, the reclaiming and redeveloping of individuals has little to do with their psychological or sociological label and everything to do with building relationships of accountability that are nurtured in a *spiritual, ethical and moral* context.

Souryal's *Probation as Good Faith* (1996:5) argues that the professional practitioner is continually working with the questions, "who are we?, what are we here for?, what is important or not important?" Community interventionists believe that, at its best, justice is a community activity that establishes answers to the problem of crime through the practice of law applied by the heart. Tracing the history of probation, Souryal locates a classic heroic anchor in John Augustus (1784-1859) who took sentenced men into his home to prevent their incarceration. There grows up around the idea of probation what Souryal calls a sense of *voluntary self-denial and mercy*. Justice in the Souryal framework is a two-way street, engaging the traffic between both the criminal and noncriminal actors. The successful probationist helps facilitate movement between the victim and the perpetrator, who have a relationship that suffers from the pain of transgression. A dialogical-spiritual act creates the probationary mind and requires the probationist to be wise but also to believe blindly in the equality and potentiality of all persons. To talk about the motivations of the contemporary probationary agent, Souryal finds that we must still use the words "heart" and "soul" (Note 1). It is the heart and soul that bridges the gulf created by the transgression.

Reconciliation for those involved in this work is a holy, or in the very least, a spiritual, activity. NYTS builds all of its models on a liberation and reconciling perspective that grows out of the best wisdom of its constituency that is evangelical, conservative, liberal, radical Protestant and Catholic. Important to the success of all its programs, NYTS incorporates Black and White feminist traditions. Like NYTS, some feminist traditions have also recognized that reconciliation is a voluntary spiritual activity requiring self-denial (Note 2). Catherine Faver's account of Emily Greene Balch, 1867-1961, a Nobel Peace Prize winner and advocate for oppressed groups, found that Balch "insisted that both spiritual qualities and practical strategies were necessary for constructive social change" (1991:351). Similar to the NYTS faculty, Balch argued that one's God concept shapes one's method for change.

Theology, then, has social consequences (Note 3). Balch's solution to problems was that they be anchored in "disinterested benevolence." This benevolence could not happen until one gave up privilege and sacrificed one's self for the good of all. Faver argues that Balch's sense of justice included a notion of quiet, friendly, self-sacrifice that created space for the hearing of all voices (Note 4). Balch's Nobel Peace Prize recognized her ability to enter into conflicting communities of discourse, create a bridge between their story-lives, and develop a mediating strategy anchored in the respective moral integrity of the parties, who then agreed to seek the common good. At their own cost, liberationist reconciling agents set a table for a family conversation that narrates, through a broken relationship between the victim and the perpetrator, a story of reconciliation.

AN EVOLVING PEDAGOGY FOR TRANSFORMATION

New ways of relating are built at NYTS through critical analyses that include inductive learning, action-reflection models and sociological theory. When students arrive in the classroom with "reasons why they are in prison" clouded in mystery, they are asked to imagine answers. Soon, answers appear: if you are good on the streets you get run over. The kids are hungry and they need shoes, so you do what you have to do.

The "I centered" responses locate the moral and practical source of action in the student while the student points a finger at society for shaping his life in this way (Note 5). The way society relates to the "I" creates the "me." All of a sudden, they realize that there is a large social conversation going on that they have not been a part of. In fact, they become rather urgent in their need to know how society works. In prison, everyone wants a new way of relating to the world, but few people come to articulate this desire. In the MPS program, students learn that, sociologically, new ways of relating require new interpretive structures. Constructing them is their work. Narrating the story of how they arrived at prison, students learn that "re-creating the self" is a community project.

Self-creation is a large task. To accomplish it, or to at least initiate a start, NYTS faculty employ a multicultural pedagogical strategy. All students regardless of their religion must read the sacred texts of his peers. The stories in the text are analyzed as the first step toward analyzing "one's own story." As teachers, it sometimes feels as if our Sing-Sing students are "discovering the self" for the first time as they become competent literary and social critics.

In the reading of sacred texts, the students discover that there are boundaries around the text, yet these boundaries have breaks in meaning when narrators come and go and historical sequencing is abandoned. Students also discover that they know something about this text that is not known to the actors in the story. From their multicultural perspectives they debate the "meaning" of the story. As they discover themselves, they also discover that life is about "a multiplicity of meanings." Together, sitting around a shared table, students further discover that knowledge is its own reward; that knowing is empowering because it is communal; that knowledge is most fun when it is shared; and that knowledge changes "meaning." They discover the joy of doing something ancient: they discover the joy of learning. Students find that their joy is rooted in the forgiveness that results from their "table talk."

The stories that their conversations unpack are their life stories. Faculty guide students into hearing and remembering each other's stories. They learn to trust each other with their stories. Often students talk for the first time in a caring group about sex and relating to lovers; about their feelings for their fathers and mothers; about their desires for their own children.

For people of faith, religion is the narrator of their story lives and the soul is the keeper of the story. Formative stories that craft moral identity are *holy stories*. As the actors in the story-books (the Bible, Koran and Torah) change their course of direction and plot their way to the end, students realize that they, too, change by going to the breaks in the boundaries and borders of their lives and by speaking and reaching through them. This is not easy work. They have to learn each other's languages and then together, faculty and students, create another language that they share.

To do this, we need to talk–a lot! Webber realized that this talk is so critical to student success that he added a day to his schedule at Sing-Sing so that he could "just sit in the classroom and listen to people talk" (Webber, 1996). It is this "third way" this other, "I-You," relational, way that we create together through much listening and talking that becomes the new structure or "sense of shared structure" that we act out of (Buber, 1970; Sumedho, 1960). We cannot share interpretative space unless we participate in the conversation that creates relationships. The NYTS student learns how relationality is constructed through language, conversation and social interaction. Once we learn how relationships are created, we can learn how to restructure them. Soul craft is time-consuming and hard work.

PFOHL'S MODEL FOR CONSTRUCTING SOCIAL STRUCTURE

At NYTS we must choose theorists carefully. We want students to argue with the theorist, so we look for sociologists whose work invites "talking back" (Gates, 1988; Willis, 1987). Most helpful are ethnomethodologists who research indigenous methods for accomplishing daily life; particularly useful is Stephen Pfohl (1975) who documents the elements of the work we do to create a "sense of shared structure." Pfohl's set of six "interpretative procedures" establishes a list of interactions between persons that forms a shared understanding of the rules that will shape their behavior. Social relationships are founded on these interactions. In a two-way process, the instructor teaches the theory and uses the theory to precipitate *normal natural* change in her students. This change must be owned by the student and come from within the conversation he creates between himself, his community of origin, society and his peers who are sitting around the table with him.

Given that sacred stories are fundamental to identity, taking Pfohl's ethnomethodological documentation of relational structuring into the inductive Biblical study mode is a *normal natural* act. The following short exercise gives the reader a taste of how the practice of faith is integrated with sociological reasoning in NYTS classrooms.

The class begins by reading a familiar story and discussing the meanings given to the story from our many traditions. In this example, the class reads and tests Pfohl's observations by rereading I Samuel 28 and by documenting Pfohl. If Pfohl is right, that people in real life do this set of six things, we should find people doing them in our story life. I Samuel 28 is traditionally described as King Saul's consultation of the *medium, witch, wizard* of Endor. Some translations call her a woman with a *familiar spirit*. In this story, we find King Saul inches away from the Philistine army, unable to communicate with God who, the story tells us, has "turned away" from him. Saul needs another way to the information he seeks and asks for a medium. Most students come to this story with an interpretation they remember from a frequently preached understanding of this story which chastises the King for disobeying God and seeking a profane creature, a medium; the King's act is punished by God through Saul's death.

After examining Pfohl, new meanings to this story emerge. It occurs to the students that long before feminism, women and men both knew that women's "profane" knowledge was prohibited by "sacred" priestly law; and that practitioners and their clients could be put to death if they were caught performing what they knew. The King's soldiers, ironically in light of Saul's persecution of the mediums and those who went to them, knew exactly where to find one. In fact, they knew the best of the lot and bring Saul to Endor. We discover that the persecuted belong to a persecuted community that was defined and created by the King's mandate.

Pfohl and other ethnomethodologists are particularly helpful for NYTS students. They encourage an indigenous pride in indigenous knowledge. Empowered by what they know, students begin to ask: What does social theory unpack for us and, what do we offer social theory? A typical unpacking of an ethnomethodological reading is similar to this:

Unpacking Pfohl's Understanding of Practices that Establish Social Structure

Reciprocity of Perspectives. Pfohl argues that a sense of social structure, relationality, could not be accomplished without our ability to interchange the places where we stand until we understand each other's assumptions. We "disregard individual differences until differences prove disruptive" to reciprocity. *Student observation: When Saul and the woman meet their first task is to interchange the places where they stand. This reciprocity of perspectives finds the woman declaring the disruptive truth about Saul, he is a persecutor in disguise, he could kill her for doing what he asks. He begs her to allow him another standpoint: he is a desperate man about to die and he needs her, and furthermore, he knows her as capable of performing the task he needs. She em-*

braces the enemy and calls up Samuel from the dead. Student accounting: The street does not leave much time for understanding the motives of the other; the street does not teach you to embrace the enemy. I have not made use of the opportunities to learn how to resist the street.

Et Cetera Assumption. We "tolerate the utterances of another" until we can assume common meaning. *Student observation: The woman decides to tolerate the demands of Saul and Saul tolerates his need of her. Samuel grumpily decides to appear and all three of them establish a common meaning for this moment: Saul has disturbed Samuel through this woman because he has no other way to divine knowledge.* Student accounting: The street teaches self-centeredness and a lack of tolerance. Often the very people we do not tolerate are the people who hold the keys to the meaning of our story. I have not made the right friendships.

Film of Continuity. We assume that our conversation together will make "what has gone on before integrally meaningful." *Student observation: Samuel explains how Saul's past shaped the present moment. The moment is judged on what happened before. Saul has no choice but to live through it even as living through it means dying. Samuel gives Saul the meaning for this moment that he seeks.* Student accounting: The meaning for this moment is the kind of death we will live.

Normal Forms. We attempt to "define the situation" thereby "normalizing the chaos" of our encounter. *Student observation: The chaos of the encounter (the woman could be put to death by the man who needs her, Saul knows he is about to die, Samuel is annoyed at being disturbed) is calmed by an agreement that this chaos is expected and normal. The situation is defined as extra-ordinary: "God has turned away."* Student accounting: It turns out that all situations are extra-ordinary ones, ones in which others help us find God.

Talk Itself Is Reflexive. We talk-talk-talk to establish the content of experience; from multiple sets of contents, we establish the "features" of our interaction. If talk is restrained in this process, the structuring task fails. All actors say what they need to say. *Student observation: When Saul attempts to speak over and past the woman, she declares, "I listened to what you said and I risked my life to obey you. Now listen to me."* Student accounting: The oppressor's narratives can suppress the oppressed's voice; all reflexive talk houses silence. We have been silenced and we have silenced others.

Descriptive Vocabularies. What "really" exists is glossed over as we move toward a common vocabulary that will practically accomplish the everyday world we want. *Student observation: When Saul confirms that he will in fact die, he decides on self-murder and refuses to eat. This sui-cidal behavior is unacceptable to the woman and to his servants who "gloss over" Saul's self-murder wish. They get him up and offer him a Passover-like meal. The woman Saul persecuted as a "witch" performs the "priestly" blessing of his death. That is what they all want, a death for Saul that has integrity. He must sit up and answer for his behavior. In the meantime, the people have gone around patriarchy and have "or-dained a woman." Student accounting:* We form the vocabulary we need around a table of people who want what is best for us; it is painful to admit that there is no way around the punishments for our behavior; it is embarrassing to remember the people we rejected, harassed and hu-miliated–people who only wanted what was best for us. We need to be forgiven so that our wounds may heal. We also need to resist an oppres-sive social order.

To the reading of texts, faculty and students bring class, race, gender and a host of other variables that unpack the context and expand mean-ing. Students read feminist analyses of gender and sexual ethics and dis-cover that the woman with "a familiar spirit" turns out to be a rather interesting character. Students discover that they have met this woman before, they know her as one of the many women who saved them. They are startled to realize that they unreflectively assumed the patriarchal interpretation of her life. They realize how easy it is to be wrong about someone. They are surprised that in the face of death she willfully bridges the chasm between Saul and God. They challenge typical inter-pretations of the text as they discover that the servants, the oppressed classes, know that her knowledge was suppressed by elite priests who did not want competition in the realm of knowing, but the people risked their lives to go to her anyway. When prophets and dreams fail King Saul, her ancient knowledge saves them both.

Through her story, students begin to talk about what it is like to be a "demasculinized/profane" man in a world of powerful, sacred, white men. What does it mean to be a Black lover, father, husband in a world that prevents achievement? How do you ever repay your wife for stand-ing by you through your life sentence? Or, what does it mean not to know your wife and the mother of your children? What knowledge do I have as a man of color that can save me, my family and perhaps even my community?

Students learn that by constructing a shared language they bridge the borders between their differences. Borders change shape and are rede-fined as they discover in this communicative process, the salvation they need. Some borders are defended when they are not convinced that they shall be saved by their alteration. We all learn that one cannot demand re-bordering. One cannot re-border by simply speaking it out loud with people *who speak like me.* Borders are reconstructed in the hidden and spiritual world of embrace–in that world where we love and seek the well-being of the other. This moment of embrace is when the other is not strange to us; when we see each other as common to each other, talk unrestrained, and co-create a new way of speaking that might not look like any language we bring to the conversation. The language of embrace radically reverses time so that we may start over and build new relationships. This language is the saving language of grace. It is a language that sociologists must come to learn if we are to understand the reconciliation process that deters recidivism.

Talking Back to Pfohl: What Incarcerated Men Have Taught Their Teachers

Through the language of grace we learn practical sociological lessons:

- All reciprocity is a potentially violent act in that it requires us to embrace the other who is, all too often, the enemy.
- We cannot avoid this embrace because we have no other way to re-create relationships.
- Relationships create the meaning that we live by moment by moment.
- Therein, all situations are "extra-ordinary."
- All reflexive talk has the potential of silencing voices; silence must be resisted so that the ultimate goal of creating a shared language, a new relationship, happens. We all answer for our obstruction of this goal. If we reach the goal it is said of us that "we died with integrity."

Once students learn how to think analytically about texts, they apply this knowledge to their story-life and the story-life of fellow students who were once strangers to them. They work at understanding the social degradation that happens on the street, between lovers and through incarceration. Once again, the empowerment curriculum teaches theory and uses theory for personal transformation.

Learning from the Sociology of Moral Indignation

Pfohl's ethnomethodological work in criminology documents the ritual work of language construction in the materializing, the making real, of a criminal identity. The individual who comes to be named a criminal is banished from commonsense and erased from memory as s/he is placed behind bars and out of sight (Pfohl, 1986). What Pfohl (1981) finds universal about crime and deviance is precisely the process that defines the offender. The person becomes a "real" offender in the "socially differentiated act of silencing" the person, when the normal ongoing process of creating and maintaining social relationships is interrupted.

Intervention into the process of criminal identity formation, then, would require intentional documentation of the act of banishment; resistance of banishment and the speaking or resistance of silencing activities. In addition, challenging or reforming the criminal identity would require the ritualistic repair of and reentry into the normal process of social relationships. This repair work, then, would point out the collective nature of identity formation as it taught the actors that the goal of social interaction is "each other."

Status Degradation Rituals

In short, there are times when the behavior of individuals, or groups of individuals, causes moral indignation in the surrounding social networks. Sociologists have long established that shame, guilt and boredom are ways society uses to address moral issues by changing individuals through the removal of particular behaviors from them, while, at the same time, keeping their egos intact.

There are many ways to replace people or groups of people with a more desirable person or social network. For example, in religious history a particular people remember that while waiting for the death of King David, Bathsheba plotted to ensure that her son, Solomon, would end up successor to the throne. Today in the United States, we create electoral processes to ensure that, if desired, we will have a regular turnover of officials. However, there are times when particular people decide that a person, group of persons, or an identity (and the memory of them) has to be totally destroyed and rebuilt. In these cases, shaming, producing guilt or promoting boredom are not sufficient acts of transformation to achieve the desired end which is a *radically new identity*. Supposedly, incarceration radically transforms people into rehabilitated members of society with radically new identities through the ultimate degradation of being labeled "unfit for human contact."

Totally replacing actions, identities, a person or a cluster of persons, outside of the normally ongoing community-based corrective systems requires a special kind of status degradation work. Harold Garfinkel (1956) calls the work of status degradation "ritual" and "ceremonial" activity that maintains its own set of specialized actions. Status degradation ceremonies serve to ritualistically replace the old with the new through carefully orchestrated events. Garfinkel found that all of the social structures and conditions for the degradation of identity are available to society. Degradation rituals were seen by him as a kind of secular "communion" that brings to the denouncing party a reinforced group solidarity. The denouncing party is empowered as the degraded person is literally destroyed and then becomes a totally new person in the eyes of the condemners whose values and virtues are successfully defended by the perpetrator's loss of identity and status.

Conditions for Successful Status Degradation

Garfinkel found that not only do the following elements create a successful ceremony, they also tell us how to "render denunciation useless" (1956, 420, Note 6). The following italicized text summarizes Garfinkel's theory and the following text indicates how the theory is used for personal transformation in an effort to cause a failure of the social degradation. A good denunciation requires:

    a. A denouncer,
    b. a perpetrator, and
    c. an event where witnesses agree with the denouncer.

The MPS program reverses these requirements as it: (i) opens its arms to the inmate and accepts him as a valuable member of society and in so doing displaces the denouncer; (ii) the inmate/perpetrator is given a respectable title: student and soon-to-be-alumni; and (iii) the witnesses to the event are expanded past the law to include community members who will now witness to his transformation. As soon as the student goes through the rigorous admissions process he joins a tight knit group of alumni who begin the work of affirming his identity and who require strict accountability for his behavior.

These are the steps to successful degradation:

- *Both the event and the perpetrator are removed from their every-day character and made to stand "out of the ordinary."* The students use normal everyday understanding of life to claim that all events are out of the ordinary and no single event can be determinative of the rest.
- *The event and the perpetrator are treated as instances of uniformity, as ongoing possibility; and, the witnesses must appreciate the characteristics of the person and the event as dialectical counterparts–as profane and sacred, for example.* The student is clear that "the me who did that is not me." The MPS faculty affirm the "out of characterness" of the event and the person. What everybody knows is that all people want to be loved and enjoy loving others. The student failed, but the student is not fundamentally a failure. He will never do this, or anything like it, again. He is not a profane being, he is back on the journey toward the Holy.
- *The denouncing agent must be identified as a publicly known actor who participates in the witnesses' lives, who feels what they feel, who sees what they see, and knows what they know.* Just as "professionals" acted publicly to incarcerate, professionals now act publicly to reclaim the person.
- *The denouncer then makes the values of the witnesses super-personal and delivers the denunciation in their name.* The MPS faculty and NYTS take on the prison system as a matter of "mission and identity." Their reputation is on the line each time they give a grade to or support the release of a student.
- *The denouncer arranges beforehand to speak in the name of these values as one of their greatest supporters.* Just as the legal system that incarcerated him did, the reconciling agent speaks on behalf of "all society"; however, the reconciling agent claims that its students are also supporters of the values society holds.
- *The denouncer leads the witnesses to experience the distance from the perpetrator.* The reconciling agent declares that the student is not an enemy to be feared and pulls the student closer to its heart as it declares separation undesirable–conferring friendship/familyhood status.
- *The denounced is then ritualistically separated from the legitimate order and placed outside of it as opposed to it and is made "strange."* The student is ritualistically matriculated and graduated, made a legitimate member of a responsible organization.

The steps towards a successful degradation are intended to announce that:

- The old identity was an accident and the new identity was there all along;
- the rightful identity has been established in the eyes of witnesses; and,
- the old identity is not changed, it is reconstituted.

Reconciliation "happens" when the degradation fails to establish a new identity (as "criminal") and reclaims an ancient one (as child of God) as the rightful identity that witnesses affirm is also theirs.

Robert Gephardt's study (1978) of the successful *forced succession* status degradation ritual within an organization's succession events, extends Garfinkel's observations to include the denouncer's use of social rules and the importance of the denouncer's knowledge of "the organization" in the success of the attempted degradation. What interests Gephardt is that the denouncing actors must display a knowledge of that which they want to replace. In other words, the actors who create succession events know what they are doing and know themselves to be potentially capable of enforcing a new organizational reality. Society, then, knows what it is doing when it builds prisons and expands the criminal justice "professional" network. Society, then, also knows what the alternatives are to incarceration.

Reversing Degradation as the First Step to Reconciliation

Self-assertion is a critical tool for empowerment and for resistance of the effects of degradation. Without self-assertion degradation is complete and people mentally, socially, culturally and physically die–they become invisible (for a classic reading see Patterson, 1982; for the role of Eros, see Tong, 1992). NYTS teaches all of its students how to claim and reclaim their rightful identity as valued members of society.

Low alumni recidivism rates are a welcome but unintended by-product of the NYTS program (O'Conner & Erickson 1997). Although all prison service programs have reducing recidivism as a goal, the NYTS program was different in that the goal was designed to create chaplains to minister to inmates inside of prison. The NYTS ministry had lasting consequences. O'Conner (1996) found that compared to a similar group of inmates released from prison, NYTS MPS alumni have a surprisingly lower recidivism rate. After 12 months, 0% of MPS alums are rearrested as compared to 30% in the larger population. After 28 months, the rates are 9% for the MPS and 37% for the non-MPS ex-offenders. George Webber (1996) argues for further studies that control for the year of alumni release. Under his directorship, significant program changes increased personal accountability between students and, Webber says, contributed to the now almost 0% recidivism of alumni. O'Conner and Erickson (1997) argue that further studies are needed to determine the fine detail of institutional, programmatic, curricular, and personal contributions to declining recidivism of alumni. Whatever these new findings will conclude, it is ultimately the men themselves who are responsible for performing the hard work of self-transformation.

In a 1996 survey of alumni, Erickson found that alumni reported the changes brought about by contact with the faculty and through expanding their education to be "personal life changes." They learned how to build community, develop their faith and construct helpful spiritual practices. One commented:

> I have good memories of the 1987-1988 class and realize it was a great turning point in my rehabilitation . . . The year at NYTS was very important to me to not lose faith and that I could and would be redeemed from that sin of the past. The faculty were important in this development. Here I was a student–a person–and not just a convict. This is very important.

Said another, "I still have a useful life to lead."

What is clear is that alumni have encountered community and have created friendships that hold them accountable to "moral living." They extend this accountability to themselves inside and outside of prison. The skills they credit to their empowerment are: the ability to *restructure* their lives, *motivate* themselves and others, *create and maintain* values through new networks of supportive people and through rooting this transformation in a *wisdom source*. Their empowerment facilitated an extensive offering of alumni sponsored classes and workshops for other inmates.

Inmates tell us that it is in the *seeing* of themselves as creators of relationships and as nurturers of others that give them strength to keep going and a sense of purpose. Their leadership role teaches them how to hold themselves and others accountable to moral community. Answering to God, friends and community for what one has done wrong has taught them how to forgive themselves and to seek forgiveness from others.

MPS alumni are continually disappointed in the prison system's inability to see their transformation. Equally frustrating is society's continued stereotyping of their identity. A common question is: "How can

I change the way people think about me?" (For an expanded discussion of how people cope with damaged identities, see Goffman, 1963.) Communities are not consistently, nor primarily, reconciling. Human beings teach each other how to be reconciling through any means we have; not the least of these are social theory and the sacred text.

NOTES

1. See also, Muldrew (1966). For sociologists to understand much about the culture of community corrections we must be conscious of modernism's redefinition of "community." Muldrew argues that the culture of reconciliation was disrupted in the late sixteenth century when the goal of community to preserve charity and love was replaced by the maintenance of commerce. Although never actualized in reality, the ideal of a love-directed community created a different understanding of sociality than the market-directed community.
2. Sing-Sing is a men's prison. However, women's prisons are actively studied. See: McDermott (1994) and Hannah-Moffat (1995).
3. The 1960s produced many liberation and feminist theologies foreshadowed in Balch's life and work. See: Russell and Clarkson (1996).
4. For an expanded discussion on how Christians taught themselves how to hear across differences, see: Irvin (1994).
5. For an example of how sociologists taught themselves to hear across differences, see: Lemert (1993).
6. For extended discussion of Garfinkel on degradation, see: Erickson (2002).

REFERENCES

Arneson, Richard J. (1985). Marxism and Secular Faith. *American Political Science Review*, 79, 627-40.

Buber, Martin (1970). I-*Thou* (Walter Kaufmann, trans.). New York: Charles Scribner's Sons.

Erickson, Victoria Lee (2002). Mapping Love and Terror: Walking the Terrain of I AM Who Is Being There. In *Surviving Terror: Hope and Justice in a World of Violence*. Grand Rapids, MI: Brazos Press.

Faver, Catherine A. (1991). Creative Apostle of Reconciliation: The Spirituality and Social Philosophy of Emily Greene Balch. *Women's Studies*, 18, 335-351.

Garfinkel, Harold (1956). Conditions of Successful Degradation Ceremonies. *American Journal of Sociology*, LXI, 420-424.

Gates, Henry Louis, Jr. (1988). *The Signifying Monkey: A Theory of African-American Literary Criticism*. Oxford, UK: Oxford University Press.

Gephardt, Robert, Jr. (1978). Status Degradation and Organizational Succession: An Ethnomethodological Approach. *Administrative Science Quarterly*, 23 (Dec.), 553-581.

Goffman, Erving (1963). *Stigma: Notes on the Management of Spoiled Identity*. New York: Simon & Schuster.

Hannah-Moffat, Kelly (1995). Feminine Fortresses: Women-Centered Prisons? *Prison Journal*, 75 (2), 135-164.

Irvin, Dale T. (1994). *Hearing Many Voices: Dialogue and Diversity in the Ecumenical Movement*. Lanham, MD: University Press of America.

Lemert, Charles. (1993). *Social Theory: The Multicultural and Classic Readings*. Boulder, CO: Westview Press. [See especially George Herbert Mead, The Self, the I and the Me, pp. 243-247.]

McDermott, M. Joan (1994). Criminology as Peacemaking, Feminist Ethics and the Victimization of Women. *Women & Criminal Justice*, 5 (2), 21-44.

Muldrew, Craig (1966). The Culture of Reconciliation: Community and the Settlement of Economic Disputes in early Modern England. *Historical Journal*, 39 (4), 915-942.

O'Connor, Thomas, Ryan, Patricia, & Parikh, Crystal. (April 16, 1996). The Impact of the New York Master in Professional Studies Program on Recidivism: An Exploratory Study. Unpublished document, Division of Ministerial Services, New York State Department of Correction, Albany.

O'Connor, Thomas, & Erickson, Victoria. (1997). Theology and Community Corrections in a Prison Setting. *Community Corrections Report*, July/August, 67-68, 75.

Pfohl, Stephen J. (1975). Social Role Analysis: The Ethnomethodological Critique. *Sociology and Social Research,* 59 (3), 243-265.

Pfohl, Stephen J. (1981). Ethnomethodology and Criminology: The Social Production of Crime and the Criminal. In Israel L. Barak-Glantz & C. Ronald Huff, editors, *The Mad, the Bad and the Different*. Lexington, MA: Lexington Books.

Pfohl, Stephen J. (1986). Criminological Displacements: A Sociological Deconstruction. *Social Problems*, 33 (6), S94-S113.

Russell, Letty M. & J. Clarkson, Shannon (Eds.) (1996). *Dictionary of Feminist Theologies*. Louisville, KY: Westminster John Knox Press.

Souryal, Sam S. (1996). Probation as Good Faith. *Federal Probation*, 60 (4), 5-10.

Sumedho, Ajahn (1960). Being Patient with Our Inability to Forgive. *Middle Way: A Journal of Buddhist Society* 71, 83-88.

Webber, George Williams (Bill), (1997). Taped Interview, December 10, at New York Theological Seminary, New York, NY.

Willis, Susan (1987). *Specifying: Black Women Writing the American Experience*. Madison, WI: University of Wisconsin Press.

AUTHOR'S NOTE

Dr. Victoria Lee Erickson is associate professor of the sociology of religion and university chaplain at Drew University, Madison, New Jersey. Portions of this paper were presented to the Sociological Practice Association's Annual Meeting in Alexandria, VA, June, 1998.

Address correspondence to Dr. Victoria Lee Erickson, Associate Professor of the Sociology of Religion and University Chaplain, President's House Annex, Drew University, Madison, NJ 07940 (E-mail: Victoria.Erickson@att.net).

Religion, the Community, and the Rehabilitation of Criminal Offenders. Pp. 249-257.
© *2002 by The Haworth Press, Inc. All rights reserved.*

The Prisoner as Scapegoat: Some Skeptical Remarks on Present Penal Policy

T. J. GORRINGE

University of Exeter

SUMMARY The article examines the claim that prisoners function as scapegoats in our society. The scapegoat mechanism, as illuminated by Girard, arises from mimesis, and this accounts for a good deal of crime, and is one of the reasons that the poor are disproportionately criminalized. In addition, it is a way for individuals and societies to deal with guilt: offloaded on to the prisoner, society no longer has to deal with it. Scapegoating, however, is a way of dealing with problems through violence. Its opposite is inclusion and the practice of forgiveness. Programs of restorative justice can begin to turn this practice from noble sentiment into penal policy. *[Article copies available for a fee from The Haworth Document Delivery Service: 1-800- HAWORTH. E-mail address: <getinfo@haworthpressinc.com> Website: <http:// www.HaworthPress.com> © 2002 by The Haworth Press, Inc. All rights reserved.]*

KEYWORDS Bible, prison, religion, community, scapegoat, inmate

At the entrance to prison they demand ID, so let me provide some. I am a priest and a theologian, and have been visiting prisons and prisoners in Britain and India since 1979. In 1996 I tried to put some thoughts down on the relation between theology and criminal justice in a book called *God's Just Vengeance: Crime, Violence and the Rhetoric of Salvation.* The main title wasn't mine: publishers always think they know better than authors. But at least one friend has told me of personal delight at receiving a card from the local bookstore which read simply: "God's Just Vengeance is awaiting you at Waterstone's." It is now pinned on the kitchen door. In this article I want to take further one or two of the suggestions floated in that work. I shall say something, firstly, about scapegoat theory; secondly about prisons and prisoners; thirdly about this theme in one great literary text; finally about present penal policy.

Let me make it clear: my experience is confined to Britain and India. I know about the United States only through the media, books like *Dead Man Walking,* and films like *Shawshank Redemption.* United States readers will obviously have to see how my remarks apply, *mutatis mutandis,* to their situation. I also have to say that I have no qualifications as a psychiatric social worker, full-time prison worker or anything of the sort. I have spent a lot of time talking to prisoners and reflecting on that as a priest and theologian, and that is it. These are my only qualifications. With these caveats, I begin.

SCAPEGOAT THEORY

Scapegoat theory has been largely developed over the past 40 years by the French cultural anthropologist Rene Girard, who has worked for much of that time at Stanford. Girard's thesis is simple (Note 1). He appeals to Aristotle for the insight that all learning happens through *mimesis.* The problem with imitation is that we all want the same thing, and this generates violence. The story of Cain and Abel is a classic story of two brothers in competition for the same goods (a "blessing," i.e., success in his enterprise), where the failure of one leads to murder. But mimesis does not just belong to ancient myths or to childhood. The nuclear arms race was a classic instance of mimetic violence whilst mimesis is one of the major motors of capitalism. As Tony Reilly, chief executive of Heinz, once said: "Once something is on TV, it turns out that everyone wants more or less the same thing." Blue jeans, Nike shoes, burgers, baked beans . . . But as we also know, capitalism presupposes competition, and even, as we often say, "cutthroat competition," violence.

Before the advent of law, and social conventions, Girard believes we have the war of all against all, as everyone competes for the goods everyone desires. In order to survive, societies have to find a way of limiting violence. This is the scapegoat mechanism. Society channels all of its pent-up frustration, anger, rage and aggression on to one single victim–the scapegoat. In the scapegoat ritual outlined in Leviticus 16 the priest lays his hands on the head of a live goat and confesses over it all of the people's sins and transgressions, "putting them on the head of the goat." The goat is then driven into the wilderness, bearing the people's iniquities away (Leviticus 16.23). It is a symbolic story of immense power.

Nothing is said in Leviticus about the role of the whole community in driving away the goat by throwing stones, though this is what happens when people are executed by stoning. Also, the goat is not killed, but simply driven into the wilderness. Girard, however, works on the assumption that the scapegoat is normally killed, and he is able to give copious examples from both Scripture and other world literature to support his case. He also illustrates, only too plausibly, how the scapegoat mechanism has functioned in world history. In European history, for example, the Jews were scapegoated, as were old women (so called "witches") and, as now, are ethnic minorities. We also know that scapegoating frequently happens within families, or other smaller communities. The scapegoat mechanism, in fact, as is already clear in Leviticus, is a way of dealing with guilt. When we feel guilty, doubt and anger are directed at ourselves: if we cannot deal with that the obvious thing is to displace it on to another. On this other is dumped all of our rage and aggression. That one is the guilty one, guilty of everything. The rhetoric of Isaiah 53 picks this up: "On him YHWH has laid the iniquity of us all" (Isaiah 53.6). In this way the scapegoat–a person, or a community, or perhaps a symbolic animal–actually saves us or delivers us from our own inner conflict, at least for a time. Girard envisages a situation in primitive society where it was repeated yearly, as, of course, Leviticus envisages. Once the murder has taken place the scapegoat can even become a divine figure since it delivers the person or community from its own anger.

But whilst the scapegoat mechanism *delivers* from violence, at the same time it *institutionalizes* violence as a way of dealing with conflict. This aggression is not absent from law. To be sure, law comes to control the blood feud and the lynch mob, but the sentiments of retributive justice–make the punishment fit the crime–cast a cool and rational veil over the scapegoat mechanism. No one realized this more clearly, or stated his opposition to it more forcibly, than George Bernard Shaw. The prison authorities profess three objects, he wrote:

> (a) Retribution (a euphemism for vengeance), (b) Deterrence (a euphemism for terrorism) and (c) Reform. . . . They achieve the first atrociously. They fail in the second. The third is irreconcilable with the first.

He then went on:

> A punishment system means a pardon system: the two go together inseparably. *Once you admit that if I do something wicked to you we are quits when you do something equally wicked to me, and you are bound to admit that the two blacks make a white.* Our criminal justice system is an organized attempt to produce white by two blacks. (Note 2)

The mechanism of scapegoating is a way of dealing with aggression by aggression. But this is true of retributive justice also. I do not say they are identical. I do, however, believe that retributive justice may be a way of scapegoating others and that, as Shaw argued, it inevitably involves violence.

THE PRISONER AS SCAPEGOAT

In turning to the state of imprisonment let me begin with a question: in the West, why is it that the vast majority of prisoners are from social classes 4 and 5? Why so few from the wealthy and educated? This question has troubled people from the time of the Hebrew prophets on. We know part of the answer: there is a high correlation between poor environments and crime. More significantly, there is the question of what we count as crime. "Crime" for the newswriter means street crime, burglary, mugging, rape, robbery, murder and drugs. But anyone who has spent time in our jails knows that the great majority of inmates are not in for sensational offences. Most are in for property offences, in themselves quite minor. And prisoners are entirely up front about their motivation in taking what they regard as their fair share of the world's goods.

Mimesis . . . We all want the same. When the goods of this world are denied to many, some will take them for themselves.

So Girard's theory has something to contribute to understanding the motivation of many crimes. However, if we go on to try to understand all violence through mimetic theory, as he does, I think we go too far. If I think of the many prisoners I have known doing time for GBH (Grievous Bodily Harm), and some of those who are serving time for murder, I find it artificial to trace everything to mimetic rivalry. I want a portfolio of explanations, and at the end of the day I will expect an inexplicable residue.

I will look to what Alice Miller says about parenting, to what Fromm says about authoritarian personalities, and above all I will look to what my own experience has taught me: that violent people are often emotionally inadequate people. This is not to patronize them. It is to say that where some of us can vent our rage and frustration in verbal or rhetorical violence, in swearing at God, like Job, or in paint, like Francis Bacon, there are many who can only vent them through violence. And the inexplicable residue? Sorry, but as they say in Yorkshire: "There's nowt so queer as folk." (I once met a farmer on a Yorkshire moor. Lovely day, I cried. He scowled: "Day's fine; it's buggers you meet." Quite). We never, with our theories, tie up, wrap up, exhaust the mystery of any other personality. All we can provide are rough approximations towards answers.

Girard has illustrated how the Jews were scapegoated in medieval Europe. In the early modern period attention switched to vagabonds, vagrants, masterless men, the poor. Between 1690 and 1850 these were hanged, transported, flogged and imprisoned in quite astonishing numbers. Society was changing with breathless speed. People were desperately uneasy about the consequences: they sought and found a scapegoat. This process, I would argue, still continues. To return to my question: why are the prisons full of social classes 4 and 5? It is not that the middle and upper classes are more moral and law abiding than the poor; rather, their filching is smarter, or even legal. Morally, for instance, which is a more serious abuse of the community: breaking and entering or using overseas tax havens? For one you may end up in the nick (and if you are unfortunate enough to live in California–three strikes and you're out–you may get life); for the other you're applauded. But wrongdoing must be punished; it must be made an example of. Someone must show that crime doesn't pay, and we know who: social classes 4 and 5.

I have never seen a United States jail, but I can tell you that the architecture of British jails is the architecture of the scapegoat. What did Leviticus say? "Drive him out into the wilderness . . ." And so these huge structures are erected with their vast walls, a wilderness of bars and keys. Of course prisons are also about surveillance, as Foucault argues; they are also about preventing escape. But prisons, as every prison chaplain will tell you, are part of the community. But just look at your nearest prison and see the degree to which that is recognized. In fact, prison architecture exists to deny that: in the rhetoric of concrete, razor wire and stone it says: those within have forfeited their right to be considered part of community. Keep out! Small wonder that anywhere there is a prison only a handful of citizens know, or want to know it; only a handful of dedicated souls enter its gates to visit. Those within are those driven out, like the goat for Azazel. They are there to pay the price for all.

Don't get me wrong: I am not sentimental about prisoners. I know they include the vicious and the crafty, and the downright wicked. But then, so do theology faculties, and churches, and businesses, and senates and Houses of Parliament. If I will not be sentimental about prisoners, neither will I be about all those "good" people outside either.

MEASURE FOR MEASURE

As we all know, England only ever produced two truly great theologians, William Shakespeare and William Blake. That Shakespeare may speak to prisoners has been shown with tremendous power by Murray Cox and Alice Theilgard in *Shakespeare as Prompter*, which records how they have used his plays with category A prisoners in Broadmoor, a hospital for the criminally insane, in England.[3] Here I want to offer my own brief commentary on the play in which Shakespeare reflects most insistently on retributive justice, *Measure for Measure*. The play is a sort of extended meditation on Romans 11.32: "God has shut up all to disobedience that God might have mercy on all." It is a passionate exposé of scapegoating logic.

In the play we have a kingdom ruled by a Duke (like Prospero, one of Shakespeare's "God" figures), who is about to leave for a time. Part of his reason for doing so is that he feels he has administered the laws too laxly, and he wants to see how his virtuous deputy, Angelo, will cope. In fact he does not disappear but only takes disguise as a friar. In New Testament terms, he does not consider his greatness something to be hung on to (Philip, 2.5) but henceforth is to be found quite literally in the underworld, "visiting the spirits in prison" (1 Peter 3.19).

No sooner has the Duke left than the laws against promiscuity are set in force with full vigor. A young man, Claudio, is condemned to death for getting his intended with child. Claudio has a virtuous sister, Isabella, about to take the veil: she is urged by the "low life" Lucio to plead with Angelo. Eventually Angelo extorts from her a promise that he will spare her brother if she sleeps with him. The Duke knows that Angelo once broke a marriage contract because the dowry promised him was inadequate: in pitch darkness this jilted lady goes to bed with Angelo in place of Isabella. But no sooner has Angelo had his pleasure then he sends a peremptory note for the execution of Claudio. Down in the condemned cells the Duke at first suggests a notorious criminal, Barnadine, be executed in Claudio's stead, but he is too drunk, "unfit to live or die." The convenient death from fever of another prisoner solves this dilemma. But soon comes the denouement: the Duke gives up his disguise, and all is made plain. The spirits in prison are delivered, including even Barnadine. All are judged, and all receive mercy.

Puritan societies are notoriously punitive societies. In Puritan England Shakespeare gives his own assessment of criminal justice, of the relation between the underworld–pimps, bawds, welfare scroungers–and the overworld–government and even the virtuous Isabella. For the most chilling line in the play is her, "more than my brother is my chastity." At the end of the play the Duke acknowledges *his* need, in asking for her hand in marriage, and she gives up her deadly principle. Angelo has proposed a logic of violence, making an example of the young and incautious and the loose living. Claudio was to be made a scapegoat. Why? Clearly because he embodied all those repressed instincts Angelo could not face up to. Shakespeare shows the hypocrisy of this strategy: unmasking it is a prelude to the establishment of a society built upon a different logic, that of forgiveness–one of his favorite themes.

GOING BEYOND SCAPEGOATING

To scapegoat is to load with sin and drive into the wilderness. It is to exclude. The opposite of scapegoating, therefore, is inclusion. I am tempted to say that it is the formation of community except that I am more and more convinced that community remains an unfinished project for human beings. As Iris Marion Young has insisted, those cosy tight communities of our old villages and towns were often also deeply punitive–and scapegoating–of those who were different. When the industrial revolution dissolved those communities it brought not only alienation, but also freedom for many. And yet–we cannot do without community, and there is no way of "rehabilitating" prisoners without it (the quotes are there because, as Shakespeare shows in his commentary on the New Testament, we all need rehabilitating). The first step in such a process is in the *practical* recognition that prisons and prisoners are part of the community, by which I mean, part of the whole fabric of society.

This is where "church" comes in. The great Swiss theologian Karl Barth refused to use the word "church" as he got older because, he said, it was so overburdened. He preferred the word *gemeinde*, community. Following the hints of his work I would suggest that what we have in the New Testament is not a blueprint for a religious society (with bishops, priest, and deacons, for example). Rather, the New Testament points to the unfinished task of the fashioning of community, and envisions a community not based on the scapegoat principle. Now this is not to say that some people should not be locked up. On the contrary, there are certainly people from whom society needs protecting (advertising moguls and military hardliners come to mind). What it is to say is that if people are locked up they are nevertheless recognized and treated *as those who continue to belong to society, as those produced by society, and therefore as those to whom society also continues to recognize a debt.* This necessarily entails ruling out the death penalty, which is the ultimate form of scapegoat penalty, the ultimate form of exclusion, and which breeds a violent and exclusionary culture within any society which practices it.

Now penal policy in Britain for more than twenty years has been committed to exclusion: to "banging up" more and more prisoners, so that we have had to return to the prison ships of the early nineteenth century, and also to the private jails which the early penal reformer, John Howard, warned were always a disaster in dealing with prisoners. Those responsible for "justice" (i.e., scapegoating the poor), in Britain, Home Secretaries, to a man play to the gallery of the tabloid press, exploiting moral panics and depicting certain individuals or groups (in Britain the child murderer Myra Hindley, and pedophiles) as uniquely vicious. Of course I have no brief for child murder or pedophilia. I do, however, want to escape the stench of scapegoating about these political pronouncements, and to see some recognition of the fact that we are all responsible for the community we live in, which includes, unfortunately, child murderers and pedophiles, just as it includes dictators immune from prosecution who are responsible for the torture of thousands, or World Bank officials who urge dumping toxic waste in the Third World.

We are all members one of another: that is the bottom line of penal policy, and it precludes scapegoating. Prisoners, in my experience, share the view that "nothing works"–they are as skeptical of rehabilitation as anyone. I beg to differ. As I think Helen Prejean illustrates so movingly, respect and acceptance work. In the concrete, and over the long haul "love" works. And so–prisons? Unfortunately, yes, though

I would change their clientele considerably. But only in vigorous inter-action with their surrounding communities–in an interaction of respect in minute particulars, as Blake urged. If we really understood that need we might begin to do something about that particular tranche of human evil we call "crime."

NOTES

1. Among his many books on the theme are *Violence and the Sacred* (Johns Hopkins, Baltimore, 1977), and *Things Hidden Since the Foundation of the World.* (Athlone, London 1987).

2. In S. and B. Webb, *English Prisons Under Local Government* (London: Longmans, 1922) p. liv.

3. M. Cox and A.Theilgard, *Shakespeare as Prompter* (J. Kingsley Press, London and Philadelphia, 1994).

AUTHOR'S NOTE

Tim Gorringe is St. Luke's Foundation Professor of Theological Studies in the School of Classics and Theology at the University of Exeter in the United Kingdom. His academic interests focus on the interrelation between theology, social science, art and politics. He published a major book offering a political reading of Karl Barth's the-ology in 1999, and he is currently working on a theology of the built environment.

Address correspondence to T. J. Gorringe, Department of Theology, School of Classics & Theology, University of Exeter, Queen's Building, The Queen's Drive, Exeter EX4 4Qh, United Kingdom (E-mail: T.J.Gorringe@exeter.ac.uk).

Religion, the Community, and the Rehabilitation of Criminal Offenders. Pp. 259-285.

Rethinking God, Justice, and Treatment of Offenders

TED GRIMSRUD

Eastern Mennonite University

HOWARD ZEHR

Eastern Mennonite University

SUMMARY The connection between religious belief, in particular how people in the West have viewed God, and retributive criminal justice practices runs deep. God has been understood to be the basis for the practices of human beings inflicting severe punitive pain upon other human beings judged guilty of violating community standards. God is understood, most of all, to be "holy" (that is, unable to countenance sin of any kind). God's holiness "forces" God to act punitively–and justifies God's agents (either in the church or in society) also acting punitively. This retributive theology dominated Western worldviews in the Middle Ages and formed the bases for criminal justice practices which began to be institutionalized during that time. However, a closer look at the founding document of the Christian tradition, the Bible, challenges such retributive theology. Biblical understandings of justice point more in the direction of restorative than retributive justice. Biblically, "justice" has to do not so much with punishment as with healing, restoring relationships, and fostering the well-being of the entire community. Present-day alternatives to retributive criminal justice are emerging which reflect the general thrust of biblical justice. These include victim-offender reconciliation programs, sentencing circles, and family group conferences. The success of such programs provides encouragement for those who hope for criminal justice practices which effect healing more than simply punitive pain. *[Article copies available for a fee from The Haworth Document Delivery Service:*

1-800-HAWORTH. E-mail address: <getinfo@haworthpressinc.com> Website: <http://www.HaworthPress.com> © 2002 by The Haworth Press, Inc. All rights reserved.]

KEYWORDS Prison, religion, Bible, restorative justice, community, punishment

According to Gorringe (1996, p. 266), Leo Tolstoy observed of the criminal justice system that "The whole trouble is that people think there are circumstances when one may deal with human beings without love, but no such circumstances ever exist. Human beings cannot be handled without love. It cannot be otherwise, because mutual love is the fundamental law of human life."

Our criminal justice system certainly is troubled by tendencies to treat some people (whether offenders or victims) without love, and the consequences are costly (Zehr, 1995). From a Christian perspective, and simply for the sake of social well-being in our society, we need to challenge those tendencies.

This paper will address three issues: (1) On what bases do people think they can deal with offenders without love? That is, what views of God, ultimate reality, and justice justify unloving (retributive) approaches to criminal justice? (2) Is it possible to construct an understanding of God, ultimate reality, and justice, based on the founding texts of the Christian tradition (i.e., the Bible), which supports Tolstoy's assertion about the fundamental law of life being love? (3) Is it possible in "real life" to approach criminal justice issues from the point of view of Tolstoy's assertion that love is foundational?

CONCEPTS OF GOD AND RETRIBUTIVE JUSTICE

Despite the widespread occurrence of inter-human violence throughout most of recorded history, few people would deny that most human beings tend naturally to avoid violence toward other human beings. Perhaps this instinct should be understood as an evolutionary, survival-of-the-species instinct; perhaps it is a necessary condition for living in human community; perhaps it should be understood as a reflection of the law of God placed in the human heart by our Creator. Regardless of the basis, in human experience we usually need some overriding reason to go against this instinct. That is, to act violently toward, especially to kill, other human beings, is serious business, undertaken because some other value, commitment or instinct overrides the tendency not to be violent.

Punishment involves, by definition, the intentional infliction of pain and the use of coercion and thus must be seen as a form of violence. Punishment by the state, then, is morally problematic as it involves the state doing things that are normally considered morally and socially unacceptable. The problematic nature of punishment has given rise to a huge variety of justifications for delivering such pain.

In the criminal justice tradition of the Western world, the overriding justifications given for violently punishing offenders, even to the point of death, have and continue to be tied to an understanding of ultimate reality which believes that this reality requires retributive justice when fundamental natural or divine laws are violated. Such "retributive justice" is seen to restore the moral balance.

Given the religious roots of Western culture, this understanding is to a large extent rooted in a particular understanding of God as ultimate reality: retribution is needed to "satisfy" the need God has that violations be paid for with pain. When someone commits a wrong, it is assumed, the central question of justice is "What does s/he deserve?" and the normative answer is pain.

So in the area of criminal justice, the issue of punishment, i.e., of authorized human beings inflicting pain (including death-dealing pain), on other human beings is a theological as well as a philosophical and practical issue. In saying that violence is a theological issue, we are using "theology" in a broad sense to refer to beliefs about ultimate reality, foundational beliefs about the nature of the universe. We are using "God" as the common human symbol for ultimate reality, whether this understanding of ultimate reality posits a personal deity or not (Kaufman, 1993).

Punishment is an issue having to do with how human beings understand the world they live in, the values by which they shape their lives. The concept of retribution or punishment as justice is an issue shaped decisively by beliefs about God and God's character (or, in non-religious language, beliefs about ultimate reality and the character of ultimate reality).

Western culture has explicitly theological roots dating back to the "Christianizing" of the Roman Empire which began in the fourth century with the first "Christian" emperor, Constantine, and was given powerful theological grounding in the work of Augustine a century later. This process continued as Western concepts of justice were decisively shaped during the Middle Ages through an interaction between Christian theology and newly-emerging concepts of law. This interaction deeply influenced Western culture as a whole and helped to reinforce a retributive view of justice.

Part of the theology underlying retributive justice, which we will summarize in very broad strokes, speaks to how God was (and is) understood. There are some key aspects of the view of God generally characteristic of medieval Europe which shaped (and were also shaped by) the emerging punitive practices of criminal justice and which continue to be foundational in present-day practices of retributive justice.

A crucial consequence of this view of God is how it provides the basis for understanding God to desire violent punishment. God's wish for violent punishment provides a crucial impetus for the overriding of our instinct *not* to kill or in other ways act violently toward other human beings.

Retributive theology sees the first, and most basic, attribute of God as holiness, or, we could say, purity, or perfect righteousness. God's holiness is such that God simply cannot countenance any kind of sin. Sin is unholiness, impurity, unrighteousness. God can have nothing to do with such blemishes. In fact, if God has direct contact with sin, God must destroy it immediately. Everything about God and God's actions must be understood as ultimately deriving from this holiness.

From this perspective, human beings know what sin is because God has provided us laws, or rules, to follow. These laws have been revealed in part through the special revelation from God given in the Bible but also through the natural awareness people have in their own hearts of what is right and wrong. Human societies construct legal structures which, to a greater or lesser degree, depending on the particular society, reflect God's laws. When human beings sin, it is because they diverge from God's laws. Since the laws come from God, the sins are ultimately against God—and they hence directly violate God's holiness. This makes God angry and punitive. The only way holiness can be satisfied is through just punishment.

God's essential nature, then, is essentially inflexible. God cannot simply choose to forgive violations of his law. God cannot respond to each case in a unique way given the unique circumstances of each sin. God is unable to act with unilateral mercy and compassion. God, rather, is constrained by holiness—again, the most foundational characteristic of God. Simply to forgive would violate that holiness and leave it unsatisfied.

Compassion without satisfaction is simply not possible for God. Since God's justice is based upon the principle of holiness, God's justice allows nothing but punishment (i.e., the giving of pain for the sake of giving pain) as recompense for sin. Otherwise, the imbalance of a universe where God's rules have been violated can never be rectified. People must get what they deserve.

Ultimate reality, then, is in this view based on an inflexible principle of holiness. God may be understood, in essence, as a personified unchanging law of holiness. Deep down, reality is impersonal and unmerciful and the universe is seen in this view as an impersonal balance. "Justice" is most fundamentally concerned with maintaining this balance. If the balance is upset, justice requires recompense to restore the balance–payment to satisfy the requirements of the balance. This payment is made through punishment, pain for pain.

When the offense is serious enough, the only payment acceptable to justice is death–hence the moral validity of capital punishment. The human instinct not to kill is overridden by the requirements of justice. God wills that humans kill other humans under these circumstances because the most important value is God's justice.

In this theological framework, the doctrine of the atonement enters the picture here. Due to the extremity of the offenses of human beings against God's law, the only way God can relate to human beings is if there is death from the human side to restore the balance. God cannot relate to human beings simply based on love and compassion; God's justice, i.e., holiness, trumps God's love. God can relate only if God's holiness is satisfied.

As it turns out, the only way this can happen is through the enormity of the death of God's own Son, Jesus, whose righteousness is so powerful that it can balance out the unrighteousness of all of humanity. Jesus' atoning death provides a way for God to relate to repentant human beings. Human beings, when they confess their own hopeless sinfulness, may claim Jesus as their savior from the righteous anger of God, anger based on human violation of God's laws. As a consequence, salvation itself does not go counter to the basic nature of the universe as founded on impersonal holiness. Salvation happens only because that holiness is satisfied through the ultimate act of human violence–the sacrificial death of Jesus Christ. The basic nature of the universe does not change, and hence the pattern of restoring the balance by punishment when violations of God's law occur remains intact.

This theology has infused the social, political and cultural life of the West in very fundamental ways going back not just to the medieval period but into antiquity. Timothy Gorringe makes a strong case for the atonement theology of Anselm of Canterbury (c. 1033-1109) providing a crucial link in applying this view of God and ultimate reality to the practice of punitive criminal justice (Gorringe, 1996, pp. 85-125; see Evans and Evans, eds., 1998, pp. 260-356). However, surely the roots of such an application of these theological themes go much further back, to the infusion of Greek philosophy into Christian thought and the extraordinarily influential writings of Augustine of Hippo (see Paolucci, 1962, especially sections I and IV).

While recognizing these ancient antecedents, we will focus on the Middle Ages in sketching the impact of retributive theology on the criminal justice practices of the West (Berman, 1983; Bianchi, 1994; Zehr, 1995). In the early Middle Ages, the church, as it struggled with the state for dominance of European society, found it helpful to utilize the law of the later Roman empire as its instrument for solidifying its authority. It merged its theology with this newly-rediscovered legal system to create canon law. Secular authorities, in their turn, followed suit.

The theology provided a notion of God's impersonal holiness and retributive response to violations of that holiness. The Roman legal philosophy was also centered on impersonal principles. Instead of being based on custom and history, law in this perspective stood alone.

Roman law assumed a central authority, thus providing a basis for "legitimate" initiation of action by a "neutral" centralized dispenser of justice. In the medieval worldview, this centralized authority (church or state) was God's direct agent.

Roman law was written law, based on principles that were independent of specific customs ("transcendent," to use theological language). As embraced by the medieval church in its canon law, it had an accompanying method for testing and developing law (i.e., scholasticism). Roman, law, therefore, could not only be systematized and expanded but could be studied and taught transnationally by professionals. This universal character helps explain its appeal and almost immediate spread to universities throughout most of Western Europe.

From the base of Roman law, the church built the elaborate structure of canon law, the first modern legal system. This was a revolutionary development. It provided the papacy with an important weapon in its struggle for supremacy both within the church and in its relationship to secular political authorities.

By providing for prosecution by a central authority, it established a basis for attacking both heresy and clerical abuse within the church. The most extreme expression of this new approach was the Inquisition in which representatives of the pope ferreted out heretics and tortured them both to obtain evidence and to settle accounts (Binachi, 1994, pp. 16-17; cf. also Hamilton, 1981).

No longer was the individual the primary victim. In the Inquisition, it was a whole moral order which was the victim, and the central authority was its guardian. Wrongs were no longer simple harms requiring redress. They were sins requiring retribution. *God's* holiness understood in terms of retributive theology, necessitates *punishment*, carried out by the human agents of God's will.

These retributive practices actually diverged greatly from the approach of the earliest Christians. In the early church wrongs were seen as against people. In Matthew 18, for instance, wrongdoers are to make it right to the victim, then the obligation is loosened in heaven. But in the new medieval understanding, wrongs came to be seen as against God, against moral order. The wrong was seen to be against the sovereign, the overall authority, and that figure was a legalistic, punishing figure. God took the place of the victim, and salvation became appeasing an angry God (Pleasants, 1996). God's punishment was portrayed as so awful that all our attention is on saving the sinner from punishment, ignoring the obligation to the victim. In this theology—as in the emerging legal system—the focus is on dealing with the offender.

Justice became a matter of applying rules, establishing guilt, and fixing penalties—without reference to needs of the victim or the relationship between victim and offender. Canon law and the parallel theology which developed began to identify crime as a collective wrong against a moral or metaphysical order. Crime was a *sin*, not just against a person but against God, against God's laws, and it was the church's business to purge the world of this transgression. From this it was a short step to the assumption that the social order is willed by God, that crime is also a sin against this social order. The church (and later the state) must therefore enforce that order. Increasingly, focus centered on punishment by established authorities as a way of doing justice.

By the end of the sixteenth century, the cornerstones of state justice were in place in Europe, and they drew deeply from the underpinnings of retributive theology. New legal codes in France, Germany, and England enlarged the public dimensions of certain offenses and gave to the state a larger role. Criminal codes began to specify wrongs and to emphasize punishment. Some of these punishments were overwhelmingly severe, including torture and death.

Enlightenment thought and post-Enlightenment practice increased the tendency to define offenses in terms of lawbreaking rather than actual harms. To the extent that harms were important, emphasis was increasingly upon public rather than private dimensions. If the state represented the will and interests of the public, it was easier to justify defining the state as a victim and giving up to the state a monopoly on intervention. Most importantly, the Enlightenment provided new objectivity in the practice of punishment.

Enlightenment and French Revolutionary thinkers did not question the idea that when wrongs occur, pain should be administered by the state. Instead, they offered new justifications for state-initiated punishment. They instituted more rational guidelines for administering pain. And they introduced new mechanisms for applying punishment.

The primary instrument for applying pain came to be the prison. The reasons for the introduction of imprisonment as a criminal sanction during this era are many. However, part of the attraction of prison was that one could grade terms according to the offense. Prisons made it possible to calibrate punishments in units of time, providing an appearance of rationality and even science in the application of pain.

In short, our current "retributive" model of justice gained ascendancy through this legal revolution starting around the eleventh century, but which was not fully victorious in many places until at least the nineteenth century. Through this process, crime came to be defined as against the state, justice became a monopoly of the state, punishment became normative and victims were pushed out. But it was not a simple matter of theology shaping emerging criminal law or vice versa. The influence went both ways, with law and theology shaping each other (Gorringe, 1996, p. 22).

Developing penal theory, based partly on Roman law, helped reinforce the punitive theme in theology–e.g., a satisfaction theory of atonement, which reinforced the idea of payment or suffering to make satisfaction for sins. Biblical interpretation was biased in that the Latin translation of the New Testament caused it to be read through the lens of Latin law. As Gil Baillie has noted, Christ's death was intended to end retribution but this reinterpretation, including "satisfaction theology," worked toward the opposite–desensitizing us to, even justifying, judicial violence (Baillie, 1995).

Retributive theology, which emphasized legalism and punishment, deeply influenced Western culture through rituals, hymns, symbols. An image "of judicial murder, the cross, bestrode Western culture from the eleventh to the eighteenth century," with huge impact on the Western psyche. It entered the "structures of affect" of Western Europe and "in doing so, . . . pumped retributivism into the legal bloodstream, reinforcing the retributive tendencies of the law" (Gorringe, 1996, p. 224). The result, at minimum, was an obsession with the retributive theme in the Bible. A kind of historical short-circuit occurred in which certain concepts were taken from their biblical context, interpreted through the lens of Roman law, then used to interpret the biblical text. The result was an obsession with the retributive themes of the Bible and a neglect of the restorative ones–a basic theology of a retributive God who desires violence.

This view is embedded in the Western criminal justice system through our modern paradigm of "retributive justice," which might be characterized like this:

1. Crime is understood primarily as a violation of the law (unchanging, impersonal), and the state is the victim.
2. Offenders must get what they deserve: The aim of justice is to establish blame and administer pain to satisfy the demands of the moral balance in which the violation is countered by the punishment.
3. The process of justice finds expression as a conflict between adversaries in which the offender is pitted against state rules, and intentions outweigh outcomes and one side wins while the other side loses.

This paradigm of retributive justice which dominates Western criminal justice is a recipe for alienation, as is readily apparent today. By making the "satisfaction" of impersonal justice ("God's holiness") the focus of our response to criminal activity, the personal human beings involved–victims, offenders, community members–rarely find wholeness. Moreover, the larger community's suffering often only increases. Instead of the healing of the brokenness caused by the offense, we usually find ourselves with an increasing spiral of brokenness. Many victims speak of being victimized again by the impersonal criminal justice system. Offenders, often alienated people already, become more deeply alienated by the punitive practices and person-destroying experiences of prisons–which are most certainly not systems built upon anything resembling Tolstoy's law of love.

A crucial step in breaking free from the destructive dynamics of violence responding to violence is to recognize that the notion of ultimate reality (drawing from a particular notion of God), which underlies the retributive justice paradigm, is a human construct. Gorringe's "archaeology" of the impact of Anselm's theology provides powerful evidence for such a recognition (Gorringe, 1996).

All theology, in the broad sense of our views of ultimate reality, is a human construct. To quote Gordon Kaufman:

> All understandings of the world and of human existence are human imaginative constructions, grown up in a particular historical stream to provide orientation in life for those living in that history. But at any given time it is always an open question whether the conceptions and values and perspectives inherited from the past remain suitable for orienting human existence in the new present: this is a question to be investigated, never a position which can simply be taken for granted. (Kaufman, 1993, p. 43)

The notions of God and ultimate reality which underlie the retributive paradigm outlined above are not set in concrete. They are the result of human reflection and human application. If these constructs contribute to brokenness instead of healing, furthering the spiral of violence instead of fostering genuine peace, they need to be deconstructed and replaced.

Ironically enough, given the roots of our predicament in "Christian" theology, if we would return to Christianity's founding documents, the writings in the Bible, we might well discover the bases for a very different understanding of justice, ultimate reality, and God. This alternative reading of the Bible provides the basis for constructing a new understanding of justice, one which is increasingly coming to be called "restorative" justice, in contrast to "retributive" justice.

To put it another way, the source of our problem might actually provide a way to overcome the problem. Dutch law professor Herman Bianchi has argued that we should apply "homeopathic theory" to our situation. It will take a dose of what made us sick to cure us. Since an interpretation of theology got us into this "illness" in the West, he argues that it will take a dose of theology to make us free of it (Bianchi, 1994, p. 2).

In what follows, we will summarize some of biblical themes which undergird a non-retributive theology. Then we will briefly discuss present-day attempts to express this alternative theology in the realm of criminal justice practice.

THE LAW OF LOVE AND RESTORATIVE JUSTICE– AN ALTERNATIVE READING OF BIBLICAL MATERIALS

To read the Bible itself on its own terms and not through the lens of retributivist theology reveals a remarkably different portrayal of God and justice. From start to finish, we find in the Bible a "logic of salvation" fundamentally counter to salvation based on satisfying an impersonal principle of retributive justice.

The Bible's "logic of salvation" time after time reveals a God whose mercy is unilateral, whose compassion takes precedence over wrath (Hosea 11:9). The act of creation itself can be understood thus–God bringing peace out of chaos. The story of Noah and the Flood concludes with God simply *deciding* to act henceforth with mercy and not destruction (Genesis 9:8-17). Abraham and Sarah are called to form a people meant to bless all the families of the earth (Genesis 12:1-3) based totally on God's unilateral gift to them of an unexpected child ("Sarah was barren," Genesis 11:30).

Abraham and Sarah's descendants are given new, miraculous life–liberation from slavery in Egypt–simply as a gift from God. The law of Moses came in the same way–simply as a gift from God. Much later, God spoke similarly through Hosea in promising to continue to love the rebellious children of Israel ("I am God and not mortal, the Holy One in your midst and I will not come in wrath," Hosea 11:9). After Israel's fall and while in exile, more such words spoke of God's persevering love and unilateral mercy (Isaiah 40-55).

The story of Jesus continues this account of God's dynamic, responsive, unilateral saving mercy. According to the Apostle Paul, the work of God to save even God's enemies (Romans 5) is an expression of God's *justice* (Romans 3:21). That is, God's justice finds expression in unilateral, life-giving mercy–mercy which heals, which restores broken relationships, which has absolutely nothing to do with punishment or retribution. Paul's understanding of God's justice as personal and restorative (not impersonal and retributive as articulated by later Christian theology) fully coheres with earlier portrayals of God's justice in the Hebrew Bible.

We will focus our further elaborations on biblical justice on one of those earlier portrayals, that recorded in the Book of Amos, set in the mid-eighth century, BCE (see Grimsrud, 1999).

"Justice" (Hebrew: *mishpat* and *sedeqah;* Greek: *dikaisune*) is a common term in the Bible. A careful examination of its usage reveals an understanding quite different from impersonal, retributive, "English-speaking" justice (cf. Dihle, 1974; and Grant, 1974).

The Book of Amos contains perhaps the most concentrated treatment of the theme of justice in the Bible. The prophet Amos confronts the people of Israel for their treatment of weak and marginalized people in their midst: "You . . . who oppress the poor, who crush the needy" (4:1).

The Israelites "trample the head of the poor into the dust of the earth, and push the afflicted out of the way" (2:6). They have corrupted the local legal system which, instead of protecting weak people, actually makes their plight worse.

Israel is in jeopardy here due to its practices of oppression and exploitation and due to its active religiosity which only makes God more unhappy with the people. "Why do you want the day of the Lord? It is darkness, not light" (5:18).

Israel's only hope is to reverse the directions of its social practices. "I hate, I despise your festivals . . . Take away from me the noise of your songs; I will not listen to the melody of your harps. But let justice roll down like waters, and righteousness like an ever-flowing stream" (5:21, 23-24). The salvation for Israel is *justice*. But it is not justice as an abstract principle, as an impersonal balancing of the universe's scales. It is God's justice–the farthest thing from punishment.

The Book of Amos does speak of impending judgment should Israel not turn to the ways of justice. However, the judgment is not called "justice." "Justice" has to do with restoration of wholeness, not with retribution.

Amos presents justice as tied up inextricably with *life*. Do justice and live, Amos asserts; do injustice and die. Justice is not an abstract principle but rather a life-force. An unjust society will die; it cannot help but collapse of its own weight.

The goal justice seeks is life for everyone in the community. Because life is for everyone, justice pays particular attention to the people who are being denied life. Justice provides for access by all to the communal "good life." None can justly prosper at the expense of others, or even in the light of the poverty and need of others.

Justice, for Amos, establishes relationships, it meets needs, it corrects wrongs. Justice is concrete, practical, and historical. It is tied to specific acts and people. It is not abstract nor ahistorical.

In Amos, as elsewhere in the Bible, the ultimate goal of God's justice is redemption (cf. the vision of the healing of Israel which concludes the book of Amos [9:11-15]). Even the judgment God brings on Israel is for that end: it is intended to correct Israel's self-destructive injustice. The threats, warnings, and judgment of God are not for the sake of punishment as an end in itself. They are not a matter of retribution, of repaying rebellious Israel an "eye for an eye." Rather, the threats and warnings offer hope of salvation, of transformation. But if Israel does not respond, God's respect for Israel's free-will will result in God allowing its collapse as a nation-state. As we well know, this is precisely what happened: Israel played power-politics to the end and succumbed to the superior power of Assyria.

The overall biblical teaching on justice parallels what we find in Amos. We may summarize the biblical perspective with the following four points:

1. *Justice is for the sake of life.* God's justice in the Old Testament is not primarily retribution but salvation, not primarily punitive but corrective. The justice of God is saving power, God's fidelity to the role as the Lord of the covenant. Hosea 2:19 makes this point clearly: "I will take you for my wife forever; I will take you for my wife in righteousness and in justice, in steadfast love, and in mercy." Other representative Old Testament texts include the following: Ezekiel 34:16; Psalm 25:9; Isaiah 1:27; and Jeremiah 9:24.

The biblical God created the earth and its inhabitants for harmonious relationships and continually acts, even in the midst of human rebellion, to effect those relationships. "The Jewish and early Christian understanding of God's justice put the primary emphasis on the divine initiative, on God's readiness to do for his human creatures what they could not do for themselves, on God's readiness to 'go the second mile' and more" (Dunn, 1993, p. 35).

In the Old Testament justice is not primarily a legal concept; rather it tends to merge with concepts such as "steadfast love," "compassion," "kindness," and "salvation." Justice has ultimately to do with enhancing *life*. In that way we imitate our life-enhancing, loving Creator.

In the New Testament, the writings of the Apostle Paul, particularly the Letter to the Romans, make similar points. In Romans, Paul states that the *justice* of God has been revealed (apart from the law) in the saving work of Jesus Christ (Romans 3). That is, God's justice is God's compassionate love which effects salvation.

2. *Justice is part of the created order.* The Old Testament connects justice and life as part of its creation theology. Old Testament theology confessed "creation" to be an act of the covenant-making God of Israel (Lind, 1990, p. 95). Therefore, the basic character of creation harmonizes with the values of the covenant love, justice, peace, compassion–that which sustains and nourishes life. The Old Testament allows for no disjunction between the creator God and the covenant-making God. In fact, creation was God's first covenant-making act. Thus, covenant values are part of the very fabric of creation.

This means that human life has meaning, purpose, and destiny. Human life originated as an expression of God's covenant-love. So all human action that is in harmony with that love has meaning and is part of the basic meaning of creation–and is thereby "just."

The creation of humankind in the image of this God means that all people need relationships–with each other and with God. The purpose of human activity is to facilitate these relationships. Since all people, simply by virtue of being people, image God and thus have dignity and value, discrimination and disregard of any human life can never be justified. Injustice severs relationships. Justice seeks to establish and/or restore relationships.

God's will has to do with all parts of creation. Nothing is autonomous from that will. The Old Testament challenges people of faith to carry out the creator's will in all spheres of human existence. Ultimately, the Old Testament makes no distinction between the order of creation and the order of redemption. The creator-God and the redeemer-God are one and the same. Faithfulness to the "creation mandate" equals living lives of love.

The heart of God's character is steadfast love, which for God means desiring the good of all people. This includes God's enemies and especially social outcasts. God's love provides the model for God's followers.

3. *Justice is not soft on evil but rather seeks to destroy evil*–as an expression of God's justice. However, this justice is rooted in God's love for all humans. God's love for enemies means that God hates that which evil does to humankind, and God works to heal its effects. Evil only ends when the cycle of evil fighting evil is broken. The Old Testament model for this is the suffering servant in Isaiah (for Christians, the precursor to Jesus), who did not retaliate but accepted all that the powers of evil could do and conquered them. This is the ultimate model for biblical justice (Lind, 1990, pp. 89-90).

God destroys evil, ultimately not through coercive force but through suffering love. This biblical theme symbolically comes to its completion in the book of Revelation, where the Lamb, Jesus Christ, wins the final battle with the powers of evil through his cross and resurrection (cf. Rev. 19:11-21; see Grimsrud, 1988).

God's love works to set right that which has been corrupted. This is justice. One way of characterizing justice, therefore, is to say that justice is how love is expressed in the face of evil. Love expressed in the face of evil acts to stop the evil and to heal its effects. That is, it is redemptive, salvific.

God's justice creates life and acts to sustain and restore life. Human justice, in the Old Testament sense, would seem truly to be justice only when it also acts to sustain and restore life. Since biblical justice seeks to make things better, justice is not designed to maintain the status quo. Indeed, its intent is to shake up the status quo, to improve, to move toward shalom.

4. *God's justice is especially concerned with the most vulnerable members of society* (see Yoder, 1987, pp. 27-37; Wolterstorff, 1983, pp. 69-72). The biblical teaching ends up emphasizing the poor and needy because in their oppression they were being excluded from community life and from the shalom God wills for everyone. This destroys community and ends up lessening the well-being of each person in the community.

Jeremiah identifies doing justice to the poor and needy with "knowing" God (22:13-16). He represents God as stating that those who "understand and know me" are those who recognize that "I am Lord; I act with steadfast love, justice, and righteousness in the earth, for in these things I delight" (Jer. 9:24). This is true for God; it is likewise God's expectation for people.

Expressing love toward one's fellow human is the inescapable condition of having communion with God. "Sow for yourselves justice, reap steadfast love, . . . for it is time to seek the Lord" (Hosea 10:12). This becomes the call to conversion: "Return to your God, hold fast to love and justice, and wait continually for your God" (Hos. 12:6).

This communal justice was not to be for the Israelites' own sake alone. The purpose for justice within Israel was ultimately worldwide justice. Even in the story of Israel's initial election in Genesis 18, a major reason given for it is to bring about "justice and right" for all humankind.

Biblical teaching redefines justice in ways that help us do justice in a largely unjust world. As Millard Lind writes, "biblical justice speaks to the world's problems of justice, and it speaks so radically (to the 'root' of the matter) that it changes the definition of justice" (Lind, 1990, p. 95). In changing the definition of justice, the biblical perspective changes the definition of the ultimate character of God.

The Bible emphatically identifies God's love with God's justice. This inextricable connection guards against rationalizing the treatment of some people as objects instead of as human beings, all in the name of "justice." Such "justice" becomes a dehumanizing power-struggle with winners and losers. And because losers are so seldom content with being losers, the battle never ends.

Holding love and justice together also guards against thinking of justice as an abstraction, separate from its function as a relationship-building, life-sustaining force. The concern for justice is people, much more than "fairness," "liberty," or "entitlements." Biblical justice focuses on right relationships, not right rules.

In this way of thinking, justice is primarily corrective or restorative. Justice seeks reconciliation and reparation. Injustice must be opposed and resisted–but only in ways that hold open the possibility of reconciliation. What happens to the offenders matters, too, if justice is the goal. Corrective justice rules out death-dealing acts, such as capital punishment, as tools of justice.

This understanding of biblical justice (and the biblical God) places a high priority on restoring relationships and social wholeness in the face of brokenness and alienation (e.g., crime). Hence, we might call it restorative justice.

We may illustrate the contrast between biblical, restorative justice and retributive justice as follows:

Retributive Justice	Restorative, Biblical Justice
(1) Rule-focused (break law)	People-focused (cause harm)
(2) Focus on infliction of pain	Focus on making right
(3) Rewards based on just deserts	Rewards based on need
(4) Separate from mercy	Based on mercy and love
(5) Seek to maintain status quo	Transforms status quo
(6) Central actors: state vs. individual	Central actors: entire community, including offender
(7) State (or God) as victim	People (shalom/peace) as victims
(8) Goal is offender paying debt to society (God); victim is (often) ignored	Goal is restoration of relationships, healing for all parties

Restorative justice is personal, relational, social, and dynamic. It stands in stark contrast with the Western retributive justice which characterizes our criminal justice practices. The contrast may be said, by some, to be so great that restorative justice is essentially irrelevant to the "real world" we now live in.

We propose, to the contrary, that restorative justice offers tremendous possibilities for "healing" even in the brokenness and alienation of today's criminal justice world. Hundreds of programs in many parts of the world demonstrate that restorative justice is not only relevant but essential. Without doubt, healing is needed–and, we believe, it is possible.

PUTTING RESTORATIVE JUSTICE INTO PRACTICE

"Human beings cannot be handled without love," Tolstoy wrote, and yet our concept and practice of criminal justice have been built upon the opposite. We have argued above that the Christian scriptures support Tolstoy's assumption that relationships are fundamental. However, a misconstruction of God's nature, formed in part through an unfortunate symbiotic interaction between law and theology during a formative period of Western culture, has caused us not only to ignore but to pervert this understanding into a retributive concept of justice. It is this retributive understanding which underpins the unprecedented rate of punishment in today's world, providing conceptual justification for the "corrections-industrial complex" or industry which is part of its driving force (Christie, 1994; Schlosser, 1998).

This concept of justice is not only morally questionable–it is counterproductive as well. James Gilligan, former head psychiatrist for the Massachusetts Department of Corrections, notes that many offenses emerge out of injustice and victimization that offenders themselves have experienced or perceive themselves to have experienced: "the attempt to achieve justice and maintain justice, or to undo or prevent injustice, is the one and only universal cause of violence" (Gilligan, 1996, p. 12). Given that, Gilligan continues:

> What is conventionally called "crime" is the kind of violence that the legal system calls illegal, and "punishment" is the kind that it calls legal. But the motives and the goals that underlie both are identical–they both aim to attain justice or revenge for past injuries and injustices. Crime and punishment are conventionally spoken of as if they were opposites, yet both are committed in the name of morality and justice, and both use violence as the means by which to attain those ends. So not only are their ends identical, so are their means. (pp. 18-19)

What would a concept of justice look like if it were based on love–that is, on respect and concern for the people involved, on a commitment to respond constructively (Claassen, 1990)? Could such a relational or restorative approach to justice not only be articulated but actually implemented?

During the past twenty-five years, a growing movement has sought to do just this. Eduardo Barajas, Jr., a program specialist for the National Institute of Corrections, has characterized it like this: "A revolution is occurring in criminal justice. A quiet, grassroots, seemingly unobtrusive, but truly revolutionary movement is changing the nature, the very fabric of our work." He argues that it extends beyond most reforms in the history of criminal justice: "What is occurring now is more than innovative, it is truly inventive, . . . a 'paradigm shift' " (Barajas, 1996).

The immediate source of this "restorative justice" movement may be traced back to two Mennonite practitioners in Ontario, Canada. Frustrated with existing criminal justice practices, trying to put into practice their religious beliefs, seeking to be practical about peacemaking, they conducted a series of "victim-offender reconciliation" encounters between two juvenile offenders and the numerous people these young men had victimized in a drunken spree. This led to the implementation of various forms of victim-offender mediation or reconciliation throughout North America, Europe and elsewhere and to the development of restorative justice theory.

From that tiny source was born a stream that is truly international in scope. Nothing comes from nowhere, though, and of course this restorative justice stream has many much-deeper sources; indeed, its exact origin is obscure. It can be traced to a variety of religious traditions. During the past several decades it has been fed by the conflict resolution movement as well as the seemingly-contradictory movements for victim rights and alternatives to prison. Feminist theory has provided an important awareness of the patriarchal nature of our structures, including the justice system, but has also enriched the stream with its emphasis on an ethic of relationship.

The stream is fed in important ways from a variety of traditional values, practices, and customs. Indeed, two of the most promising forms of restorative justice today–Family Group Conferences and Circle Sentencing, come directly from aboriginal or indigenous values adapted to the realities of modern legal systems.

In contrast to the "retributive" paradigm of justice outlined earlier in this paper, the concept of restorative justice underlying these approaches might be summarized like this:

1. Crime is primarily a violation of, or harm to, people and relationships.
2. Violations create obligations. The aim of justice is to identify needs and obligations so that things can be "made right" to the extent possible.
3. The process of justice should, to the extent possible, involve victims, offenders and community members in an effort to mutually identify needs, obligations and solutions.

The restorative justice concept can be framed in a variety of ways, but two ideas are fundamental: restorative justice is *harm-focused* and it promotes the *engagement* of an enlarged set of stakeholders. Most restorative justice can be seen as following from these two concepts.

Restorative justice views crime first of all as harm done to people and communities. Our legal system, with its focus on rules and laws, often loses sight of this reality, that crime is essentially harm; consequently, it makes victims at best a secondary concern of justice. A harm focus, however, implies a central concern for victims' needs and roles. Restorative justice, then, begins with a concern for victims and how to meet their needs, for repairing the harm as much as possible.

A focus on harm also implies an emphasis on offender accountability and responsibility–in concrete, not abstract, terms. Too often we have thought of accountability as punishment, that is, pain administered to offenders for pain they have caused. In reality, this has very little to do with actual accountability.

Little in the justice process encourages offenders to understand the consequences of their actions or to empathize with victims. On the contrary, the adversarial game requires offenders to look out for themselves. Offenders are discouraged from acknowledging their responsibility and are given little opportunity to act on this responsibility in concrete ways. The "neutralizing strategies"–the stereotypes and rationalizations that offenders use to distance themselves from the people they hurt–are never challenged.

However, if crime is essentially about harm, accountability means being encouraged to understand that harm, to begin to comprehend the consequences of one's behavior. Moreover, it means taking responsibility to make things right insofar as possible, both concretely and symbolically.

The principle of engagement suggests that the primary parties affected by crime–victims, offenders, members of the community–are given significant roles in the justice process. They need to be given information about each other and to be involved in deciding what justice in this case requires. In some cases, this may mean actual dialogue between these parties. In others it may involve indirect exchange or the use of surrogates. In any case, engagement implies involvement of an enlarged circle of stakeholders as compared to the traditional justice process.

In highly simplistic form, the three central questions of the retributive justice paradigm might be characterized like this: "What laws have been broken? Who 'done' it? What do they deserve?" The comparable questions for a restorative approach then might be these: "Who has been hurt? What are their needs? Whose obligations are they?"

"What does the Lord require?" asks the Hebrew prophet Micah, and begins the answer like this: "To do justice . . ." But what does justice require? The latter question is central to restorative justice. What does justice require for victims? For offenders? For communities?

Out of the traumas of victims' experiences come many needs. Some of these have to be met by victims themselves and their intimates. But some of their needs are best addressed by the larger society, especially the justice process.

Victims badly need what might be called somewhat ambiguously "an experience of justice." This has many dimensions. Often it is assumed that vengeance is part of this need but various studies suggest that this is not necessarily so. The need for vengeance often may be simply the result of justice denied.

The experience of justice seems to include public assurance that what happened to the victim was wrong, that it was unfair, that it was undeserved. Victims need to know that something is being done to make sure that the offense does not happen again. Often they feel the need for some repayment of losses, in part because of the statement of responsibility that is implied. So *restitution* and apologies from an offender can play an important role in the experience of justice.

Victims also need *answers*; in fact, crime victims often rate the need for answers above needs for compensation. Why me? What could I have done differently? What kind of person did this and why? These are just a few of the questions that haunt victims. Without answers, it can be very difficult to restore a sense of order and therefore to heal.

Another area is sometimes termed *"truth-telling"*–opportunities to tell their stories and to vent their feelings, often repeatedly, to people that matter: to friends, to law enforcement people, perhaps even to those who caused this pain. Only by expressing their anger and by repeatedly telling their stories can many victims integrate this terrible experience into their own stories, their own identities.

Also important is the need for *empowerment*. In the crime, an offender has taken power over victims' lives–not only of their body and or property during the incident itself, but over their subsequent emotions, dreams and reality. Indeed, many victims find that, at least for awhile, the offense and the offender are in control of their psyche. That is profoundly unnerving. Without an experience of justice and healing, this, too, can last a lifetime.

Offenders, we have argued above, need to be held accountable, but in ways that encourage empathy and responsibility. However, they certainly have other needs as well. Instead of isolation, offenders need encouragement to be reintegrated–or integrated–into the community. They also need opportunities for personal transformation. This implies focus on developing competencies (instead of the usual focus on deficiencies). It requires that they have an opportunity to have their own needs–including the harms and sense of victimization that may have led to their actions–addressed.

Although retributive justice is done in the name of the "community" (which in effect means the state), in actuality the human community of those affected by the crime is left out of this process and its needs addressed only abstractly, if at all. Fears and stereotypes are heightened rather than addressed. People are encouraged to view things in simple dichotomies–them and us, guilty or innocent–rather than appreciate the rich nuances of real-life people and situations. Worst of all, perhaps, when the community is left out of the justice process, important opportunities for growth and community-building are missed.

Judge Barry Stuart, an early developer of Sentencing Circles, notes that when conflicts are processed right, they provide the means to build relationships between people and within communities; take this away, and you take away a fundamental building block of community and of crime prevention. Communities have needs as well as responsibilities that must be addressed (Stuart, n.d.).

To address these needs, a diverse set of practices has emerged in various communities. Most work in a cooperative relationship with the existing justice system, receiving referrals from it. Many are designed to provide alternative sentencing options or alternatives to arrest or prosecution. Others, such as those which work with severe violence, may be primarily designed to assist the healing of victims and offenders, with minimal impact on legal outcomes. Most, however, involve some form of victim-offender conferencing. That is, they involve an opportunity that is provided for a facilitated dialogue between victim and offender, often with a written restitution agreement as part of the outcome.

Three examples of restorative-oriented alternatives which have emerged include the following: (1) the Victim Offender Reconciliation Program (VORP); (2) Family Group Conferences (FGC); and (3) Sentencing Circles (SC).

1. *Victim Offender Reconciliation Program.* In North America, the leading form of victim-offender conferencing, at least until recently, has been called the Victim Offender Reconciliation Program (VORP) or Victim Offender Mediation (VOM). In its "classic" form, it is operated in cooperation with the courts but often housed in separate non-profit organizations. Upon referral of a case by the court or probation service, trained volunteers separately contact victim and offender to explore what happened and determine their willingness to proceed. If they agree, victim and offender are brought together in a meeting facilitated by the volunteer mediator who serves as a neutral third-party. In this meeting, the facts of the offense are fully explored, feelings are expressed, and a written restitution contract worked out. This contract and a brief report then go back to the court or referring agency. If it is to become part of a sentence, it must receive final approval of the court, then becomes a condition of probation.

   In its original form, VORP predominately handled property offenses such as burglary. Increasingly, however, programs are being designed to handle cases of violence, including offenses such as rape and homicide. Offenses like this, of course, require special precautions and procedures and so VORP is today taking many forms.

2. *Family Group Conferences.* Recently, new forms of conferencing are emerging, new applications are being tried, and new lessons are being learned as a result of two approaches originally rooted in indigenous traditions.

   Family Group Conferences (FGC) emerged in New Zealand (and soon were adapted in Australia) in the late 1980s as a response, in part, to the concerns and traditions of the indigenous Maori population. The Western-style juvenile justice system was widely recognized to be working poorly and many Maori argued that it was antithetical to their traditions; it was oriented toward punishment rather than solutions, was imposed rather than negotiated, and left family and community out of the process.

   In the new juvenile system adopted in 1989, all juvenile cases with the exception of a few very violent crimes are diverted from police or court into FGCs. New Zealand Judge Fred McElrea has called it the first truly restorative approach to be institutionalized within a Western legal framework (McElrea, 1994).

Instead of a court hearing, a youth justice coordinator facilitates a conference which includes victims and offenders, though families of the offender are an essential ingredient as well. Not only do families help to provide accountability and support but advocates argue that it empowers the family as well. Caregivers involved with the family may be invited and a youth advocate–a special attorney–is included to look out for the legal concerns of the offender. Victims, too, may bring family or supporters. Moreover, the police (who are the prosecutors in this legal system) take part in the meeting.

The meetings are not only large but include parties with divergent interests and perspectives. This group is expected to come up with a recommendation for the entire outcome of the case, not just restitution, and they must do this by a consensus of the group! Even more startling, they actually manage to do so in most cases. Family Group Conferences are working well enough that many judges and other practitioners have called for their adaptation to the adult system in New Zealand and pilot projects are under way there.

3. *Sentencing Circles.* Sentencing Circles (SC) have developed as an effort to take seriously the traditions and concerns of indigenous peoples (see Ross, 1996). Until recently they have operated primarily in Native Canadian or "First Nation" communities, but in Minnesota and other places they are being applied to a variety of settings, including inner-city neighborhoods and the workplace.

Sentencing Circles take a variety of forms. Usually, though, they work in conjunction with the formal legal process to provide forums for developing sentencing plans while at the same time addressing community-wide causes and problems. SCs bring together offenders, victims (or their representatives), support groups and interested community people to discuss what happened, why it happened, and what should be done about it. Discussions are apparently wide-ranging and aim toward a full airing of facts and feelings and consensus about solutions.

While the "punishment" or sentence of the offender is worked out here, primary emphasis is on healing of victim, offender, and (significantly) community. According to Stuart, the principal value of the approach is the impact on communities: "In reinforcing and building a sense of community, Circle Sentencing improve[s] the capacity of communities to heal individuals and families and ultimately to prevent crime."

These emerging practices imply a radically different approach to justice for offenders, one that emphasizes an accountability that Australian criminologist John Braithwaite (1998) calls active rather than passive responsibility.

Critics point out that if restorative justice is to be taken seriously, it will need to expand its analysis of offender needs to encompass an understanding of rehabilitation. Drawing upon the "What Works" tradition in rehabilitation (Levrant et al., 1999; Bazemore, 1998; Crowe, 1998), we suggest the following as essential building blocks of restorative or relational rehabilitation:

1. Restorative rehabilitation is victim-focused. Treatments and therapies are not conducted in isolation from understanding of impacts on, responsibilities to, and concern for, victims.
2. Treatment is not viewed as an entitlement–as may happen in the current model–but rather as part of accountability to victims and the community and as a form of social exchange.
3. Treatment is contextualized, focusing upon integration and the creation or strengthening of social bonds rather than isolation.
4. Interventions are tailored to the profiles and personal characteristics of individual offenders. For example, levels of service are matched to the level of risk; intensive services to low-risk offenders are often not only ineffective but often backfire. High anxiety offenders do not respond well to confrontation, and offenders with below-average intellectual abilities do not respond well to cognitive skills programs.
5. Interventions are designed to identify and change the criminogenic needs of offenders and, except for individuals not suited to it, are rooted in behavioral or cognitive-behavioral treatment models.

Tolstoy's assertion suggests that justice needs to be redefined in new terms, if not explicitly in the language of love, then in the language of peace and respect. Criminologists Richard Quinney and John Wildeman, set the context like this:

> From its earliest beginnings . . . the primary focus of criminology has been on retribution, punishment, and vengeance in the cause of an existing social order . . . rather than a criminology of peace, justice and liberation. . . . If crime is violent and wreaks violence on our fellows and our social relations, then the effort to understand and control crime must be violent and repressive. (Quinney and Wildeman, 1991, pp. 40-41)

However, such an approach only intensifies the spiral of violence leading to greater violence. What is needed is something which *breaks* the cycle of violence. Quinney and Wildeman suggest that finally a peacemaking school of criminology is beginning to emerge.

We have argued in this paper that such a peacemaking approach to criminal justice is indeed needed. This peacemaking approach must take seriously (and vigorously critique) the philosophical and theological roots to retributive criminology. However, we are suggesting that the *deepest* roots of Western theology, found in the Bible, are indeed fully compatible with new, peacemaking approaches to criminal justice. Tolstoy would be pleased.

REFERENCES

Baillie, Gil (1995). *Violence Unveiled: Humanity at the Crossroads.* New York: Crossroad.

Barajas, Eduardo (1996). Moving Toward Community Justice. In *Community Justice: Stiving for Safe, Secure, and Just Communities* (pp. 1-7). Washington, DC: National Institute of Corrections.

Bazemore, Gordon (1998). Restorative Justice and Earned Redemption. *American Behavioral Scientist, 41.*6, pp. 768-813.

Berkovits, Eliezer (1969). *Man and God: Studies in Biblical Theology.* Detroit: Wayne State University Press.

Berman, Harold J. (1983). *Law and Revolution: The Formation of the Western Legal Tradition.* Cambridge, MA: Harvard University Press.

Bianchi, Herman (1994). *Justice as Sanctuary: Toward a New System of Crime Control.* Bloomington, IN: Indiana University Press.

Braithwaite, John and Philip Petit (1990). *Not Just Deserts: A Republican Theory of Criminal Justice.* Oxford, U.K.: Clarendon Press.

Braithwaite, John (1990). *Crime, Shame, and Reintegration.* Cambridge, U.K.: Cambridge University Press.

Braithwaite, John (1998, November). Principles of Restorative Justice. Plenary presentation at the International Conference on Restorative Justice for Juveniles, Ft. Lauderdale, FL.

Christie, Nils (1994). *Crime Control as Industry: Toward Gulags, Western Style.* New York: Routledge.

Claassen, Ron (1990). Prerequisites for Reconciliation. In *VORP Volunteer Handbook* (pp. 10-11). Akron, PA: Mennonite Central Committee.

Crowe, Anne H. (1998). Restorative Justice and Offender Rehabilitation: A Meeting of Minds. *Perspectives: A Journal of the American Probation and Parole Association,* 22.3, pp. 28-40.

Dihle, Albrecht (1974). *Greek and Christian Concepts of Justice.* Berkeley, CA: The Center for Hermeneutical Studies.

Dunn, James D. G. (1993). *The Justice of God: A Fresh Look at the Old Doctrine of Justification by Faith.* Grand Rapids, MI: Eerdmans.

Evans, Brian and G. R. Evans, Eds. (1998). *Anselm of Canterbury: The Major Works.* New York: Oxford University Press.

Gilligan, James (1997). *Violence: Reflections on a National Epidemic.* New York: Vintage Books.

Gorringe, Timothy (1996). *God's Just Vengeance: Crime, Violence and the Rhetoric of Salvation.* New York: Cambridge University Press.

Grant, George Parkin (1974). *English-Speaking Justice.* Sackville, New Brunswick: Mt. Allison University Press.

Grimsrud, Ted (1988). Peace Theology and the Justice of God in the Book of Revelation. In Willard M. Swartley (Ed.), *Essays on Peace Theology and Witness* (pp. 135-153). Elkhart, IN: Institute of Mennonite Studies.

Grimsrud, Ted (1999). Healing Justice: The Prophet Amos and a "New" Theology of Justice. In Ted Grimsrud and Loren J. Johns (Eds.), *Peace and Justice Shall Embrace: Power and Theopolitics in the Bible* (pp. 64-85). Telford, PA: Pandora Press.

Hamilton, Bernard (1981) *The Medieval Inquisition.* New York: Holmes and Meier Publishers.

Kaufman, Gordon D. (1993). *In Face of Mystery: A Constructive Theology.* Cambridge, MA: Harvard University Press.

Levrant, Sharon, Francis Cullen, Betsy Fulton, and John Wozniak (1999). Reconsidering Restorative Justice: The Corruption of Benevolence Revisited? *Crime and Delinquency,* 45.1, pp. 3-27.

Lind, Millard C. (1990). *Monotheism, Power, Justice: Collected Old Testament Essays.* Elkhart, IN: Institute of Mennonite Studies.

McElrea, F. W. M. (1994). Restorative Justice in Practice. In Jonathan Burnside and Nicola Baker (Eds.), *Relational Justice: Repairing the Breach.* Winchester, U.K.: Waterside Press.

Mica, Harry (1995). Victim Offender Mediation: International Perspectives on Theory, Research, and Practice. *Mediation Quarterly ,12.*

Paolucci, Henry, Ed. (1962). *The Political Writings of St. Augustine.* Chicago: Henry Regnery.

Pepinsky, Harold E. (1991). *The Geometry of Violence and Democracy.* Bloomington, IN: Indiana University Press.

Pleasants, Julian (1996). Religion That Restores Victims. *New Theology Review, 9*.3, pp. 41-63.

Quinney, Richard and John Wildeman (1991). *The Problem of Crime: A Peace and Social Justice Perspective.* Mountain View, CA: Mayfield Publishing Company.

Ross, Rupert (1996). *Returning to the Teachings: Exploring Aboriginal Justice.* Toronto: Penguin.

Schlosser, Eric (1998). The Prison-Industrial Complex. *The Atlantic Monthly, 282.*6, pp. 51-77.

Stuart, Barry (n.d.). Alternative Dispute Resolution in Action in Canada: Community Justice Circles. Unpublished paper. Whitehorse, Yukon: Yukon Territorial Court.

Wolterstorff, Nicholas (1983). *Until Justice and Peace Embrace.* Grand Rapids, MI: Eerdmans.

Yoder, Perry B. (1987). *Shalom: The Bible's Word for Salvation, Justice, and Peace.* Newton, KS: Faith and Life Press.

Zehr, Howard (1995). *Changing Lenses: A New Focus for Crime and Justice.* Second edition. Scottdale, PA: Herald Press.

Zehr, Howard (1997). Restorative Justice: The Concept. *Corrections Today, December*, pp. 68-70.

Zehr, Howard (1998). Justice as Restoration, Justice as Respect. *Justice Professional*, 11, 71-87.

AUTHORS' NOTES

Ted Grimsrud teaches theology and peace studies at Eastern Mennonite University, Harrisonburg, Virginia. Prior to joining the EMU faculty, he served for ten years as a Mennonite pastor in Oregon, Arizona, and South Dakota. Grimsrud holds an MA in peace studies from Associated Mennonite Biblical Seminary and a PhD in Christian Ethics from the Graduate Theological Union. He is author of *Triumph of the Lamb: A Self-Study Guide to the Book of Revelation* (Herald Press, 1987) and *God's Healing Strategy: An Introduction to the Main Themes of the Bible* (Pandora Press, US, 2000).

Howard Zehr is a professor of sociology and restorative justice at Eastern Mennonite University in Harrisonburg, VA. Dr. Zehr served for 19 years as a director of the Office on Crime and Justice for Mennonite Central Committee US. His book, *Changing Lenses: A New Focus for Crime and Justice*, has been a foundational work in the growing "restorative justice" movement. As a result, he lectures and consults internationally on the theory and practice of restorative justice and the Victim-Offender Reconciliation Program (VORP), which he helped pioneer. Dr. Zehr has also worked professionally as a photographer and photojournalist. His primary interest currently is in the use of photography and interviews for documentary work. He has written most recently *Transcending: Reflections of Crime Victims* (Good Books, 2000).

Address correspondence to Dr. Ted Grimsrud, Associate Professor of Theology and Peace Studies, Eastern Mennonite University, 1200 Park Road, Harrisonburg, VA 22802.

Index